The Last Soviet

Alexander Lukashenko's Belarus

Stewart Parker

Order this book online at www.trafford.com/07-1373
or email orders@trafford.com

Most Trafford titles are also available at major online book retailers.

© Copyright 2007 Stewart Parker.

All rights reserved. No part of this publication may be reproduced, stored in a retrieval system, or transmitted, in any form or by any means, electronic, mechanical, photocopying, recording, or otherwise, without the written prior permission of the author.

Note for Librarians: A cataloguing record for this book is available from Library and Archives Canada at www.collectionscanada.ca/amicus/index-e.html

ISBN: 978-1-4251-3527-0

We at Trafford believe that it is the responsibility of us all, as both individuals and corporations, to make choices that are environmentally and socially sound. You, in turn, are supporting this responsible conduct each time you purchase a Trafford book, or make use of our publishing services. To find out how you are helping, please visit www.trafford.com/responsiblepublishing.html

Our mission is to efficiently provide the world's finest, most comprehensive book publishing service, enabling every author to experience success. To find out how to publish your book, your way, and have it available worldwide, visit us online at www.trafford.com/10510

Trafford PUBLISHING www.trafford.com

North America & international
toll-free: 1 888 232 4444 (USA & Canada)
phone: 250 383 6864 ♦ fax: 250 383 6804 ♦ email: info@trafford.com

The United Kingdom & Europe
phone: +44 (0)1865 722 113 ♦ local rate: 0845 230 9601
facsimile: +44 (0)1865 722 868 ♦ email: info.uk@trafford.com

10 9 8 7 6 5 4 3 2 1

Acknowledgements.

I would like to thank all of the people who have helped me with this project, either by supplying information and support or by simply putting up with me whilst I talked about little else for the last three years. Particularly to Elaine Oxley, Gareth Thomas, Demi Parker, and to my long-suffering Mother, and 'Bobby'.

I would also like to especially thank all of the Belarusian people I interviewed* and talked to about their country, but particularly Aleg Litvinovich, and Sergei 'Koresh' Kurashov, as well as Alyaksei Mazhukhou and Zoya Kolontai.

President Lukashenko's speech to the UN in 2006 is reproduced in full as an Appendix, with the kind permission of Oleg Morozov, Second Secretary at the Belarusian Embassy in Washington DC.

I am profoundly grateful to Stephen Reid who actually suggested I write this book, and who also has helped enormously with proof reading and editing. The cover photo is used by permission of Peter at 'Abdymok.net'.

This book is dedicated to my son.

---

* The interviews were all qualitative with no set questions. People were encouraged to freely discuss their country, President Lukashenko, and whatever issues were pertinent to them.

Contents.

A Short Note on Language: 6

Introduction: 7

1. A Brief history of Early Belarus: 8

2. The October Revolution: 12

3. The Creation of Soviet Belarus: 19

4. The 1930's. Collectivisation and Industrialisation: 25

5. The Great Patriotic War: 32

6. Rebuilding and Recovery of the Belarusian Soviet Socialist Republic: 1945-1985: 38

7. Perestroika, Glasnost and the End of the Soviet Union: 45

8. Alexander Lukashenko: A Short Biography: 52

9. Belarus in Transition 1991-1994: 56

10. Alexander Lukashenko's Consolidation of Power: 64

11. The Economy Under Lukashenko: 75

12. Social Policy in Alexander Lukashenko's Belarus: 85

13. Human Rights in Belarus: 103

14. International Affairs: Belarus and the World: 121

15. Elections and the Belarusian Opposition: 170

Conclusion: The Historical Choice of Belarus: 194

Appendix. President Alexander Lukashenko's Speech to the UN Assembly in 2005: 200

Notes: 205

Bibliography: 246

A Short Note on Language.

'Belarus' is not the only commonly used name for this country. Yet it is the correct one for the republic as it stands today. Historical names such as 'White Russia', and alternative spellings, including 'Byelorussia' certainly have been more commonly used in differing periods. However in this book, *Belarus* will be the common name for the republic and its territory.

Belarus historically has had various nationalities living within its frontiers, and as such language has developed with broad and often competing influences.

Minsk for example, the capital city of Belarus, is the Russian name, whereas in Belarusian it is 'Miensk'. Russian, Polish, Yiddish and Ukrainian have all had influence on the Belarusian language over time, and to further complicate matters, Belarusian can be written in two different alphabets.

For the purpose of this book I will use the most familiar language, and recognised spellings; which usually are the Russian ones. Significantly for the spelling of Lukashenko, who in Belarusian is 'Lukashenka'.

Introduction.

Alexander Lukashenko became president of the Republic of Belarus in 1994. His actions since then have earned him both praise, and criticism. Despite being elected he has been called a dictator, with subsequent elections denounced as fraudulent, and in 2004 the US Secretary of state Condoleezza Rice included Belarus in her list of 'Outposts of Tyranny'.

Lukashenko himself has been called both a fascist and a communist, and thus frequently compared with Hitler, and Stalin. His external criticism is severe, and internal opposition claim that they are persecuted, and even that their activists have been 'disappeared'.

Despite these claims, Lukashenko enjoys genuine support in Belarus, and is also widely admired in Russia. His nickname of *Batka* translates as 'father'.

Belarus maintains a social welfare system of free education and healthcare, state pensions from the Soviet era are still paid on time, the economic crises that hit Russia, and the other former Soviet states have been largely avoided in Belarus.

The Belarusian economy has not been artificially buoyed by privatisation, and Lukashenko removed the IMF commission to Belarus, calling them "*swindlers*".

Belarus is not a garrison state or an island, entry and exit are relatively simple, but there is no mass exodus from this small nation of ten million people to its free market neighbours. In fact in 2001 more people immigrated to Belarus than left it.

This book is not intended to serve as an apology for Lukashenko, or as an indictment of him, but rather to examine and tie together the many loose ends of this largely unexplored and unexplained part of modern politics and world affairs. Few genuine attempts have been made to examine the politics and realities of Lukashenko's Belarus, the history, and the reasons for actions, policies and indeed criticisms. What is the nature of 'opposition', who creates the criticisms and why?

In fact the majority of criticism of Lukashenko comes from abroad. The myth of absolute government control of the media in Belarus will also be explored. Due to the often-external nature of this criticism; and even funding of internal opposition this book will frequently compare the policies and system of Belarus with those of the nations who chastise it.

A nation, or indeed an individual cannot be understood without examining their history, and this is particularly the case in nations 'born' from larger entities. The former colonies in Africa, and the newly created sovereign nations of the Balkans cannot be studied without reference to the British Empire or Yugoslavia. This is also the same for the former Soviet republics.

Belarus has a relatively short history as a nation, and most of its key development was as a Soviet Socialist Republic. For this reason the first part of this book will deal with the historical development of Belarus, and the influence of the Soviet Union on the Belarusian people and culture.

All too many opinions of Lukashenko are formed with little knowledge of him, or of the history of Belarus. Frequent comparisons are made with Poland, despite a different culture, history, and social structure.

What effect then has Lukashenko had on Belarus, how is it performing in the economic and social field? What are his methods, and are they justifiable? This book intends to examine these questions, particularly in comparison with the other former Soviet and socialist countries. Has Lukashenko taken a step back? Or is his approach progressive and positive?

Chapter 1. A Brief History of Early Belarus.

"Belarus, with its clean lakes, natural forests, with the unplundered natural economy is attracting avid interests from all sides".[1] A.G. Lukashenko

Where is Belarus? This question is one I have been asked by many people as I have begun researching this book. Compared to other nations of the former Russian Empire and Soviet Union, such as Finland, the Baltic states, Kazakhstan or Ukraine, Belarus is certainly unfamiliar to most in the West.

Belarus is a landlocked country that lies between Poland and Russia. It is comparable in size to England and Scotland combined, or to the US State of Kansas.

Belarus occupies a strategic geographic position in Europe, and historically has served as the 'gateway' to invasions of Russia from the West, and to Europe from the East.

Despite a very brief declaration of independence in 1918, Belarus as a sovereign nation has only existed since 1991. Before this Belarus has been a fought over and frequently occupied territory. Poland, Lithuania, Russia, and Germany have all occupied Belarus.

As part of the Soviet Union, the Belarusian Soviet Socialist Republic achieved its present borders, and though it was not independent of Moscow, Belarus has been represented at the UN since 1945. Only the Belarusians and Ukrainians were so honoured out of the constituent republics of the USSR. The history of the nation of Belarus is inextricably linked to the Soviet Union. This is a vital factor for understanding the current direction and outlook of this country, and indeed its president.

Although Belarusian culture has survived from the Middle Ages (Slavs becoming dominant in Belarusian lands in the eighth and ninth centuries AD) it has not been a nationalist culture. The Belarusian people historically having been absorbed into one nation or another only began to develop their own united desire for statehood in the late nineteenth century.[2]

This developing politicisation in Belarusian territory reflected the general 'enlightenment' throughout the region. Despite having no formal border the Belarusian people had remarkably kept a unique identity within the lands of their various occupiers. The most significant example of this is that when Belarus was part of the Grand Duchy of Lithuania, all affairs of state were officially conducted in the Belarusian language.[3]

Lithuania and Poland formed a 'commonwealth' in 1569, which saw the introduction of a Polish influence in Belarus. This ultimately led to the vying for power between the Catholic and the Eastern Orthodox churches.

By the 1700's the Russian Empire was clearly becoming the dominant political, and military force in the region, and when Polish lands were re-partitioned between 1772 and 1795 all Belarusian land fell into the hands of the Russian Empire.

The Russian Empire was multi-ethnic, and multi-cultural, encompassing many nationalities, and religions. However it was also chauvinist, enforcing Russian law, language, and Eastern Orthodox Christianity on its subjects.

A significant factor in the make up of the Belarusian culture and people was the creation in 1791 of the 'Pale of Settlement'. This was a slice of land running down the western border of the Russian Empire in which Jews were permitted to live. Those Jews who had not converted to Christianity (which was almost all of them) were restricted to this area of Russia.

It was Catherine the Great who created the Pale of settlement, as a compromise between those in her government who wanted the wholesale expulsion of the Jews, and those who recognised the need for the mercantile class that most Jews had become.[4]

The 'Pale' covered almost all of the current Belarusian territory, as well as parts of what are now Lithuania, and Ukraine.

Over the following century, the 'Pale' was altered to include more land taken from Poland, and some large cities which were inside the 'Pale' were excluded from it; significantly Kiev in Ukraine, which expelled its Jews in December 1827.[5]

By 1900 Belarus was still largely a rural society; industrialisation was slow across most of Russia, but particularly in Belarus. Some urban development had taken place, with the large towns and cities becoming busy centres of trade. Jews became the majority ethnic group within Belarusian cities, with Yiddish being the most spoken language.[6]

The underdeveloped nature of the Belarusian land, and economy, meant that co-operation and bartering were essential for survival.

Though the type of work was ethnically divided, the Belarusians, and the Jews were inextricably tied. The Belarusians primarily worked the land, and sold or exchanged their produce for the clothes, boots etc. that the Jews manufactured.[7]

The importance of this was notable, particularly when the Nazis occupied Belarus in 1941 they found little anti-Semitism, and indeed great resistance to their policies. With one German officer reporting that the people of Belarus actually considered the Jews to be: *"as much of a human being as the Belarusian"*.[8]

However before the massive tragedy that was the German invasion in 1941, there was another colossal event that was to shape the history of Belarus. This one coming from the east, the Russian October Revolution of 1917.

Chapter 2. The October Revolution.

"Our grandfathers and forefathers have their biographies and destinies linked to the October Revolution, we regard their deeds and achievements with respect".[1]
A.G. Lukashenko.

Belarusian history, though long, has for the most part been a history of a people with no control over their own destiny. Whether Belarus 'belonged' to Lithuania, Poland or the Russian Empire was almost insignificant to the lives of the Belarusians themselves.

The sudden collapse of Imperial Russia, and the revolution that followed changed all of that. Although Belarus was to be a constituent part of a larger state, this time the Soviet Union, its unique identity was finally acknowledged.

In order to understand the significance of the October revolution and its consequential influence on Belarus and Alexander Lukashenko, it is important to understand the aims of this revolution. This was not a simple peasant revolt or an accident of circumstances.

Lenin and his 'Bolshevik' party were following a strict and detailed revolutionary theory. Communism, as formulated by Karl Marx and Friedrich Engels in the 19th century is entirely revolutionary in its goals and methods, as such the followers of this doctrine were dedicated activists, and in the case of the Bolsheviks led by 'full time, professional revolutionaries'.

The success of this revolution and the subsequent emergence of communism as a major force in international politics throughout the twentieth century was quite remarkable in light of the conditions that prevailed in the Russian Empire at the time.

How could a theory such as Marxism, which advocated the complete overturn of all established society, and even the 'withering away of the state' have come to such pre-eminence in the Russian Empire?

How could the works of Marx, often complicated economic theories and philosophical concepts, written in an often unsatisfactorily translated and lengthy prose be made accessible and agreeable to the barely literate minority class of workers in Russia?

Also, how could a Marxist revolution have taken place in a country that barely had a working class, which is so vital to the overthrow of capitalism? As written by Marx, and Engels in their book, the 'Manifesto of the Communist Party' in 1848: *"not only has the bourgeoisie forged the weapons that bring death to itself; it has also called into existence the men who are to wield those weapons- the modern working class- the proletarians"*.[2]

This is particularly key in the case of introducing communism to Belarus, a country that, as we have seen, had almost no industry in 1917, and significantly where the Belarusian people themselves were in fact a minority in the vital urban areas.

The answers to these questions are complicated, and are subject for debate, and indeed books of their own. However it is clear that a large amount of the appeal of communism in Russia came primarily in reaction to the harsh living conditions of the 'masses' as opposed to the perceived, and often genuine wealth and opulence of the landowners and monarchy. Indeed the wealth in Imperial Russia was extremely concentrated, as were access to education, healthcare, land and decent housing.

Relations between the poor and the rich were especially strained in the Russian Empire, as compared to Western Europe. The Russian aristocracy was also hugely reliant on the Tsar for both financial support and political recognition.

The backwardness of the Russian Empire is highlighted by the fact that the mediaeval system of serfdom carried on in Russia until 1861. This system allowed landowners to pay their workers literally nothing at all in return for any crops grown. The Serf was simply allowed to work the aristocrat's land.

Serfdom was ended in response not to any sense of social conscience, but because the Russian aristocratic lifestyle incurred such a level of debt that by 1861 two thirds of the private landlord's serfs had also been mortgaged along with the land.[3]

The combination of this system, that two generations of rural Belarusians had lived under, and official anti-Semitism, which was felt in the towns, meant that the 'workers and peasants' needed little agitation in Belarus.

The 'Bolshevik' party was not the only revolutionary group in Russia, nor did the workers and peasants themselves universally approve its vision of society. Indeed the Bolsheviks had emerged as a faction of a larger organisation, the Russian Social Democratic Workers Party.

This party originally being formed in 1898 in Minsk, as an attempt to unite the various Marxist revolutionary groups. The party split in 1903 over issues of discipline, professionalism and the degree to which the party should co-operate with other revolutionary groups. Lenin emerged as the undisputed head of the Bolshevik, or 'majority' faction. Whilst the less hard-line Menshevik (Minority) faction, was headed by Julius Martov, with initially, Leon Trotsky prominent in its leadership.

Revolutionary groups throughout the Russian Empire were many, and varied. Key differences included attitudes to violence, democracy, and of huge importance, nationalism.

The Ukrainians and the Poles for example, had a long history of statehood, with well established national symbols, identity and culture. When their lands were drawn into the strong Russian Empire the nationalists were simply waiting for signs of weakness before attempting to break away. Parallels can easily be drawn here between the crumbling Russian Empire watching helplessly as its composite nations broke away in 1917, and that of the ailing USSR around 1990 failing to keep its constituent republics and satellites under the control of Moscow.

Significantly at both of these times the reaction of Belarus, or rather the inaction that followed, indicates no strong sense of statehood, or of the ability to 'go it alone'.

In the period from 1900 to 1917, nationalism can be seen to be a phenomena that failed to truly unite the Belarusian people, in the same way as it did in other countries in this time of patriotism and imperialism leading up to the First World War.

In a study of the Belarusian population from 1897, it was noted that some 98% of the ethnic Belarusian population lived in settlements with no more than 2000 inhabitants.[4] It is unsurprising therefore that a sense of nation and statehood did not take hold, particularly in light of the earlier mentioned ethnic divide between town and country.

Within Belarus the revolutionary organisations were numerous, though the largest were those espousing Marxist, and anti-imperialist ideals. The major parties were: The Autonomous Jewish Bund, The Bolshevik and Menshevik Social Democrats, and the Belarusian Socialist Hramada, (meaning assembly).

What these parties had in common, and what was able to inspire both urban and rural Belarusians was not the promise of an 'independent homeland' of Belarus, but rather the lure of socialist egalitarianism across the region.

The First World War on the eastern front was not quite as static as that in the west. This resulted in a slow, but steady push eastwards by the German army (the Russians still achieving occasional success against the Austro-Hungarians). By late 1915 one third of Belarus was under German occupation, increasing to two thirds in October 1917.[5]

This slow eastern drive, was a combination of German military preparedness, and the poor performance of the Russian army.

In a bid to restore discipline the Tsar named himself commander in chief of the army in September1915, and thus made himself personally responsible for the defeats of the army, as well as the plight of the peasantry and the lack of industrial development.

This ultimately left the Tsar in an untenable position as head of state, because the revolutionaries now no longer feared the army, but were in a position to rely on it for support.

In March 1917 the army in the Russian Imperial capital of Petrograd (renamed from St. Petersburg after the outbreak of the war due to its Germanic name.) mutinied. The Tsar sent troops from Mogilev in Belarus with orders to put down the mutiny, but instead, upon arrival they joined its ranks. Russia now truly began to 'collapse' leading to two distinct revolutions within the same year, as well as the abdication of the Tsar, and the end of 300 years of the Romanov dynasty.

The first revolution occurred in February, and the hastily formed provisional government struggled to impose its authority over the elected soviets (councils) of workers and soldiers. The Bolsheviks would not co-operate with the provisional government, firstly they did not recognise its authority or status, and secondly because they sensed the time and opportunity was at hand to seize power themselves.

Despite this internal turmoil and the Tsars abdication on March 15th, Russia was still at war with Germany and her allies. The provisional government wanted to continue the war, whereas the vast majority of Russians now wanted peace. Here was Lenin's chance, and he took it, by declaring *"all power to the Soviets!"*

By allying himself with the established popular councils, Lenin was able to quickly consolidate his and his party's position, and assume control of Russia.

These revolutions did not make an initially significant impression on Belarus. This was primarily due to the fact that the majority of the country was still under German occupation and the rest under martial law, in effect since August 1914.

What did occur was a curious situation whereby the increasingly marginalised provisional government declared sovereignty for nationalities amongst it's core principles; at almost the same time as Lenin declared the same in his 'April Thesis' and yet Belarus was not able to exert its authority as a nationality.[6]

In March of 1917 with the political situation in turmoil, and both German and Russian troops occupying Belarusian territory, a conference was held in Minsk, with the main parties and national organisations present. Statehood was the key issue, but this was almost inextricably linked to the success of the Bolsheviks in Petrograd. The Russian Social Democrats were able to have an enormous amount of influence over proceedings due to their clear rise to dominance within the workers and soldier's soviets. Also the charisma and clear message of Lenin was something that many other parties simply lacked. Although the conference did declare itself in favour of becoming a republic, this was under the proviso that it would become an autonomous part of the newly formed Russian Democratic Republic.[7]

This very same theme was a key part of Alexander Lukashenko's 1994 election campaign, and subsequent policy. The Belarusian/Russian union advocated in 1917, and again in 1994, were strategic, in terms of the fact that Belarus was unable to be self sufficient in either case; and it was also formed from a socio-political position. In 1917 this was the identification with the socialist movement gaining ascendancy in Russia, whilst in 1994 it was an identification with the notion of 'Pan Slavism' and acknowledgement of the Russification of Belarus which had taken place over the previous seventy seven years. It is of note that in neither case was the issue of national sovereignty offered away, but rather a union of mutual benefit was proposed (The 1994 Belarusian/Russian union is discussed further in chapter 14).

The Bolsheviks officially assumed power in October 1917, and began issuing orders to the army to negotiate a truce with the Germans and their allies. As a means to further their control across the vast territories of the former Russian Empire, they initiated worker's and soldier's soviets, maintaining their hold on power by sharing it with the people.

These soviets were the first chance that most citizens of the former Russian Empire had been granted to take part in any form of government or decision making. The fact that the soviets were strongly controlled by the Bolsheviks was barely noticed, and almost unimportant in the revolutionary fervour of 1917.

It was on November the seventh 1917 that the Bolsheviks officially claimed power in Minsk. At the time the Bolsheviks in Belarus, failed to mention Belarusian independence in their plans. This caused a reaction from the other Belarusian parties, who could see that they were being marginalised, and also concern from the Germans, who still had conflicting territorial demands.

A curious situation then arose whereby the Central Powers and the Bolsheviks signed the Brest Litovsk treaty on March the third. In which the Germans agreed to take no part in creating states on former Russian territory, in exchange for a significant slice of that territory, and peace on the eastern front.

On March the 25th under German occupation, an independent Belarusian state was declared. This state was very short lived, due mainly to the way it was declared in direct violation of the far more important Brest Litovsk peace treaty. Also with the collapse of Germany and her allies in 1918, Poland was freed from occupation and granted independence.

Poland had territorial claims on parts of Belarus going back to 1569, and with Russia descending into civil war, the Belarusian independent state had no allies, and little popular support to ensure its survival.

Historian David R. Marples summarised the 1918 Belarusian republic thus: "*It was a product of World War I rather than the Russian Revolution and died an inevitable death*".[8]

The Bolshevik government was in an unenviable position. They had many enemies, not only the pro Tsarists, and nationalists, but also from other socialist groups, who disagreed with what they saw as a strict and dogmatic position. Added to this there was enormous civil unrest that was fuelled by the abundance of firearms provided by the collapse of the army. The new government also faced hostile foreign powers eager to prey on a weakened Russia, or those who simply opposed the establishment of a workers state. The result was that Russia in 1918 was plunged into a particularly bloody civil war.

The concessions made by the Bolsheviks at Brest Litovsk meant little to Poland, who in February 1919 invaded the newly proclaimed Belarusian Soviet Socialist Republic (BSSR). The war that followed was brutal and fluid. The Red Army rebuffed the Poles all the way back to Warsaw before being beaten back to Minsk. The 1921 treaty of Riga established a new border for the Belarusians, which split the country almost down the middle. The Polish took the western half, and simply incorporated it into Poland, whilst the Bolsheviks re-established the BSSR in the east.

Chapter 3. The Creation of Soviet Belarus.

"The Soviet Union, despite all mistakes and blunders of its leaders, was the source of hope and support for many states and peoples".[1] A.G. Lukashenko.

In March 1918 the Bolsheviks changed the national capital from Petrograd to Moscow, as it was in a far safer, and more strategic central location. Also in the same month the Bolsheviks changed their name to the 'All-Russian Communist Party (Bolsheviks)'.

By 1921 the Russian Civil War was all but over. The 'White' armies aiming to overthrow Communism had failed to co-ordinate their offensives, and the 'Reds' held onto power. The Civil War also acted as a warning to the fledgling Soviet State, that other nations took seriously the threat to their ruling elites that a socialist or communist government posed. The tragedy of the First World War had led many 'ordinary people' to question the wisdom of their leaders, and indeed the whole social order. Trade unions and socialist parties sprang up around the industrialised world, and frequently looked to the Soviet Union for inspiration. For example the Communist Party of the USA was formed immediately after World War One in 1919, and the British Labour Party formed its first government in 1924.

During the Russian Civil War as well as fighting the 'White' forces, the Bolsheviks also had to contend with anti-communist 'intervention forces' sent to Russia by the armies of Britain, France, Japan, and the USA. This came in addition to the Polish invasion of 1919, and also the occupation of Ukraine, Azerbaijan and Georgia by the German and Turkish armies in 1918.[2]

The 'intervention' was unable to bring about the downfall of the new communist government, but did cause significant damage to Soviet infrastructure, and military emplacements. For example the British in 1919 scuttled five Russian navy submarines at Sevastopol, to prevent them being 'captured' by the Red Army.

Following the Civil War the Bolshevik government had consolidated power in Russia, Ukraine, Belarus (although partitioned with Poland), Georgia, Armenia, and Azerbaijan. The last three nations were united into the short-lived Transcaucasian Soviet Socialist Republic. These Soviet Socialist Republics were all then united in December 1922 by the official establishment of the Union of Soviet Socialist Republics. Although allowed limited national autonomy they were all required to follow the Marxist political line of the ruling Communist Party. This had all been obtained at a terrible cost, around 13 million people had died during the civil war.

Marxism is not a nationally exclusive doctrine. Indeed the goal of communism is the overthrow of the exploiting classes, in the name of the workers, wherever they may be. Hence the final sentence in Marx and Engels' manifesto reads: "*The proletarians have nothing to lose but their chains. They have a world to win*".[3]

The goal of a world revolution was still at the forefront of the Soviet leadership's mind despite the foreign intervention during the civil war. It is also of note that the Polish fought particularly bitterly against the Red Army in 1919-20, which was viewed as much as victory for Polish nationalism over international socialism as it was a military success.

The significance of this to Belarus was high. The new Soviet government wanted to develop Belarus, both materially and culturally, in order to provide a direct and positive contrast to the fate of the western/Polish half of Belarus. One of the first steps was in key personnel. The Russian Bolsheviks were slowly replaced throughout 1921-22 by reliable Belarusian communists.[4]

At this time a popular slogan, coined by Josef Stalin was; "*National in form, socialist in content*".[5] This was how the Communist Party envisioned the Soviet Union, and indeed one day the world, with religious and national distinctions falling away to be replaced by a common and harmonious Soviet socialist culture.[6]

However in the 1920's religious and national distinctions were very open, and in light of the civil war, often very raw. The Soviet government spent the next decade redrawing the map of eastern Europe, trying to marry up the ethnic majorities with the correct republic. As a result the narrow strip of territory around Minsk which had constituted the Belarusian Soviet Socialist Republic (BSSR) was expanded in 1923, 1924 and 1926. This resulted in the population increasing threefold from that of 1921.[7] The Belarusian towns of Vitebsk and Gomel had their districts expanded, which meant that by 1927 the eastern border of the republic had been established just as it remains today.

The ethnic composition of Belarus remained varied, but roughly proportional to that in Tsarist times, however with two notable differences. Firstly the Polish minority had mostly lived in western Belarus, and as such now lived in Poland officially. Secondly the urban/ rural ethnic split had all but disappeared under communism.

With the Belarusian peasants no longer 'tied' to the land, and Jews allowed to live wherever they wanted, unforced migration took place in Belarus for the first time in over 100 years!

The result was a Belarusian urban population of approximately 40% by 1926.[8] This migration from country to towns also had economic consequences. The turmoil that had hit Belarus since 1914 had been particularly acute. The First World War, occupation, Revolution, the Polish invasion and civil war had all left their mark. The predominantly Jewish urban population in Belarus had been strongly affected by this upheaval, and indeed by Soviet distrust of private traders. As a result many in urban areas were unable to find work, and as an example, in Gomel in the early 1920's Jews made up 70% of the unemployed.[9] As a result of the civil war, and population migration the Soviet Union was seriously threatened with starvation. Many farms had been destroyed, and the Red Army's grain seizures in the civil war had not left a positive impression on the peasantry, particularly in the South, and Ukraine. Lenin's solution was twofold: the New Economic Policy (NEP), and re-settlement of the land by the urban unemployed. As a result the Soviet government published in 1925 and 1926 a journal entitled 'The Jewish Peasant", and established two organisations dedicated to the voluntary settlement of 'Jewish Toilers' on the land.[10]

The attempts to resettle the land with former town dwellers were not particularly successful, but the NEP certainly was. The NEP was a departure for the communist government from the traditional Marxist position on private trade. Lenin had to convince many doubters within his own party that the NEP was necessary, although as he stressed, only temporarily. Lenin's argument was that Russia was under developed and thus not ready for an immediate launching of socialism. However allowing this small amount of free trade in the country was as much a matter of necessity as it was of policy. Throughout the 1920's the NEP was proving to be a great success, by the year 1926 agricultural production had reached the pre revolutionary level, with grain production actually being higher on less land.[11] This achievement was made by relaxing the tight economic controls in the agrarian sector, but also through redistribution of the land. Meaning that peasants were now tilling their own land, and not enriching a landlord at their own expense.

This early period of Soviet power was characterised in the BSSR by ethnic migration, agrarian recovery, and Belarusian cultural development. The republic adopted a new constitution on the 11th of April 1927, partly in response to the NEP, and consolidation of communist rule, and also in recognition of the national development, and expansion of Belarus. The Belarusian State University was established in 1921, and in 1922 an Institute of Belarusian Culture was established in Minsk. At the same time a Minsk State University Library was opened, later renamed the Belarusian State Library in 1926. These progressive developments were essential both to a socialist ideology, but also to the development of a republic which was soon to industrialise.

In stark comparison, was the plight of the Belarusians living in Polish territory. Whilst the government in Moscow was striving for socialism and appeasing its national constituents, the Polish were re-asserting their statehood, and following a strong nationalist line. Despite being supported by the USA and UK, Poland was warned against establishing arbitrary rule over the territories in the East. US President Woodrow Wilson stipulated at the conclusion of the First World War that the re-established state of Poland should only include territories that had, *"indisputably Polish populations."*[12]

British Prime Minister David Lloyd George all but condemned Polish expansion in Lithuania, Ukraine and Belarus, noting that the Polish government was simply applying Polish nationality by force to the peoples in its eastern territories.

Against the Polish trend, communist sympathy, and indeed party membership, was rising throughout the Belarusian area. This culminated in strikes and peasant uprisings in 1928, causing a period of unrest lasting until 1932, when the Polish army forcefully pacified the Belarusian villages.[13]

The Belarusian towns were spared no indignity either, the city of Brest on the western most tip of Belarus, lost its significance as a centre of trade, its canals and railway networks fell into disrepair, and under-use. The Soviet historian Nikolai Kudrayashov noted that the Polish not only held back the cultural development of its Belarusian territory, but also that of its economy.[14] This was not only a blow to the Belarusian population, but also to the economic development of Poland as a whole.

By the mid 1930's the Polish government had launched an all out campaign in its Belarusian, and Ukrainian territories to enforce Catholicism. Across western Belarus one hundred and forty Orthodox churches were simply closed.[15] In the Polish census of 1931 any Belarusian Catholic was counted as being of Polish origin, regardless of their understanding of Polish culture, or language.

September 13th 1935 saw the Polish government scrap all laws to protect ethnic minorities as established by the League of Nations (forerunner of the UN), the reason given being that Polish laws were adequate. Two months later a large concentration camp was established on Belarusian territory at Bereza Kartuska, for the internment of 'socially dangerous elements'. This included leaders of Belarusian workers unions, and members of the Belarusian intelligentsia.[16]

The Polish campaign against the 'Eastern Provinces' culminated in 1938 with a presidential decree on the relations between the government and the Orthodox Church. The result of this decree was the confirmation of the dominant theological and political role of the Catholic Church in Poland. A notable result being the new law that no Orthodox citizens of Poland would be entitled to own land.[17]

The Eastern half of Belarus was also to face a radical change in the 1930's. Lenin had died in 1924 leaving no obvious successor. What followed were political intrigues and manoeuvres, temporary alliances and betrayals. The result of which was the rise to dominance of the Georgian born Josef Stalin, General Secretary of the Communist Party of the Soviet Union. Significantly, Stalin also held the post of 'People's Commissar for Nationalities Affairs' from 1917 to 1923, and had written the book, 'Marxism and the National question', published in 1913. This work was praised by Lenin, and hugely influential in his policies towards the constituent republics of the USSR. Stalin had effectively taken control of the communist party and the USSR by 1928.

Shortly after Lenin's death, Stalin declared a strategy of 'socialism in one country'; this was in contradiction Trotsky's 'permanent revolution' and was intended to lead by example, the success of the USSR would give revolutionaries and progressive people across the world support and verification for their ideas. However, Stalin had learnt the lessons of the foreign 'intervention' during the civil war, and the savage defence of their homeland by the Poles. He argued that socialism could not be delivered by force to other nations, but must prove itself as a success. The result of this was the five-year plans. The economy was to be strictly centralised and controlled to make specific achievements within this time frame. Huge industrialisation programmes were to be launched, and speculation in the countryside would be brought to heel by the ending of the NEP, and the introduction of collectivisation.

Chapter 4. The 1930's: Collectivisation and Industrialisation.

"Collective farms must be preserved as they are the units which will always protect humans and help them. They are both political and administrative units, everything relies upon them today".[1] A.G. Lukashenko.

Stalin's drive to create a modern, industrial socialist country within a single generation was a bold step. The backward state of Russian industry combined with a countryside recovering from serfdom meant that the development needed was huge, and the fledgling USSR was required to make huge sacrifices to achieve these goals. The role of the industrial working class is of prime importance to Marxists, and thus industrialisation was to be grand, and rapid. Historian Ian Grey summarised the first, 1928, five year plan, as being not only a hugely ambitious industrial, and agrarian task, but also as being *"a challenge to the Russian nation;* [that] *summoned the people to a life of heroic endeavour"*.[2]

The plan certainly was challenging, and the cost of failure was not to be considered.

The Belarusian Soviet Socialist Republic, having been ravaged by war, certainly had a lot to gain from the planned development, but equally was required to undergo monumental upheaval to achieve it. Indeed Belarusian agriculture was yet to reach its pre First World War production levels. The situation was such that in the late 1920's Belarus was importing twice as much grain as it had needed to in 1913.[3]

The NEP achieved its initial aim, which was to release the country from the threat of starvation, but also allowed elements of the free market to return to Soviet lands. This created a situation where by 1927, almost three million peasants no longer owned any land, this was approximately 35% of the total peasant population.[4]

Who then owned the land, and was in a position to acquire it from other peasants? The answer to this question was to form the most controversial element of Soviet collectivisation. Under the NEP, a new higher class of peasant had emerged, those with larger, or more profitable areas of land, who were able to bring financial pressure to bear on their neighbours, and increase their smallholdings. The very basis of communist support in the countryside was the injustice of many peasants working for a few landowners, and yet ten years after the revolution such a position was re-emerging. Throughout the Soviet Union approximately six per-cent of peasants managed to enrich themselves so. This class of 'higher peasants', who by 1926 were in control of 20% of the marketable Soviet wheat,[5] were to be known in the USSR as the 'Kulak' class.

In order to achieve socialism, and also to free the towns from the financial manoeuvring and whims of the Kulaks, Stalin and the Communist Party established themselves two goals in the countryside, firstly collectivisation, and secondly the 'liquidation of the Kulaks as a class'.

The relatively backward nature of Belarusian agriculture meant that the definition of a Kulak was stretched to accommodate the middle peasants too. Despite less than five per-cent of peasant households being defined as Kulak in 1927, almost 15 per-cent of the same peasant households were marked for 'de-Kulakisation' in the early 1930's.[6] This was in part due to the governments desire to remove all vestiges of the free market, and also as a means to push peasants into the collective farms.

Benefits to collectivisation however certainly existed, even for the individual peasants. Machine Tractor Stations were established, wherein agricultural machinery could be used by the collective farmers, and instruction given in its use and maintenance. This was seen to be a direct and clear benefit for the rural workers in supplying the foodstuffs for industrialisation. The leap forward was obvious, and Soviet propaganda made a great deal of the Russian peasant having finally left the middle ages and entered the twentieth century within the period of one five year plan.

The collective farms were also more than simply a base for large scale agricultural production. The collectives also contained schools, and provided access to colleges, as well as being host to simple medical clinics. The collective farms created a semi-urban environment in a rural setting. Despite the hardships the Belarusians collectivised at an accelerated pace. In some areas 86% of Belarusian peasant households had collectivised by February 1930.[7] Despite only a 57% average for the USSR as a whole.[8]

Collectivisation was not actually compulsory, joining was up to the individual, but as the collective farms were established and prospered, the benefit was obvious. During the initial period of collectivisation significant numbers of peasants in the USSR had actually left collective farms, and it was propaganda and economics, not force that was used to entice them back.

The drive to collectivise was officially completed in1937. The expropriation of property from the Kulaks was also accompanied by their relocation to remote areas of the USSR, where they would be able to work, but never again pose any threat to the new government and its plans. The justification for this used by the government, and its supporters was that in the USSR some 80% of the population lived in the countryside, and to allow a rural bourgeoisie to exist would have prevented any establishment of socialism. Such methods were harsh, but to the new Soviet government, the Kulaks represented a potential 'fifth column' within the country would naturally oppose the construction of socialism. This was particularly important in the late 1930's with Fascism establishing itself as a political force in western Europe, with the destruction of the USSR as one of its core principles.

National interests and cultural development were now made clearly subordinate to those of the greater Soviet whole. With power being held in Moscow, this meant a greater Russian dominance in the fields of language and arts. The Belarusian intelligentsia, persecuted in Poland, also found themselves suspect in the BSSR, as any kind of national sentiment, and aspiration was deemed to be of a potentially counter-revolutionary, and anti-Soviet nature.

Belarusian poet Janka Kupala, and the President of the Belarusian Academy of Sciences, Usievalad Ihnatouski attempted suicide (Ihnatouski successfully) rather than face a Soviet trial for their parts in alleged 'National Democratic' attempts to remove Belarus from the Soviet Union.[9] The validity of these cases has never been proven, but the message was clear that the Belarusian Soviet Socialist Republic was to be Soviet and socialist first and Belarusian second.

The optimism of the 1920's, and the upsurge in Belarusian culture and language, was certainly brought to an almost halt in the 1930's. The reality of the work required in constructing socialism required dedication and sacrifice. The gains promised by the Revolution had their price, significantly in terms of any 'national deviation'. The Belarusians were to become increasingly 'Russified' from this era on. The Marxist goal of eliminating national, and religious differences was, like collectivisation, to be pushed through at an accelerated pace, with Russian language to serve as the first language of all Soviet citizens.

Some historians, and Belarusian nationalists regard the actions of the Soviet government in the 1930's as being a 'genocide' against the Belarusian culture and people. An example given by Jan Zaprudnik (1993) is that of Belarusian writers.128 of them having being arrested by 1937. The Writer's Union of Belarus subsequently was dominated by writers who wrote in Russian.[10] In 1933 a language reform was passed by the Soviet government that sought to more clearly define the Belarusian language. The result, unsurprisingly, was that the Belarusian language was made closer to Russian. Also the use of the Latin alphabet for Belarusian words was officially replaced with Cyrillic. The language reform also negated the use of Belarusian at higher official places, and even within higher education.

The prime goal of the first five-year plans was the development of heavy industry. The collectivisation of agriculture was to feed this, and the removal of nationalist sentiments was to lay the ideological foundation. Indeed mass migration occurred across the vast territories of the USSR as new industries were founded, and diversity in language, and ethnic schisms were certainly obstacles to the completion of industrialisation.

The BSSR faced an enormous task in industrialising. As an area neglected by the Tsar's government, and ravaged by war, the republic lacked almost all of the basic infrastructure required to develop heavy industry. Particularly considering the ambitious nature of the first five-year plan, which called for more than a tripling of total industrial output. The response from the government was to send qualified workers and specialists from across the Soviet Union to Belarus. As well as this human materiel, tonnes of metal, oil, and coal were imported. Significantly the vast majority of the specialists sent, came from Moscow, Leningrad (as Petrograd was renamed in1924) and Kharkov.[11] This is an important fact, as it meant that the first major migration into Belarus was primarily from Russian cities (Kharkov lies on the north eastern tip of Ukraine bordering Russia, and has a large ethnic Russian population).

As with collectivisation the Belarusians made progress quickly with the task of building industry where none had previously existed. The first five-year plan period saw the successful completion of seventy nine large scale industrial enterprises. A further seventy four factories were built on the basis of older, smaller workshops. To help in powering all of this a large hydroelectric power station was built in the Mogilev region. The result was an over fulfilment of the plan, with industrial output reaching 4.8 times that of 1927.[12] This increase was also noted to be well beyond the average industrial increase throughout the USSR, but as historian David Marples notes, the fact that there was almost no industry in Belarus prior to 1928 must be a factor.[13] The fact that this was achieved however, should not be played down. Having such a rudimentary base means that statistical improvement was inevitable with investment, but the scale of the industrialisation was certainly impressive in its own right.

Significantly, the USSR was also borrowing very little foreign capital, and it was the severe hardships endured and labour of the workers that earned the achievements. The Soviet propaganda machine emphasised that the fruits of the labour would justify the sacrifices being made. Propaganda justified, and verified communist methods, by comparing the huge advances in the USSR, in contrast to the terrible economic depression occurring in the capitalist countries. The ruthless methods of the Poles in suppressing their Belarusian and Ukrainian territories also were used to highlight the investment that the USSR was putting into all of its peoples. Despite the increase in the urban population, and industrial sector, Belarus still remained overwhelmingly an agricultural society, albeit a collectivised one. Factories employed three times as many people as they had done previously, but of the total population, workers still made up less than six percent. The trend toward urban growth looked set to continue with each five-year plan, and as the collective farms became more efficient, this growth seemed sustainable. However in 1939, one of the most significant products of the Great Depression was to change all that.

Hitler had been elected in 1933, in a Germany crippled by war reparations and torn with internal strife. Hitler's notorious anti-Semitism provided a scapegoat for Germany's war defeat. He was elected on an ultra nationalist platform, his promises were to make Germany strong, through the removal of racial enemies, and the destruction of Bolshevism. On September the first 1939, Hitler invaded Poland, seventeen days later, as the Polish resistance crumbled, the Red Army entered eastern Poland, and re-occupied western Belarus and Ukraine.* Conflict between the German, and Soviet forces was postponed by the mutual non-aggression pact signed earlier in the

---

* Territory occupied by Poland following the 1919 invasion.

year.

The non-aggression pact, and partition of Poland are controversial events. Anti-Soviet writers refer to the pact as an alliance, whereas the Soviet line, and the reality, is that it was purely a manoeuvre to gain time to prepare for the inevitable war with fascism. What is significant however is that the Red Army entered Poland after the Polish army was essentially defeated, and certainly did not split the Polish defence, nor did the Red Army occupy any areas that were regarded as Polish before 1919. Indeed the official reason given for the Red Army's entry was: *"To protect the life and property of the population of west Ukraine, and west Belarus."*[14]

The arrival of the Red Army was greeted enthusiastically by most western Belarusians, as they had lived under direct persecution in Poland: with around ten thousand Belarusians having been imprisoned during the thirties for belonging to 'communist groups'.[15]

The Soviet authorities were quick to reunite Belarus and set about 'Sovietising' the western half too. At this time, the original border between the two halves remained closed, as each half was at markedly differing levels of development, plus the process of 'de-Kulakisation' and the rooting out of anti-Soviet elements in western Belarus had not yet begun.

Two groups had very different feelings on now coming under Soviet rule. Firstly the Poles, who had been landowners and bosses, were now likely to feel the backlash of their governments nationalist policies. Secondly the Jews of western Belarus, who had been spared Nazi occupation. Jewish life was developing well in the USSR, with the establishment of a Jewish Autonomous Region near the Manchurian border in 1934. This autonomous region attracted Jews from across the Soviet Union, and even from around the world, however Jewish life in the Belarusian towns was firmly established, and many Belarusian Jews remained in the BSSR.

The rate of 'Sovietization' in western Belarus was set deliberately slower than the previous five year plans. Lessons had been learned by the government, and also the western Belarusians had been notably welcoming of the new regime. The Soviet government set about eliminating unemployment, as well as establishing the essential social and economic structures for the establishment of socialism. Schools were built, and the Soviet system also created vocational training schools and specific trade schools. Education was viewed as a right in the Soviet Union, and not just for children. In order to complete vast industrial expansion, and improve agricultural efficiency, all of the people required at least a rudimentary education, and also new skills.

Communism is a progressive ideology, and as such the role of women was given greater importance and recognition in the Soviet Union than in other countries of the time. Significantly pre-school child care centres were opened, enabling women to be freed from their traditional domestic, and child rearing role. It should be noted in a study of Communist Albania, historian James S O'Donnell observed that the workload of women was often simply doubled. The career did not replace household tasks, but was added to them.[16] It could also be argued that the same is true of many women's lives in the 'free world' even now in the twenty first century.

Nonetheless the working people of western Belarus *"responded with enthusiasm and initiative to the concern shown by the new authorities"*.[17] The slower pace of change, with its positive effects was the prime reason for such sentiments. Over three thousand large farms were expropriated by the government and re-distributed to the peasants that worked them. The fact that this usually meant taking the land from Polish landowners, and giving it back to Belarusians made this a particularly popular policy. The majority of this confiscated land became collectivised. Western Belarus elected its own National Assembly in 1939, with 96.7% of the voters choosing unification with the USSR..[18] This level of support and the 'backwardness' of the west Belarusian nation and economy allowed for a repeat of the early years of the BSSR with cultural growth, and a raising of both the national, and a Soviet consciousness. Thus it can be seen that in the Communist Party's strategy, there appears to be a consistent element in its dealings with the 'nationalities'. Areas that had been subject to 'Great Russian chauvinism' or 'bourgeois rule' were firstly encouraged to recover their own identity, before being united by the greater socialist ideal. The re-unification of Belarus best illustrates this, but it must also be noted that the time scale was incredibly short. Nationalities were 'pushed' in all fields of their development at a particularly accelerated pace.

Chapter 5. The Great Patriotic War.

"Belarusians have never divided the Victory between nations and states. It is indivisible. Every participant of the anti–Hitler coalition made a weighty contribution in bringing nearer the long–awaited day".[1] A.G. Lukashenko.

The Second World War is known in the former Soviet countries as the 'Great Patriotic War' and for them it began in 1941. The border between the Soviet Union and Germany and her allies stretched some 3,720 miles from the Baltic to the Black Sea. War between the Soviet Union and Nazi Germany was all but inevitable. Not only are communism and nazism at opposite poles of the political compass, but also the Nazis believed they were already engaged in a racial war against the Jews, and other 'sub-humans' who threatened to 'pollute' their society. Amongst these sub-humans were the Slavs. The Nazis often termed communism, 'Judeo-Bolshevism', and referring to the 'living space' (lebensraum) policy in the east, one Nazi propaganda poster read, *"The Russians must die, that we may live"*.[2]

The controversial non-aggression pact of 1939 between the two governments gave Hitler the opportunity to invade western Europe, whilst Stalin moved his border with Germany dramatically to the west. Even Winston Churchill, who was an avowed anti-communist saw the strategic significance of the non-aggression pact to the Soviet Union. He declared on the first of October 1939: *"That the Russian armies should stand on this line was clearly necessary for the safety of Russia against the Nazi menace"*.[3]

At 03:45 on June the 22nd 1941, Nazi Germany and her allies invaded the Soviet Union. The declaration of war being delivered an hour later. The war began with a simultaneous massive air and artillery bombardment clearing the way for the huge ground assault of around five million troops. For Belarus the invasion was particularly shocking. Situated directly on the border with the third Reich, Belarus felt the unexpected and immediate impact of artillery and bombing when other parts of the Soviet Union weren't even aware that they were at war. The German Army Group Centre had the task of capturing Moscow, and the first obstacle in their way was the Belarusian Soviet Socialist republic. The German advance was swift, and the battle hardened German forces were able to brush away the majority of the initial Soviet resistance. A notable exception was right on the border at the fortress of Brest. The Germans hoped to capture this fortress within the first hour of the invasion, but were met by stiff resistance, and a siege began. Fighting went on until the end of July, by which time the Germans had occupied almost the entire BSSR. The eastern cities of Gomel and Mozyr held out until December, but by the end of the year Belarus was entirely under German control. The Soviet authorities, despite the panic and confusion at the outbreak of hostilities, managed to evacuate one and a half million people, as well as dismantling and transporting over one hundred factories and enterprises. At this time there was also the execution of political prisoners who could not be evacuated, and whom the Soviets feared would become agents of the Nazis.

The people trapped behind German lines in Belarus were uncertain of what this new occupation would bring. The German occupation of 1916-1918 had been largely conducted in a decent and peaceable manner, certainly in contrast to the subsequent Polish invasion. However it would soon become clear that the Germans were not to be benevolent or even passive liberators. The German plan for Belarus extended far beyond the military ones. Re-settlement areas for the overpopulated German cities were to be in the east, specifically Poland, Ukraine and Belarus. Nazi 'racial doctors' decreed that up to 25% of Belarusians may be of enough racial purity to be 'Germanised' whilst the remainder (Some Seven and a half million people) were to be "*destroyed*".[4]

What was for certain was the fate of the large Belarusian Jewish population. At the end of July 1941 as well as prisoner of war camps, the Nazis established a Jewish Ghetto in Minsk. This ghetto had over 100,000 inmates, and over the course of the year large numbers of European Jews were 're-settled' into this ghetto.[5] The Minsk Ghetto was headed by Yefim Stolerovitch, he recounted after the war that though the Germans did find individual collaborators that, "*they were the exception and not the rule. The dominant characteristic of the Belarusian population was one of friendship and sympathy toward the Jews*".[6]

An example of this sentiment was seen on the 21st of July 1941, when the Germans roped a group of forty five Jews together in a pit and then ordered thirty Belarusian prisoners of war to bury them alive. The prisoners of war refused, and subsequently the Germans shot all seventy five.[7] Such a gesture, although futile, showed the result of the long history of co-operation in Belarus, coupled with the success of the communist's anti-racist education. This was in stark contrast to the overt anti-Semitism that was reported by the Germans in Polish, Baltic and Ukrainian territories.

Heinrich Himmler himself visited the Minsk ghetto in 1941, and as a result of observing the shooting of one hundred Jews, he was physically sick. The problem, he decided, was not the action, but rather the method. Later the same day he was to visit a mental asylum, where the patients were to be murdered too. Himmler acknowledged the demoralising effect on soldiers of shooting prisoners on a daily basis, so a new 'more sanitised' technique was required. The hastily created solution was for two concrete bunkers outside of Minsk to be filled with the patients, and dynamited. The results were disastrous, with injured and maimed mental patients escaping across the countryside.

However the concrete bunkers gave the Germans the idea, which was to become policy, of using poison gas. Two days later, in Mogilev, eastern Belarus, around thirty mental patients were successfully murdered when they were locked in a room, into which car exhaust fumes were directed. As mentioned earlier, the German vision for Belarus did not limit genocide to the Jews. Yet there was also to be 'Germanisation'. The Belarusian nationalists, ironically, seemed to be the most likely to be spared, and fall into this category. Under the auspices of the Germans the nationalists organised themselves into a 'Belarusian Mutual Aid Society', which opened schools, and established a paramilitary 'Belarusian Defence Corps'. The nationalists used these organisations for anti-Soviet propaganda, and began flying the white, red, white flag, and displaying the 'Pahonia'* emblem.

These efforts were significant by their intention to separate Belarusian from Russian life. Education was compulsory for all children between seven and fourteen, with the strict exception of Jews, whilst Russian language texts were also banned. The nationalists were essentially used by the Germans to promote Belarusian life and culture with a western European, or Germanic outlook as opposed to a Slavic or Soviet one. The collaborators however were very few, and the occupation of Belarus was predominantly characterised by hostility, and particularly by guerrilla warfare. The 'partisan' movement sprang up sporadically throughout late 1941. The Communist Party of the BSSR

---

* Pahonia- A knight on horseback emblem. First used by the Grand Duchy of Lithuania in 1366.

created a directive on the first of July, 'Concerning the development of partisan warfare in the rear of the enemy'. Two days later Stalin addressed the nation in a speech broadcast to the whole of the USSR by radio in which he said: "*In the occupied region, conditions must be made unbearable for the enemy and all his accomplices. They must be hounded and annihilated at every step, and all their measures frustrated*".[8] Spontaneous partisan units did spring up, many formed from the nuclei of isolated groups of soldiers cut off behind enemy lines by the speed of the German advance. Stalin wanted the partisan movement to be co-ordinated, and needed the intelligence that they could supply. In order to achieve this the security service, the NKVD, was given the task of supplying the partisans, as well as ensuring their loyalty to the Soviet regime. In some areas, notably in Ukraine, partisan groups formed who would fight both the Germans, and the Soviets. The German policy in the occupied areas was one of absolute domination, with extreme brutality and violence towards the civilian population, as both warning, and reprisal. If a German soldier were murdered or military equipment stolen the authorities would frequently take hostages from the local population, and just as frequently simply murder them. This was to play a huge part in the destruction of German plans in the east.

One of the better known examples of German methods in Belarus is that of the village of Khatyn. This village was burnt to the ground in 1944 by the German Army, the villagers first being rounded up and locked in a church, and burnt to death along with the entire village. Alexander Lukashenko described this ethnic murder in 2004 as being, "*an unhealed wound in the heart of our Motherland*".[9] The village of Khatyn is just one example of what was a painfully clear message, that despite the propaganda of the nationalists, the Germans felt no compassion for Belarusian statehood, or indeed the Belarusian people. Partisans in Belarus were hugely effective, they were able to make use of the vast Belarusian forests and marshes for concealment, and by 1943 there were 75,000 partisans active in Belarus,[10] who controlled some 60% of the territory.[11] In this same year the partisans managed to assassinate the German 'General-Kommissar' in charge of Belarusian territory Wilhelm Kube.

1943 was a turning point in the war, the once mighty German forces were now being pushed over to the defensive. The Germans Sixth Army in Stalingrad surrendered on February the 2nd. Whilst the

Atlantic war had turned against the U-boats, and in North Africa the German Afrika Korps surrendered on May the 12th.

The over-stretched Germans looked to the occupied territories as a means to prop up their war machine. Young Belarusians were sent west as forced labourers, and recruiting began to raise an 'anti-Bolshevik Belarusian army'. The infamous SS also recruited, and coerced 'volunteers' from Belarus who went on to form part of the 30th Waffen SS Grenadier division. This unit was used primarily against Partisans, but in the face of the Red Armies advance the Germans moved them to France, to fight the French resistance instead. The Germans were well aware of the 'unreliable' nature of coerced troops, particularly in the east where retribution from the Soviet authorities was severe for those who had collaborated, and even for those who had been passive. The Belarusian nationalists and collaborators were led by Radasłau Astrouski, a man who frequently changed his allegiances in a long career of opportunism. He was evacuated to Germany in 1944 along with his family, and after the war he emigrated to the USA, where he established the Belarusian Central Rada to serve as an anti-Soviet 'government in exile'.

By 1944 there were over 300,000 partisans fighting in Belarus, their numbers buoyed by the brutality of the German occupation, and pending liberation. July the 3rd 1944 saw the Red Army force the Germans out of Minsk and twenty-five days later the frontier city of Brest, was re-taken. The liberation of Belarus had been carried out in a massive Soviet offensive code-named 'Bagration', which combined the efforts of more than 1.7 million Soviet troops, together with the partisans of Belarus. Soviet troops captured Berlin and Germany unconditionally surrendered following Hitler's suicide on the 3rd of May 1945.

The destruction wrought on Belarus was immense, in terms of human life, and of infrastructure. Over 2.5 million Belarusian civilians were killed in the war, with the latest estimates showing that one in three citizens of the republic died. This is startling for such a small country, as it is more than the British, US, and French casualties combined.[12] The war also decimated the Jewish population of Belarus. With 80,000 being interned in the Minsk ghetto, where many died due to the terrible conditions, (space was limited to six square feet per person). Survivors of the ghetto had been sent to the Sobibor concentration camp in Poland where some six thousand Belarusian Jews were gassed. The Ghetto itself had been 'liquidated' by the Germans on the

21st of October 1943, with 2000 Jews who could not be transported west being murdered in 'gas vans' at Maly Trostinec East of Minsk.[13] Every city in Belarus had been destroyed by savage fighting, and the German 'scorched earth' policy. Added to this, some six hundred villages had been burned to the ground by the Germans and many, like Khatyn, burned with their residents. It is notable that two hundred of these villages simply ceased to exist, with life never returning to them. The population of Belarus took thirty years to regain its pre-war level.[14]

Chapter 6. Rebuilding and Recovery of the Belarusian Soviet Socialist Republic: 1945-1985.

"Only cohesive and strong-minded people could win in the most atrocious war in mankind's history, survive all the adversities and severities of the post-war devastation, raise the ruined factories and plants, towns and villages".[1] A.G. Lukashenko.

The Second World War had ravaged and then split Europe. The gains of the Red Army were transformed into areas of Soviet political influence and ultimately control. The countries of Eastern Europe fell under Soviet occupation, and as they sought to rebuild themselves post war, they almost inevitably moved towards a socialist path.

Stalin did not want to see bourgeois states on the borders of the Soviet Union, who could be potentially hostile, in what was to become the 'cold war'. Hence countries like Poland, who had shown themselves to be anti-communist found themselves with 'puppet' Socialist governments. The Soviets held no illusions as to the loyalty of these new satellite states, and a significant Red Army presence was maintained in each.

The situation in parts of the USSR was similar. Areas that had been occupied by the Germans and their allies were regarded with some suspicion, and investigations were carried out by the NKVD. The welcome that the Germans had received in some areas (particularly the Baltic states and western Ukraine), combined with collaboration, and even armed assistance had not gone unnoticed. The situation in the Ukraine, with its strong nationalist movement was so severe that it took until the early 1950's for anti-Soviet partisans to be eliminated by the NKVD and Red Army. The German retreat from Belarus had also seen an exodus of collaborators. The Belarusian nationalists and their families fled west, rather than attempt to explain their actions to the NKVD.

The Waffen SS troops from Belarus surrendered to the US 3rd Army in France. These troops together with other collaborators, and those forced labourers in Germany who chose not to return to the USSR were re-settled in the US, Canada, and Australia. The leadership of the Belarusian pro-Nazi 'Central Rada' primarily settled in the USA, where they simply continued their anti-Soviet propaganda.

Rebuilding the BSSR was of great importance to the Soviet Union.

Agricultural output was desperately needed in a country still under strict food rationing. Plus the necessity of establishing order in the satellite countries of eastern Europe, required a great deal of assistance and aid from the USSR. Belarus and Ukraine were critical for this, in that both republics were on the immediate borders of Europe. Railways, canals, and roads were repaired and constructed to carry material west, and also to transport dismantled German industry back to the USSR.

The resistance shown by Belarus during the war was rewarded with separate representation at the newly formed United Nations. The reason given by Stalin for the necessity of both the Belarusian, and Ukrainian Soviet Socialist Republics, to sit alongside the Soviet Union at the UN was *"because of the devastation they suffered and their input into beating Nazi Germany"*.[2] Historians question the actual reason behind this demand, with some speculating that it was out of concern for the upsurge in nationalism exhibited during the war. However it would appear more likely, considering Stalin's usual approach to dissent, that he sought not to placate the nationalists with such flattery, but rather that he saw an opportunity for two guaranteed pro-Soviet votes within the UN. Winston Churchill surprisingly supported the idea, going so far as to say, *"my heart goes out to White Russia"*.[3] President Roosevelt, despite being more amiable to Stalin, disagreed, and had to be talked around by Churchill. One of the stronger arguments that could be put forward in favour of entry to the UN for Belarus was the contribution of the partisans to the overall victory. Partisans in Belarus killed, captured or wounded half a million Germans.[4] In comparison, German losses in the African, and Italian campaigns combined were less at around 411,000.[5]

After the war, Belarus had little time to rest. The Soviet construction campaigns of the thirties were started afresh. Industrialisation began, again from nothing, whilst collectivisation had to be carried through in western Belarus. Collectivisation of this region took until 1952 to be completed.[6] Over four thousand 'Kulak' families were also deported during this period.[7] Confirming that despite the defeat of a foreign enemy was still to be no tolerance of internal ones. As well as these perceived 'class enemies' there were also very real armed enemies in the form of anti-Soviet terrorists, primarily made up of nationalists, and former collaborators. In western Belarus the NKVD carried out operations against, and liquidated *"814 anti-Soviet and armed bands"*.[8] These groups were found to be primarily Ukrainian and Polish nationalists as well as some former collaborators and criminals. In the period from the end of the war until Stalin's death in 1953, Belarus was characterised by intense rebuilding, and 'Sovietization'. The development of any national culture was perceived as being of secondary importance, and deviation from the centralised Soviet system was comparable to *"collaborationism during the war"*.[9] Like the death of Lenin, almost thirty years previous, Stalin's death created a power vacuum. Stalin had no evident successor, and there were already factions emerging within the leadership. The immediate aftermath saw a vying for power between the various Politburo members, particularly the former head of the NKVD, Lavrenti Beria, and Moscow Party Chief, Nikita Krushchev. Attempting to gain support, and promote themselves amongst the party nomenclature, concessions once again were given to the development of national interests. In Belarus a plenum of the party was held in June 1953, which intended to replace the head of the Belarusian Communist Party, N.S. Patolichev (who was a Russian), with his Belarusian deputy M.V. Zimiavin. The Russification of the Belarusian party was announced in a speech by Zimiavin at the Plenum to have been a mistake. Historian Jan Zaprudnik notes that in this speech Zimiavin highlighted the fact that despite an ethnic Belarusian population of 81%, they represented only 66.2% of the party organs.[10]

Despite this complaint, and the observation that all official business in Belarus was conducted in Russian, Zimiavin was unable to depose Patolichev. This was in part due to the fact that within the Belarusian party there were many deputies and workers who had been appointed for their Marxist-Leninist position, and 'reliability'. Also within the party there were grave concerns regarding the promotion of national interests that may work against the overall Soviet concerns. Russians of course had also assisted Belarus greatly in its industrialisation. Whilst propaganda portrayed the Red Army that liberated Belarus as being the Russian people coming to the aid of Belarusians.

By the end of 1953 Krushchev had outmanoeuvred the powerful but feared and unpopular Beria. Beria himself was shot, although the circumstances are disputed as to where and by whom. Krushchev began a process of relaxing the ideological leadership exercised by Stalin over the USSR, attempting to gain quick popularity by granting concessions; even to the Kulaks. Despite being Ukrainian, Krushchev had no intention of stopping the Russification of the nationalities.

Within Belarus former partisans rose to dominate the administration, with Kiril Mazurov, a former political instructor and partisan leader becoming first secretary of the Communist Party of Belarus between 1953 and 1965. Mazurov had a long career within the Soviet political system, and was a dedicated communist. He also believed that the Belarusian language ought to be preserved. At the 40th anniversary celebration of the BSSR in 1959, Mazurov gave his speech in Belarusian. Nikita Krushchev berated him during an intermission declaring that he *"couldn't understand a damned thing"*.[11] At the newly rebuilt Belarusian State University, Krushchev continued with: *"The sooner we all start speaking Russian the faster we shall build Communism"*.[12] The fact that Mazurov was able to go unpunished for showing this potential deviation from the Central Committee's policy says more about the high regard with which the partisans were held, rather than the liberalism of Krushchev.* The Partisan leaders were genuine heroes to the Belarusians, and the other Soviet nationalities too. Communist power was particularly secure and stable in Belarus throughout the post-war years. The state policy of the Soviet Union frequently mirrored or met with the approval of the Belarusian Republican interest. The reasons for this are complex, but what is important is that of the large military losses of the Soviet Union during the war, the ethnic Russians made up the larger part. This equates with the huge losses endured by Belarus. Secondly it should be noted that the Belarusians could directly associate the development of their Republic with the support from their Russian neighbours. The Soviet leadership knew that with Belarus lying on the western frontier it would be the first experience of the Soviet Union for many western and satellite state visitors. This meant that rebuilding in the Belarusian cities was impressive, with wide boulevards, grandiose war memorials, and large parks etc.

Mazurov himself was destined to advance through the party structure, leaving Belarus, and working in the Central Committee of the Communist Party of the Soviet Union in Moscow between 1964 and 1978. The man who succeeded him as first secretary of the Belarusian

---

* This is also contrary to Communist theory.

Communist Party was Pyotr Masherov, regarded to be Mazurov's leading Protégé. Masherov was another prominent former partisan, with an impressive war record. Formerly a schoolteacher, Masherov had taken to the woods following the German invasion and established an active partisan group. Masherov was loyal to the Soviet cause, and was awarded the highest award of the state, the title: 'Hero of the Soviet Union' in 1944. The Masherov era from 1965 until his death in 1980 is regarded as being a time of great growth and prosperity in Belarus. Masherov was a truly popular leader, and despite the 'stagnation' which affected the USSR under it's new leader Leonid Brezhnev*, the BSSR continued to grow in industrial and agricultural production.

The BSSR managed to more than double its gross industrial output between 1970 and 1980, again outstripping the other republics, and well above the all union average.[13]

Belarus had once again developed a successful industry from almost nothing, and additionally it was outperforming the other Soviet Republics. This was a source of great pride for the Belarusian people, with frequent reference being made to this success by Masherov and other party leaders.

Masherov gave a speech at the 25th congress of the Communist Party of the Soviet Union where he specifically praised the achievements in his own republic. In his report he declared that in the period of the last five year plan Belarusian national income had been raised by 47% with gross output ahead of predicted figures at 64%, and the plan had been achieved almost half a year early.[14] Despite the success of the Belarusian economy, and the praising of its people, Masherov made no great concessions to Belarusian language or culture. Indeed during the Masherov years the publication of books in Belarusian as opposed to Russian declined from 87% in 1960 to 12% in 1980.[15] This was representative of the general mood and direction in Belarus to become a showcase example of a Soviet Republic, as descried by historian Jan Zaprudnik as: "*Policies aimed at creating a new historic community- the Soviet people*".[16]

The drive toward creating a Soviet mindset and not a national one was particularly successful in Belarus. The leadership, predominantly

---

* Leonid Brezhnev served as General Secretary of the Communist Party of the Soviet Union from 1964 until 1982.

from the wartime partisans were easily able to illustrate the connection between nationalism and the crimes of the Nazis and their collaborators. Coupled to this the 1933 language reform had contributed to the creation of a 'Russified' Belarusian national character. National pride in Belarus was overwhelmingly a pride in Soviet Belarus, and its recent achievements. Whilst the Ukrainians and Russians had their folk heroes, generals and Cossacks, the Belarusians had the partisans and living examples to revere such as their athletes and cosmonauts. In an official guide to the BSSR the Belarusian national character was described as being: *"Courage and staunchness, modesty and industry, and a keen sense of internationalist duty"*.[17] These are typical Soviet era values and ideals, found in most propaganda and information books of the time. However it is notable that this national character is described as having been formed out of the Belarusian struggle for sovereignty and equality predating the 1917 Revolution. Thus Belarusian history, it is argued, naturally lent itself to the establishment of a socialist consciousness, and *that* is the true Belarusian culture and identity.

Masherov was a committed communist and as head of the Belarusian Party apparatus he worked so hard that in the Brezhnev administration there was concern that he may even be a nationalist! This concern however, was unfounded, and his hard-line approach to Soviet policy illustrates this. For example he was opposed to the 'peaceful co-existence' and 'détente' foreign policies regarding the struggle against imperialism and capitalism as being no area for compromise.

As the Brezhnev era reached its twilight years the stagnation in Soviet development had slowly led to an increase in corruption amongst the party officials. Masherov was an exception to this, he was honest and direct, and his popularity with the Soviet and particularly Belarusian people stemmed from this. In 1980 Masherov published his book 'Soviet Belarus' in which he openly criticised the arrogant and conceited party leadership. His criticism was carefully worded along Marxist-Leninist principles and showed his loyalty to the cause, but not to Brezhnev. Pyotr Masherov died in October 1980 when his car collided with a truck, despite having a police escort. His unexpected death and the unusual circumstances created rumours that Masherov was a potential candidate for leadership of the USSR, and that his death was a KGB operation to keep the ruling clique in power.

Many Belarusians look upon the Masherov period with nostalgia.

The industry of the BSSR was diverse and by Soviet standards of good quality. As well as producing the 'Belarus' tractors which sold all over the world (and still do), Belarus also produced precision instruments, particularly in the scientific and military fields. In the 1980's Belarus was able to boast that of the important fields of scientific research the Belarusian *"Academy of Sciences, which comprises 32 research centres, holds leading place, not only in the USSR but also in the world"*.[18] By this time the social field had also seen huge investment, with the establishment of just under 10,000 schools and 30 institutes of higher education.[19] Minsk itself had around 200 libraries.[20] Education was a source of great pride in the BSSR, as before the 1917 revolution there had been almost complete illiteracy. A survey in 1982 found that 87% of the population aged over seven used libraries regularly, describing the reading of books in Belarus as *"a universal need"*.[21] Free public services such as healthcare and education was a constitutionally protected right throughout the Soviet Union, and in Belarus this created an educated and able workforce in one of the most politically stable climates within the USSR. Belarus however was clearly becoming an exception to the rule. The eighteen years of stagnation under Brezhnev, enabled by the re-introduction of rank and privileges under Krushchev had taken their toll. Disillusionment and cynicism were the prevailing attitudes of people throughout the USSR. To further complicate an already difficult international and domestic situation Brezhnev, in almost his last act before dying of a heart attack in 1982 made the decision (without discussing it with the Politburo) to send Soviet troops to Afghanistan to support its Revolutionary Government.

The instability of the Soviet Union was exacerbated in 1982 by the typical power vacuum and struggle that followed the death, or downfall of any of its leaders. After Brezhnev the former KGB chief Yuri Andropov took power, but died in 1984, to be replaced by Konstantin Chernenko, who himself died in 1985. What followed was to lead to the most significant era of change for the USSR since the Great Patriotic War. On March 11th 1985, Mikhail Gorbachev was elected General Secretary of the Communist Party of the Soviet Union.

Chapter 7. Perestroika, Glasnost and the end of the Soviet Union.

"The break-up of the Union of Soviet Socialist Republics will undoubtedly occupy one of the leading places on the list of geopolitical catastrophes".[1] A.G. Lukashenko.

Like the end of the Russian Empire before it, the collapse of the Soviet Union in its final years was predictable, and almost inevitable. When Hitler had described the USSR of 1941 as a *"rotten structure"* which *"one good kick would send crashing down"* he had been all too wrong. However by 1986 he probably would have been right.

Mikhail Gorbachev took power over a very unstable and disaffected Soviet Union, with the political apparatus becoming increasingly polarised between 'hard-liners and reformers'. Gorbachev believed that some reform was necessary to revitalise the Soviet economy, and referred to Lenin's New Economic Policy as justification for the introduction of competition in industry. The communist hard-liners were appalled, as Gorbachev sacrificed one of the October Revolution's greatest achievements, the guarantee of full employment in the USSR. In return for citing Lenin use of the NEP, the hard-liners quoted Lenin back, from his book, 'What is to be Done?' Lenin had declared: *"The only choice is- either bourgeois ideology or socialist ideology. There is no middle course".*[2]

Ultimately Gorbachev's reforms were acknowledged by most, to be necessary to save the USSR from immediate economic collapse, and breaking apart. Gorbachev was also generally popular with the people, as he was young (the only leader of the Soviet Union to have been born after the Revolution), healthy, and also he promised to withdraw Soviet troops from Afghanistan.

The policies of *perestroika* (reform) and *glasnost* (openness) did not strike Belarus a destabilising blow, as could be seen in the collapse of the Soviet satellite states of eastern Europe. Instead in Belarus a re-evaluation of history took place, people were able to openly discuss their history, without the threat of being accused of anti-Soviet activity. The Stalin era was of great importance to the people of the USSR, as it had been a time of great progress with victory in the war, and also one that had seen de-Kulakisation and the purging of the party apparatus. Krushchev's clumsy denunciation of Stalin at the Communist Party's 20th congress only added to the difficulties in assessing this era. Stalin had gone from being untouchable, to unmentionable. The victims of trials and purges were rehabilitated, many posthumously, but no real study of the time had been conducted in the Soviet Union. Glasnost changed this, and people were encouraged to write of their experiences in an attempt for understanding and genuine openness within the USSR. The 110th anniversary of the birth of Stalin in 1989 gave rise to a wave of arguments and debates concerning his role in Soviet history. A booklet was published with a collection of such sentiments as expressed in letters to Soviet periodicals, and the comments of Belarusians are enlightening. The general theme of these letters is one of a questioning of the methods of Stalin, but not of the Soviet cause. One writer from Minsk is concerned with the inherent risk of leadership personality cults, whilst another asks the question, to what degree the Soviet people are *"Stalin's heirs"*.[3] These comments are notable in a collection of letters from all over the Soviet Union which express either complete support of Stalin personally, or damning criticism of him, and what he stood for. The Belarusian letters are distinctly abstract, and almost philosophical compared to the emotional and dogmatic submissions from the other republics. This is an indication of the level of success of the policy of creating 'Soviet citizens' and not Belarusians in the BSSR.

Despite this there still existed a national intelligentsia who longed for autonomy from Moscow, and watching the emergence of independence movements in the neighbouring Poland, Ukraine and Baltic states chose nationalism as a means to this end. This resulted in the founding of the Belarusian Popular Front (BPF) in late 1988.

Another contributing factor to the foundation of and support for the BPF was the Chernobyl Nuclear power station disaster in 1986. On the 25th and 26th of April 1986 the fourth reactor at the Chernobyl nuclear power station needed to be shut down for routine maintenance, at the same time an experiment was to be carried out into the effectiveness of the reactors backup safety generators. In a series of errors the power level was reduced too rapidly, requiring the control rods to be pulled out further than normal. The cooling water pumps were then turned on at too high a rate necessitating the complete removal of the control rods, meaning the reactor was now running in a highly unstable state. The water turbine was switched off, and the resulting heat rise caused the water to boil, with large pockets of steam forming in the pipes. The reactor operators now realised the scale of the problem facing them and pressed the emergency shutdown button, and tried to manually re-insert the control rods. However the slow rate of the rod insertions coupled with their poor design meant that the nuclear reaction was increasing all the time, and had generated such energy that the control rod channels warped, with the rods themselves jammed about a third of the way in. The fuel rods then began to melt as the power rose further, and a huge steam explosion occurred, blowing the lid off the reactor, and also a hole in the roof. The sudden introduction of oxygen provided by the open ceiling ignited a graphite fire, and radioactive gases freely passed out into the atmosphere.

The immediate reaction to the disaster was woefully inadequate. The reactor operators did not have access to precision monitoring equipment, and were not aware of the colossal scale of the radioactive poisoning, nor did the fire crews who put out the blaze. Only 24 hours later when two people had died and over fifty more were hospitalised with radiation sickness did it become clear that a catastrophic leak had occurred. This delay meant that areas surrounding the reactor were evacuated much later than would have been recommended. Although Chernobyl was located in northern Ukraine, the prevailing wind on the day meant that 60% of the fallout was carried into Belarus. The Soviet authorities had not only under prepared the plant for such an event, but also kept it secret as it happened. The first indication that there was a problem came from abroad, when Swedish nuclear plant workers in a routine safety check were found to have radioactive particles on their clothes. The following inquiry discovered that the Swedish reactor was fine, and that the particles had been carried north from the Soviet Union.

It was at this point that the new Soviet leader and advocate of 'openness' had to acknowledge that something terrible had occurred. It took eighteen days for Gorbachev to publicly speak of the disaster, and in his speech he was angrier with certain *"Western politicians"* who he accused of attempting to *"defame the Soviet Union"*.[4] This was a notable lapse in Gorbachev's attempts to introduce openness in Soviet political life. Historian David Marples summarises the effect of Chernobyl on Soviet society thus: *"Chernobyl was directly responsible for the de-*

velopment- albeit gradually- of a more open society, which eventually spread to Belarus, the republic most affected by the radioactive fallout".[5]

It took almost three years for the full scale of the disaster to be announced, and the Soviet authorities were also slow in recognising its impact on Belarus. By 1990 only 4% of the funds allocated to dealing with Chernobyl had been given to Belarus.[6]

A 'cultural Chernobyl' occurred in 1988 with the discovery of mass graves in the Kurapaty forest North of Minsk. The graves themselves were discovered by archaeologist Zyanon Paznyak, who soon went on to become head of the BPF.

Paznyak is a Belarusian nationalist, and his immediate declaration was that the graves were those of victims of Stalin in the 1930's. The Soviet government had little chance in the era of perestroika to simply ignore the discovery of mass graves, or to 'cover it up'. A government commission was established with the specific function of exhuming the bodies, finding witnesses and uncovering the truth about Kurapaty.

The Kurapaty revelations were deeply unsettling to the BSSR and even the USSR as a whole. If the people were indeed victims of Soviet purges, then it was possible that the unpunished perpetrators were still alive. The inquiry was followed with great interest by Belarusians and for the first time Soviet policy towards Belarus was questioned on a mass scale. The commission that headed the inquiry was made up of a broad spectrum of 'experts' and concerned individuals. Paznyak himself sat alongside the representatives from the government, and the KGB, as well as former partisans and other war veterans.

The commission uncovered the following facts: There were around 510 separate burial places with between 50 to 60 people per grave. Making an approximate total of 30,000 dead. The bodies were all found to have a single bullet hole to the back of the head (a method of execution employed by both the Germans and NKVD). The Forest was also noted to be of around 40 years of age, meaning it was probably planted after the war. NKVD records were also found to be lacking in any reference to the Kurapaty victims, (although the NKVD did not keep records of all burial sites). The Commission also had eye witness reports of the executions, and in a contested verdict declared that the dead were indeed murdered between 1937 and 1941 by Stalin's NKVD. As stated, the verdict was not unanimous; indeed several questions were raised, with some members refusing to sign the official conclusion. Former partisans and others testified to the Germans carrying out executions of German and Polish Jews in the area. Another factor was that former partisan, Maria Osipava confirmed that there was no forest at Kurapaty until after the war. The significance of the forest being post war is that the NKVD were particularly unlikely to carry out such a mass murder in open fields by a major city.[7] The evidence both for and against the Kurapaty mass graves being victims of Soviet rule have strengths and flaws. The real truth may never be known, but the majority of the evidence, and the strength of the popular opinion questioning the ailing Soviet government meant that the accepted view was that Kurapaty represents victims of the Stalin regime, and not of the Germans. The issue of Kurapaty was not over however, and in 1993, the case was re-examined by the independent Republic of Belarus' government in light of doubts over the original findings. What was certain however was the impact of both Chernobyl, and Kurapaty on the Belarusian consciousness. It had become clear that the Soviet Union was no longer the superpower it had once been, and despite the achievements of the BSSR, the rest of the Union was crumbling.

Belarus in some ways was a victim of its own success. Before the revolution, Belarusian territory was the most illiterate area in Europe. The Soviet years established schools, universities, libraries, and cultural institutions. The Belarusian people became highly educated, and had a high level of political awareness. The political education of all Soviet citizens took place from an early age, with youth organisations such as the 'Pioneers' and the 'Komsomol' instilling Soviet patriotism and a simple understanding of Marxism-Leninism. Of course as the introduction of glasnost allowed a greater degree of questioning of the system, it became clear that the Soviet hierarchy was not following the egalitarian rhetoric it espoused. Perestroika's economic policies too were an obvious compromise with the principles of Karl Marx's book 'Capital'.

The Gorbachev years introduced a revival in national interests across the Soviet Union, and Belarus was no different. Again the issue of the Belarusian language was raised. In 1990 the Supreme Soviet of the BSSR finally conceded to declaring Belarusian the official language of the Republic. This was seen as a huge success for the BPF, and was also interpreted as a move towards greater independence from Moscow. Indeed in the subsequent elections to the Supreme Soviet in Belarus, members of the 'pro-democracy bloc' stood and were elected, taking 14% of the seats. This may seem a small number, but the impact was huge. Across the Soviet Union the constituent republics were all undergoing political turmoil, with independence high on their agendas.

Stanislav Shushkevich became the elected National Deputy for Belarus in March 1990, and immediately set about creating a coalition of anti-'conservative' politicians. Amongst this coalition were communists, industrialists, agrarians and the BPF.

The BPF were unique in this group in that they not only called for independence from the USSR, but also sought the introduction of 'Western style democracy', and the introduction of a market economy. The Belarusian declaration of independence did not come of its own accord, but rather after the declarations of Lithuania, Ukraine, and most significantly, Russia. The fact that Russia had withdrawn from the USSR meant that effectively the head had been removed from the body. It can be noted that once again Belarus failed to take the initiative in the issue on its own sovereignty, as had happened at the end of the Russian Empire. On the 27th of July 1990 the BSSR declared independence from what was left of the USSR. The Communist Party was still the dominant faction in the Supreme Soviet, and the republic still retained its Soviet system. This however changed a year later following the disastrous attempted coup in Moscow by communists, hoping to preserve Soviet government, and restore the Soviet Union. Belarus saw mass demonstrations against the political violence in Russia, but as a final nail in the Soviet coffin, Mikhail Gorbachev resigned as leader of the Communist Party and his final decree in August 1991 was to declare a suspension of all Communist Party activity. Following Gorbachev's lead, Belarusian Prime Minister Viacheslav Kebich officially suspended the Communist Party of Belarus on August the 28th 1991. This left Belarus in a political limbo, whilst neighbouring Republics simply broke away and declared themselves independent, Belarus still functioned as a Soviet Socialist Republic. An extraordinary session of the Supreme Soviet of Belarus was held on September the 17th, lasting two days, and resulted in the promotion of Shushkevich to chairman speaker of the parliament, and a full proclamation of independence.

The Soviet economy had been built around the entire Union, and going it alone was a hard option for most of the republics. In an attempt to protect each new nation from total economic collapse, a new union was created, this time called the Commonwealth of Independent States (CIS). The CIS was created in Belarus at a country house in Belavezha. The chief architects of this commonwealth were the Russian President Boris Yeltsin, Ukrainian President Leonid Kravchuk, with Stanislav Shushkevich representing Belarus. The Belavezha Accords could only officially declare the end of the Soviet Union after each of the constituent governments had voted to adopt them. The vote in Belarus was all but unanimous, with only one member of the Belarusian parliament voting against the final dissolution of the Soviet Union. That one member was Alexander Lukashenko.

Chapter 8. Alexander Lukashenko: A Short Biography.

"Belarus is our common home and everyone should feel warm and comfortable here. All of us are united by the noble goal – strong and prosperous Belarus".[1]
A.G. Lukashenko.

Alexander Grigoryevich Lukashenko was born in August 1954 in the village of Kopys. This lies in the Orsha district of the Vitebsk region in eastern Belarus. This area lies very close to the Russian border, and along with Gomel in the south east is notable for its predominant use of the Russian language. Lukashenko was raised by his mother only, it is known that his father had fought in the Great Patriotic War, but not why he left his family. Lukashenko would not have been unique growing up in the 1950's without a father as the losses in the war had devastated many families. Kopys is an urban settlement, but the Lukashenko's were a peasant family. Lukashenko credits his hard working nature, and perseverance to the experience of growing up under tough circumstances, with a high level of responsibility placed on him from an early age. Despite the guarantee of employment and education in the USSR, hard work was still required to survive.

Lukashenko has always been a keen reader, and took his education very seriously, as well as developing a competitive nature in the field of sports. He graduated from the Village Alexandria Secondary School, before going on to study history at the Mogilev Pedagogical Institute. He graduated in 1975 with teaching qualifications in both history and social studies. After graduation Lukashenko served two years in the Soviet frontier troops of the KGB. The frontier troops were particularly respected and trusted soldiers, working as they did right on the borders of the USSR. Lukashenko served as a 'zampolit' (political instructor) and held the rank of lieutenant. The zampolit was responsible for the morale of the unit, and also for the continued education of the troops, particularly in ideological areas. Lukashenko served two years in this role, at a time of great advancement and prosperity in Belarus. As such, Lukashenko held Pyotr Masherov in high regard, and would later describe him, along with Felix Dzerzhinsky[*], as one of his *"heroes"*.[2]

---

[*] Felix Edmundovich Dzerzhinsky (1877-1926): Bolshevik revolutionary and first head of the Soviet security services.

Lukashenko served two years in this position, before being asked to work for the Komsomol (Communist youth organisation) where he held various posts, culminating in his running of a chapter in Mogilev for a year. During this period Lukashenko also worked for several Communist Party bodies including the all-union society 'Znanie' (knowledge), with which he would continue to be actively involved until the dissolution of the Soviet Union. Lukashenko went back to the military in 1980 serving until 1982 in the Soviet Army. Upon leaving the army Lukashenko became vice director of a factory that specialised in construction materials. He then returned to education and graduated from the Belarusian Agricultural Academy in 1985, with further qualifications in agricultural science, and economics. Lukashenko acted upon his agricultural qualifications, and began work on the 'Udarnik' (shock worker) collective farm holding the post of vice chairman. All the time he was in these jobs he also kept active politically and served as the party secretary for the farm. His hard work paid off in 1985 when he was appointed director of the 'Gorodets' collective farm in the Mogilev region. It was from this position that Lukashenko was able to gain recognition, both as a man who could get things done, and who also earned the respect of his fellow workers through the hard working example he set. This recognition led to his being elected as a deputy to the Belarusian Supreme Soviet in 1990, and the real beginning of his full time political career. Lukashenko was always active and committed in whatever endeavour he undertook. He was also noted for independence in ideas and initiative, and actually earned himself two reprimands from Communist Party organs for his honesty and outspoken opinions on the running of the country. It is interesting to note that the only political party Lukashenko has ever been a member of is the Communist Party of the Soviet Union. Following its suspension in 1991, Lukashenko did not attempt to 'change his colours' or claim allegiance to any newly emerging party. Lukashenko is certainly a 'Soviet man' in that he strives for egalitarianism and equality, and firmly believes in the value of labour. Hence he found himself becoming increasingly at odds with the Soviet bureaucracy, whom had developed in its last years into a self-serving new privileged class.

One of the first actions undertaken by Lukashenko as a politician was to create a group within the parliament called 'Communists for

Democracy'. This was at the time of the ascendancy of the Belarusian popular front; and the increased toleration of factions within Soviet politics. Lukashenko's faction wanted to maintain the Soviet Union, but ensure it was governed following truly democratic lines. Significantly this would have meant a less centralised approach to government, and greater national autonomy for the constituent republics. However time was running out for the USSR, and Lukashenko's faction came too late to have significant influence.

Following the dissolution of the USSR, Lukashenko briefly returned to his collective farm, but could not stay out of politics for long, particularly in light of the enormity of the changes occurring in eastern Europe, and the former USSR. Lukashenko's outspoken opinions, and criticisms came from a firm ideological base. He could not tolerate corruption or hypocrisy. His political education had been the classic texts of Marxism, extolling egalitarianism and the principles of a nation run by, and in the best interests of its working people. However as the Soviet Union was collapsing it was clear that the bureaucratic elite lived better than the people they represented, and this situation was exacerbated by the events of 1991 that replaced an all encompassing welfare state, with absolutely nothing.

As privatisation swept Russia, and the first elements of the new forms of corruption this created hit Belarus, parliament created the 'Supreme Soviet Commission for Investigating the Activity of Business Entities Created under the Bodies of State Administration'. This was better known as the 'anti-corruption committee'. Lukashenko was elected to be the chairman of this committee in 1993. This was the post that singled out Lukashenko as a true contender for leadership, he proved himself to be firm in his convictions, and unafraid of the consequences of striving for the truth. He gained himself a reputation of being incorruptible. This combined with his espousing of Soviet principles gained him recognition, trust and support from a majority of Belarusians. Which ultimately led to him securing 80% of popular the vote for the post of president in 1994.

Alexander Lukashenko is married to a schoolteacher named Galina Rodionovna who works in the Mogilev region. They have two sons, Viktor, and Dimitry. Lukashenko has taken a firm position on the notion of a 'first lady'. His principle is that the people do not elect a president, *and* their partner. Commenting on the opposition in the run up to the 2006 presidential election he said, *"those who want a 'first lady' should elect them*".[3] Alexander Lukashenko does not live with his wife, firstly as she has remained in her job in Mogilev, and secondly due to the huge workload that Lukashenko has taken on. He is involved in almost every facet of state administration, and maintains an incredibly busy schedule. He has admitted to not being able to be a 'family man' because of his position, and in regard to family life has admitted, "*I'm not an example to follow*".[4] Despite this Lukashenko does keep a close watch on the activities of his sons. Viktor Lukashenko studied diplomacy at the Belarusian State University and after working with the Belarusian Foreign Ministry went on to work as a national security advisor to the President. Lukashenko's second son Dimitry, at the time of writing, is in military service. In a 2007 interview Lukashenko also hinted that he has a young third son, but has kept him out of the media spotlight.

Lukashenko is a keen sportsman, ice hockey in particular, but he also played on a parliamentary football team. Lukashenko's passion for ice hockey is his most well known pastime, and he has played in matches against the Detroit Red Wings, Sweden, and various Belarusian and Russian teams. As part of his commitment to the people of Belarus, Lukashenko has a record kept of every day's activity; his schedule can be viewed by anyone.

Chapter 9. Belarus in transition: 1991 to 1994.

"At that time, I think many of my MP colleagues' eyes opened and they regretted having voted for the disintegration of the Soviet Union. Alas history cannot be reversed: what has been done, cannot be undone".[1] A.G. Lukashenko.

Following the Belavezha agreement nothing changed overnight in Belarus, but quickly the first problems of independence became clear. Young BPF activists proudly waved the white/red/white flags of the Grand Duchy of Lithuania, as a sign of freedom from the Soviet red banner, largely unaware of the heritage of the flag, or its adoption by the Nazi collaborators during the war. The BPF however were not deliberately attempting to offend the older generation, but were harking back to the 1918 republic of Belarus, as being the first legitimate republic, and not the Soviet one that replaced it.

As well as the adoption of replacement state symbols, the new government also set about applying a programme of 'de-Russification'. Minsk for example was renamed 'Miensk', and the Belarusian language was applied wherever possible in an official context. The BPF did not represent the wishes of the majority of Belarusian people, or of the parliament, they were simply the most enthused by independence. The result was the promotion of Belarusian culture and language, at the expense of the political and social reality within the country. Belarusian simply was not the dominant language in the republic, and enforcing it was perhaps a noble attempt to preserve it, but counter productive in the actual life of the country. By 1989 some Belarusians simply didn't speak it at all, particularly in eastern Belarus. It is also notable that of a population of around 10 million in Belarus some 1.3 million were ethnic Russians.[2] Inter-marriage of Russians and Belarusians was also commonplace, further diluting the Belarusian cultural identity. The nature of the Soviet Union was such that people from one republic may study, or work in another, and families would not necessarily all live in their republic of origin. After 1991, people found that to visit their families or to return home, they needed visas, and often bribes to cross the new borders.

The economic trauma of independence was also critical, as the centrally planned and directed materials and payments simply ceased. Belarusian industry required fuel imports from other republics, and many of the products of Belarusian industry were merely components of items assembled elsewhere, particularly in the case of military contracts. The difficulties faced by industry were great, as fuel supplies went into private hands, and prices were permitted to rise with no safeguards, or guarantees. Moreover Belarusian manufacturers now had to compete with Western companies, who frequently used lower paid workers in the 'third world' to keep costs down, and were also prepared to take early losses to 'break into' this huge new market. The result was obvious to workers in all the former Soviet republics, the free market and competition meant a wealth of choice, but unemployment and the end of state run social welfare systems gave little opportunity to enjoy this. The Belarusian economy, once a source of pride, was now in decline. The gross output fell by 14% between 1989 and 1993, and the ending of state price controls led to a decline in real wages to 15% of their 1990 value.[3] There was also a huge downturn in the production of fuel and even food. The energy issue was also acute, as Belarus did not have enough natural fuel deposits in its territory to be anywhere near self-sufficient. Instead Belarus needed to look elsewhere for its energy supply. The obvious answer lay in Russia, which has large oil, coal and gas reserves, and the pipelines in place to satisfy Belarusian needs. However the Russian government was aware it could demand higher prices from western Europe than its struggling neighbour. The result was Belarusian pipelines transiting gas to Poland and beyond, and Belarusian plants continuing to refine Russian oil, at a time when the Russian government had decided to actually reduce consumable supplies of fuel to Belarus.

The leadership of Belarus was split over the issue of some kind of conciliation with Russia. The BPF were adamantly opposed to any kind of reliance on Russia, and within the still predominantly communist government there were differences of opinion. The government itself was essentially unchanged from the Soviet time, and as such there still existed the 'hard-line' elements, and the 'democratic opposition'.

The more conservative communists wanted stronger integration with Russia, which was hoped would lead to the restoration of the Soviet Union. There were also concerns over the absolute free fall of the Russian economy as it attempted to crash through reforms in all areas as quickly as possible. The Belarusian communists were aware that such changes could not easily be undone. What actually occurred in Belarus was a much slower introduction of any kind of reforms than happened in other former 'Eastern Block' states. The government seemed reluctant to attempt to seriously resolve its mounting problems and it entered a phase of inaction. The BPF also seemed to be losing influence as Belarus dug in for a slow and cautious transition.

Privatisation occurred in Belarus, but on a very limited scale. There is some confusion over the issue of privatisation in Belarus. Western media usually portrays Lukashenko as hostile to, or even as having reversed privatisation and thus being the sole reason that the Belarusian economy has failed to 'reform'. This however is simply not the case. In the years 1991-1994 before the presidential elections the government of Belarus privatised only 308 enterprises, and as historian David Marples notes, this represents only 2.1% of the country's work force.[4] This is a negligible degree of privatisation, and the reasons for this lie with the Belarusian people and their history.

The Soviet Centre of Public Opinion Research carried out one of its last surveys throughout 1989 to 1990, and reached interesting conclusions on Soviet citizen's attitudes to economic reform. What became clear was that the Soviet model had become deeply unpopular, and that saving the Soviet Union's command economy would probably have been against the wishes of many of its people. What also came out of the survey was that the Slavic republics of Russia, Ukraine and Belarus were less enthused with the idea of dramatic economic reform, than other Soviet Republics. In attitudes to private property (in the sense of land and businesses) 53% of Belarusians thought it to be positive, compared to 70% in Estonia. Belarusians also stated a distrust of stock supported industry, with only 19% claiming to be willing to buy shares, as opposed to 44% in Georgia. These attitudes were not only restricted to industry. In regards to the collective farm system for example, only 23% of Belarusians wished to independently farm their land. In Moldova the figure was 57%. Belarus having the lowest percentage throughout the entire USSR.[5]

Soviet statistics and opinion polls are always open to question, however this research is enlightening and appears to be reliable in the scale of antipathy and in some cases hostility that the survey found, and included in its results. The reasons for this possibly go deeper than the propaganda of the Soviet system, Dimitry Lvov* postulated a theological reason. He stated that the western European and also North American capitalist system is underpinned by protestant ethics. Namely the *"eulogising of wealth and prosperity"* with an underlying postulate of individual salvation. He argues that this is at odds with the values of Eastern Orthodoxy, which holds all men equal before God, with salvation being for everyone, or for no one. Lvov concludes that to the Orthodox Church, *"unlike in Western ethics, collectivism is the supreme value"*.[6]

This conclusion certainly seems to explain why the Slavic countries of Russia, Ukraine, Belarus, Serbia and Bulgaria all were cautious in their attitudes to, and often the implementation of economic reforms. The fact that Russia had a determined and strong president in the form of Boris Yeltsin would explain why Russia plunged headlong into economic upheaval, whilst the bureaucratic, and indecisive Belarusian government were not willing or able to act independently of the popular will. As Russia's radical reforms picked up speed, so too did Belarus allow more price liberalisation, however the conservative elements in the government would not relinquish price controls over bread, meat, dairy produce, children's goods, public utilities or transport. Despite this restraint the direction of policy was clearly moving away from the command economy of the Soviet Union. The often-contradictory policies and declarations of the Belarusian government led to various opportunities for exploitation by entrepreneurs both at home and abroad. The policy of limiting price rises effectively maintained shortages in Belarus, and thus established a thriving black market. At this time price rises in the other Soviet republics were almost out of control, which created a huge financial incentive for corruption as goods manufactured in Belarus could sell for much more in Russia or Ukraine. This led to the laundering of state money into the private sector, and subsequently created a wealthy stratum of businessmen and officials. As one example the MAZ truck factory in Minsk absorbed some 1.5 billion US dollars worth of state money, that ended up in private hands or bribes over the first three years of the 1990's.[7]

Corruption was rife throughout all of the former Soviet Union. Although in Belarus less state industry and land was being sold by the

---

* The Academic-Secretary of the Department of Economics at the Russian Academy of Sciences.

government, the government themselves were becoming both the rulers, and owners of the country. The situation in Russia was becoming known as 'oligarchic capitalism', and Belarus was slowly, but surely heading in the same direction. It is estimated that the equivalent of some 15 billion US Dollars 'left' the country between 1991 and 1994.[8] The people of Belarus suffered greatly in this period, hyperinflation set in and throughout 1992-1994 prices increased 432 times despite price regulation. Market reforms were allowing flagrant disregard for the law, and the worst elements of capitalism were flourishing in Belarus. Living standards fell, and the income disparity in Belarus increased hugely. The Belarusian people employed by state run enterprises could not be guaranteed they would be paid on time, and yet the luxury of the managers and corrupt politicians was increasing by the day.

Who held the ultimate power in Belarus was not clear, the old Soviet system was still in place, with a Council of Ministers and a parliament. Added to this was the waning though still noisy influence of the BPF. The key political players in the Belarusian leadership were considered to be Kebich, Shushkevich, and Paznyak. However these three men had very different opinions on the key issues of ties with Russia, the economy and democracy. Of the three Paznyak was the most concerned with the ideal of Belarusian nationhood. He was, and remains an anti-communist. His key positions which he fought for were the promotion of the Belarusian language, independence from Russia, and for a free market economy. Paznyak was able to campaign for these in a relatively comfortable position as he was seen as the 'opposition' leader and thus not responsible for the corruption and price rises. The collapse of the Soviet Union seemed to give credibility to his criticisms of communism and its centralised economy. However, Paznyak's vision of Belarusian statehood and ambitions did not always coincide with those of the population at large; indeed by many he was considered an extremist.

Stanislav Shushkevich headed the Belarusian parliament after 1991. He was in favour of market reforms, but also closer co-operation with Russia and Ukraine. It was Shushkevich who had signed the Belavezha protocol dissolving the Soviet Union, and instituting the CIS in its place. Shushkevich had close relations with both the reformers, and the conservatives, and this led to the concern that Shushkevich was an opportunist seeking to consolidate his position. In the words of Dimitry Bulachov, the then head of the Legislative Committee of Belarus: "[Shushkevich is] *constantly manoeuvring among the political groups*".[9] The concern of many in the parliament was Shushkevich's lack of a clear ideology or programme, and his attempts to galvanise support for him personally, from influential politicians.

Viacheslav Kebich was a man of firmer beliefs. Kebich had grave concerns about crash reforms, but was not a hard-line communist as often portrayed. Kebich held nostalgia for the Soviet times, and methods, but according to the Supreme Soviet's Deputy Uladzimir Hyrbanov: "*For some time, if ever, he has not believed in the communist idea*".[10] Kebich was the chairman of the Belarusian council of ministers, and as such was in frequent conflict with Shushkevich. The Council of Ministers and Parliament were meant to work in accord, however they became dominated by opposing forces. The parliament being for the most part pro-reform, whereas the Council of Ministers were decidedly Conservative.

Belarusian politics had hit a period of stagnation almost immediately following independence, and it became clear that a solution was required to the problem of the two highest bodies of power cancelling each other out. The result was the adoption in 1994 of a new constitution, which had as its most important article the creation of the new post of 'President of the Republic of Belarus'. This post was to bridge the gap between Parliament and the Council of Ministers. Elections were to be held later in the year with Kebich as favourite, closely followed by Shushkevich, with Paznyak as a 'dark horse' outsider. A total of nineteen candidates put themselves forward for the post, amongst them, the head of the Governments anti-corruption committee: Alexander Lukashenko.

Lukashenko was virtually unknown outside of parliament, his one notable achievement in the period of 1991-1994 was the revelations of corruption against seventy senior government officials. Significantly this included Shushkevich himself. The accusations were that senior state officials had been misappropriating state funds for themselves, or their interests. The charges against Shushkevich could not be proved, but the scale of the corruption within his government, and the worrying amount of hard currency 'disappearing' from the treasury led to a vote of no confidence in Shushkevich. He lost the vote and stepped down, but was still prominent in the Belarusian political arena thanks to the high public profile he had previously gained as speaker of the parliament.

The electoral system for the new presidency was inspired by those used in western Europe. First the prospective candidate had to obtain the signatures of seventy parliamentary deputies, or 100,000 people in support of their application.

After a week of signature verification, the campaign was to begin. On the election day at least 50% of the electorate must vote, with the winning candidate receiving at least 50% of the votes cast. If there was no clear winner in the first round, then the two leading candidates would compete in a second round of elections.

The advantage held by Kebich was obvious, with his connections within the Council of Ministers he was easily able to gain seventy parliamentary signatures. Shushkevich also retained influence in the parliament and was well known to Belarusians, plus the corruption scandal had not damaged his reputation too seriously. After the first stage of collecting signatures, the 19 prospective candidates had been reduced to six contenders. These were Kebich, Shushkevich, Paznyak, Lukashenko, plus the communists Alexander Dubko, and Vassili Novikov.

The first stage of voting did not result in an outright winner, and the results took most people by surprise. Lukashenko had polled 45.1% of the vote, followed by Kebich with 17.4%. After that came Paznyak with 12.9%, Shushkevich 9.9%, Dubko 6% and Novikov with 4.6%. This meant that the 'run off' second round was to be between Kebich and Lukashenko. The success of Lukashenko was not predicted either within Belarus or abroad. It had largely been expected that, as in the other former Soviet Republics, one of the old party 'nomenclatura' would have taken power. Kebich was notably shocked, not having expected to have almost lost in the first round. The people of Belarus had certainly responded to the early forays into privatisation and 'reform' with a certain amount of protest voting, but the individual support for Lukashenko was undeniable, and impressive. This was confirmed in the second round of voting on July 10th. Seventy per-cent of the electorate turned out, and 80.1% of those voted for Lukashenko. This amounted to 4.2 million votes out of a potential 5.2 million.[11] This election victory was huge, and in contrast to subsequent referenda, and elections, international observers, governments, and Belarusian political parties did not attempt to imply any unfair practices had taken place.

What had driven 80% of the population to vote for Lukashenko? He was relatively politically inexperienced compared to his main rivals, and at 39 it was noted that he was almost a full generation younger than the other candidates. Lukashenko's campaign had been simple yet effective. As a known 'anti-corruption crusader' he was able to restore some faith in a government that had lost the trust of the people. Lukashenko promised to bring in a 'clean' government, and bring to trial those who had misappropriated state funds. He also campaigned to maintain the pay, benefits, and working conditions of those in the public sector. Lukashenko did not campaign from a position of halting or reversing economic reforms, but instead for a re-assessment of the benefits and costs to the state, and its people.

Another vital issue in Lukashenko's campaign was that of forming a union with Russia. The BPF was horrified by this suggestion, and accused Lukashenko of trying to incorporate Belarus into the Russian Federation. There were also Russian nationalists who voiced the same opinion as the BPF, and suggested the only acceptable union would be that of Belarus being 'absorbed'. However in reply to this Lukashenko said: *"We cannot accept this approach. Such a 'reunification' will inevitably lead to negative impacts for the historical development of the Belarusian people as a nation"*.[12] Despite repeated rebuttals of this nature, and even asking, *"why not raise the question of Russia to be incorporated into Belarus?"*[13] Lukashenko is still often accused of surrendering Belarusian sovereignty by the Belarusian opposition and nationalists.

What was clear however was that Lukashenko's policies were genuinely popular, that he had 'his finger on the pulse' of public opinion, and that he was a politician that they were willing to trust. Crash reforms had resulted in crashed economies in eastern Europe, and Lukashenko's union with Russia made historical as well as economic sense. Lukashenko had the backing of over 80% of the people, but he had no political party. Following the election, the real struggle for power was to begin.

Chapter 10. Alexander Lukashenko's Consolidation of Power.

"The bearer of power is not a master, he is a servant of the people".[1]
A.G. Lukashenko.

President Lukashenko had a difficult and almost unique situation to contend with on his election to office. He had his supporters, but had not been from one of the political parties or movements. Thus he had no 'shadow cabinet' and also was not in a position to rely on support from either Parliament, or the Council of Ministers. The aim of this chapter is not to discuss the actual policies of Lukashenko, they will come later; but rather to explain the circumstances and events that transpired in order for him to be able implement these policies.

When the position of president had been approved in the constitution, it had been seen as a way for settling the wrangles between Shushkevich's Parliament, and Kebich's Council of Ministers. With neither winning the election it appeared that the position of president would simply add to the confusion, and inaction. As covered, Lukashenko was elected to the presidency as an outsider. He had popular support, but was not a part of the ruling former Communist Party nomenclatura who still held sway in Belarusian politics. Therefore Lukashenko's first political moves were aimed at securing support within the bodies of government, the Parliament, and the Council of Ministers. Lukashenko picked his 'cabinet' predominantly from former supporters and advisors of his chief rival Viacheslav Kebich, as well as his own close supporters. What this meant initially was that very little had changed by the end of 1994. The old nomenclatura maintained their power, with quite simply a different man at the top. Kebich himself even eventually came over to support Lukashenko, and at the time of writing is a vocal supporter of Lukashenko in the Belarusian parliament.

Added to this former communist support, Lukashenko also engaged the pro-reformers, although he advocated a cautious approach to reform himself, Lukashenko was not averse to using the talents of those who clearly supported it. One example being the new foreign minister Uladzimir Senka, who was decidedly Western in his outlook, and thus quite at odds with Lukashenko's proposed union with Russia. However Senka was very useful to the new president's cause at this stage, as he was a professional and respected diplomat. Likewise the new head of the national bank Stanislav Bahdankevich, was widely perceived to be pro-market reforms, which Lukashenko had not entirely dismissed, but certainly did not embrace. Bahdankevich resigned from his post in August 1995, when it became clear that neither he nor Lukashenko were flexible in their respective time scales for, or degrees of market reform.

Replacing Kebich as the Prime Minister of Belarus was Mikhail Chigir. The new Prime Minister had not been part of Lukashenko's campaign, but was well known and respected for his work in the allocation of government funds and grants in the agrarian sector. Lukashenko is a realist, and his choice of Prime Minister, and cabinet show this. He was setting about a programme that was not as popular in the organs of power as it was with the people of the country. Lukashenko made concessions initially in order to assure a smooth transition of power, one example being a promise to Chigir, that he would be allowed to make independent economic decisions.

Throughout 1995 and 1996 Lukashenko used his presidential authority to secure his position in power. He appointed a new head of the state security service (still called the KGB in Belarus), and also promoted his supporters within the hierarchy of the army.

This was not a difficult task, and certainly was no coup d'etat. The military and police were, and remain one of Lukashenko's most loyal bases of support in the country. This comes in no small part from the respect held for him as a former serviceman.

The next issue that needed to be settled was that of the parliament. The parliamentary deputies had been elected in 1990 for a five-year term, and Lukashenko declared that their mandate had run its course and the time for new elections was due. (This parliament was the same one that Lukashenko had investigated in the course of his anti-corruption commission post).

Lukashenko declared the existing legislature to be *"obstructive and dishonest"*.[2] The parliamentary newspaper, the 'People's Gazette' had in fact been critical and dismissive of the new president since the election, in what appeared to be a deliberate campaign to lessen his authority and standing. Lukashenko found that in order to begin his programme he could not rely on the parliament, and thus used the constitution to take the power directly to the people. In April 1995 Lukashenko called his first referendum. The timing of this referendum was also significant. Lukashenko chose the same day as the parliamentary elections for the vote. This was a double edged decision. On the one hand if the voters were in favour of Lukashenko's proposals they could also register their disapproval of their parliamentary candidate; but the converse was also true. If the people were as shocked with the referendum as the parliament was they could vote overwhelmingly not only against the referendum itself, but the President too.

The referendum asked the people four questions. The first three were issues of national history and 'direction'. The final question was a direct challenge to the parliament, they read:

1. *Do you agree that the Russian language should have an equal status with Belarusian?*
2. *Do you support the proposal about a new state flag and state symbols of the Republic of Belarus?*
3. *Do you support the actions of the president directed towards economic integration with Russia?*
4. *Do you agree with the need to introduce changes to the Constitution of Belarus anticipating the pre-term dissolution of the Supreme Soviet by the president of Belarus in cases of systematic or gross violations of the constitution of Belarus?*

The whole referendum was aimed at asking the Belarusian people essentially one question, what kind of leadership did they want? The state symbols in question were the old Grand Duchy of Lithuania's flag and emblem. Lukashenko had commented that these symbols were *"alien to Slavs"*,[3] and advocated instead to revert to the Soviet style flag and emblem, minus the hammer and sickle. As discussed earlier the vast majority of the development of Belarus came as a Soviet Socialist Republic, and the proud history of Belarus was primarily attached to the Soviet years, and the Great Patriotic War in particular.

The joint national language question was more an issue of common sense than it was political in a country where Belarusian was not the most spoken language of the population. The question of support for Lukashenko's policy towards Russia came on the back of parliamentary criticism. The parliament considered Lukashenko to be too pro-Russian, and yet he had been elected on a promise to make closer ties with Russia. This question, if supported, was a challenge to the parliament: who were they representing, the Belarusian people or themselves?

The BPF, unsurprisingly, were outraged at the proposition to replace the national symbols and flag. Paznyak interpreted the whole referendum as being an attempt to surrender state sovereignty to Russia. In protest Paznyak and his supporters declared themselves to be on hunger strike and promptly sat on the floor of the parliament and refused to leave. Quite how this was supposed to resolve the problem, or allow genuine debate is unclear, but what it did achieve was a slight delay in the referendum. The BPF had promised after the presidential election to give Lukashenko a hundred-day period of grace. They would not criticise his policies, and see which direction he took. Clearly the direction displeased them.

Paznyak's BPF however were not truly the 'opposition party', and as had been reflected in the votes, nor did they represent the popular sentiments of Belarusian people. Paznyak had only received 12.9% of the vote, but in what has become a feature of Belarusian politics the nationalists are few, but vociferous. The hunger strike and 'sit in' at the parliament was resolved by police intervention. The head of the Parliamentary security force visited Paznyak and his supporters and informed them that they had to leave the building due to information about the possibility of a bomb having been planted somewhere inside. This probable ruse failed to convince the protestors, and nor did the subsequent search carried out by police bomb disposal experts. No bomb was discovered, and at 03:00 the day after the protest began the protestors were physically removed from the parliament by a substantial security force. The striking deputies certainly were forcibly removed, but their claim to have received severe beatings seems unlikely considering the fact that they were allowed to return to sit in the parliament the following afternoon. The first confrontation between parliament and president had been damaging for the reputations of both, and drew criticism from abroad. This was in notable contradiction to the Western response to President Yeltsin's resolution of his own stand-off with Russia's parliament. Yeltsin had attempted to illegally disband the parliament and then had its building shelled by tanks in order to force his programme through. This resulted in the deaths of at least 180 people and the wounding of over 400 more.[4] For this act Yeltsin was rewarded with the granting of around 40 billion US dollars in IMF grants and loans*.

The referendum passed without further incident with the people voting in favour of all four of Lukashenko's proposals. The results were as follows: On the equal status of Russian language, 83.3% said yes, the new flag and symbol was supported by 75.1%, on continuing integration with Russia 83.3% approved, and most importantly on the President being allowed to dissolve parliament 77.7% agreed. The presidency had passed its first test comfortably.

The parliamentary election however was another matter. Turnout to the elections was abysmal, the behaviour of the parliamentary deputies over the referendum, and the vote of support for the President left many apathetic to the parliament itself. At the first attempt only 18 deputies were elected, voter turnout being too low to register the minimum requirement of 173. It took a further three rounds of voting to finally elect a legal working parliament. Significantly Paznyak narrowly lost his seat, and the BPF failed to secure even one. The parliament was now mostly made up of independent candidates. The Communists and Agrarians were the only two parties to secure more than one seat. Clearly the party political system in Belarus had failed to inspire the confidence of the people. This can be traced back to an element of nostalgia for the stability and success of the BSSR under single party rule. Also the huge influence that the BPF had held in the early years of independence could be seen to be out of proportion with its popular support. Their subsequent protest to protect state symbols that were rejected by some 75% of the population showed how far the BPF's position was from that of the country. Also the BPF's hunger strike and obstruction of parliament by only 14 deputies lost it a great deal of respect and credibility.

The new parliament's speaker was Myachyslau Hryb, who was noted to be an opponent of Lukashenko's policies, and had taken over from Shushkevich before the presidential elections. Hryb saw to it that the Constitutional Court (which acted as a check on the president's power) was staffed by his supporters, and was led by his ally, Valeri Tsikhinya. The Constitutional Court had become the best place for reformers and nationalists to look for support in fighting the President. Throughout 1995 Lukashenko had support from the ma-

---

* In 1995 the World Bank and IMF suspended any loans to Belarus citing the lack of economic reforms.

jority of the new parliamentary deputies, and of course the electorate, but still Hryb and Tsikhinya rejected his decrees.

With the Belarusian Popular Front no longer represented in the parliament, nationalist reformers sought the formation of another political party, that could advocate privatisation, and 'Western looking' policies in the parliament. This resulted in the creation of the United Civic Party, and was headed by the former head of the National Bank, Stanislav Bahdankevich. Within the parliament Bahdankevich formed a coalition with other economic reformers entitled 'Civic Action'. This group was essentially a more moderate version of the BPF, and conditionally supported the President (So long as he followed a their programme of reforms).

The early years of Lukashenko's rule was characterised by this ongoing struggle with the parliament and state bodies. Actual policy making was proving to be very difficult. This was a typical characteristic across all the former Soviet Republics, but particularly in Russia, Ukraine and Belarus. Indeed it was only Yeltsin in Russia who had managed to ensure full parliamentary support, and as mentioned this was achieved through the use of armed force. It is also important to remember that this period in Belarusian politics saw intense conflict, not simply over policy or ideology, but also out of the various organs of government attempting to gain ascendancy over one another. Yet again the Belarusian parliament elected a new speaker, this time Semyon Sharetski the leader of the Agrarian Party since 1992. Sharetski, like Lukashenko was a former collective farm manager, but had distanced himself from the communist faction in the parliament. Sharetski as speaker, was suddenly in a position of great responsibility, and like the speakers before him, he was aware that if he were able to achieve a pre-eminence of parliamentary authority over that of the president, he would become the de-facto leader of Belarus. Such was the nature of post Soviet politics, where an all-encompassing political system that oversaw most aspects of everyday life, was replaced with chaos. Communist Party hierarchy and discipline no longer mattered, and political intrigue was the best method of promotion, political survival and quite often wealth too.

Lukashenko under these circumstances found himself in a position where he wanted to carry through the programme he had been elected upon, but was unable to circumvent the intrigues of the parliament and Constitutional Court. The answer lay in the one area he could rely on, the Belarusian people themselves. In order to achieve a working government Lukashenko and his advisors drafted amendments to the 1994 constitution, and the proposed changes were to be put to referendum. Lukashenko had already earned the right to dissolve parliament, but did not do so; instead he asked for the peoples support to restructure it. The amendments were ambitious, and although they maintained a democratic structure were certainly aimed at underscoring the fact that the ultimate power in the country was to lie with the President.

What Lukashenko wanted to put to referendum, had to be approved by the parliament first. Under the circumstances it was unlikely that parliament would agree. Parliament issued its rebuttal in July 1996, when seven different political parties and factions accused Lukashenko of wanting to establish a dictatorship. They argued that the President's intention of amending the constitution was unconstitutional. Sensing an opportunity to be once again seen and heard, the BPF joined forces with the United Civic Party and the Belarusian Social Democratic Hramada in calling for the impeachment of the President.

Lukashenko was however undeterred, and set about making plans for the referendum. One new innovation was the creation of an 'All Belarus Peoples Assembly'. This was to be comprised of 6000 representatives from various regions across the whole country, who would debate policy and the strategies for achieving these. Lukashenko would go on to describe the Peoples Assembly as *"an open talk with the people, a direct and effective form of participatory democracy"*.[5] What was becoming clear was that Lukashenko had tired of arguing with the parliament, and instead was going to discuss with the people what they wanted, and then ask the parliament the question of why weren't they carrying out the wishes of the electorate. This polarised the deputies; although Lukashenko was clearly consolidating his power at the expense of the parliament, he was also trying to implement a programme that had been voted for by 80% of the people. In September 1996 a group of 60 deputies signed a statement in support of the President's proposals. This led Sharetski to attempt the consolidation of his own position by manoeuvring anti-presidential deputies into positions of power and responsibility within the parliament.

Sharetski as speaker and Tsikhinya as head of the constitutional court were able to rally support from some deputies against the President's proposals, however the communist faction in parliament was the hardest to guarantee support from. The communists generally supported Lukashenko's line, but were equally concerned about losing their own influence under a revised constitution. Sharetski appealed to the communists for support by playing on this fear, and describing the referendum as anti-democratic. Lukashenko in turn described Sharetski, Tsikhinya and their supporters as *"nationalist radicals"* and *"fascist swindlers"*.[6]

Tsikhinya in October engineered a motion to counter Lukashenko's referendum on a new constitution with yet another referendum on the abolition of the post of president. The Belarusian Supreme Soviet voted 88 to 84 deputies in favour of this new referendum. The parliament was almost evenly split. Those who voted for the referendum were not all necessarily those against the President, as how the public would vote was predictable. Meaning that voting for the referendum could have actually served to strengthen Lukashenko's position.

Lukashenko had already gathered the support of 110 deputies for his proposals, and then made his appeal to the people. Lukashenko argued that the constitution in place was drafted by the parliament, and there had been no input from the people themselves, and furthermore they had not been asked to approve it. Lukashenko also equated this constitution with the corruption and deprivation of the immediate post Soviet years. Lukashenko emphasised that the new constitution would not be self serving for any branch of power, but would be to the benefit of all Belarusians.

The date for the referendum was set to be the 24th of November, and that month saw appointments and dismissals within the government and protests on the streets of Minsk. Mikhail Chigir also resigned as Prime Minister.

The situation was descending into chaos and Belarusian government was almost ceasing to function due to its own internal squabbling. On the 20th of November Boris Yeltsin telephoned Lukashenko requesting that Russian Prime Minister Victor Chernomyrdin come to Minsk and negotiate a solution. Lukashenko agreed and the following day he, Chernomyrdin and Sharetski talked into the night for over ten hours.

The following morning a compromise was reached. Lukashenko

conceded to making the referendum non binding. Whilst Sharetski agreed to stop appealing to the Constitutional Court for support against presidential decrees. Further to this a Constituent Assembly was to be created to draft the new constitution, it was to have 100 delegates of whom the parliament and president could choose half each. The chairman of this assembly was to be Lukashenko.

The Parliament then failed to give support to this compromise, and as such Lukashenko dropped his promise to make the referendum non binding. This meant that the vote on November the 24th was to become a vote of confidence in the president. The final referendum asked seven questions, including parliament's proposal to remove the office of president, they were:

1. *Should the national holiday of Belarus be changed from 27th of July (independence from Soviet Union) to 3rd of July when Belarus was liberated from Nazi Germany?*
2. *Do you support the new constitution offered by the president, which would extend his term of office from five to seven years; permit him to appoint half the members of the constitutional court and the electoral commission, in addition to a new upper house of sixty senators, while the number of seats in the parliament would be reduced to110?*
3. *Do you support the unrestricted buying and selling of land?*
4. *Should the death penalty be abolished?*
5. *Do you support the draft referendum offered by the parliamentary deputies that would abolish the office of president and invest authority in the cabinet headed by a prime minister?*
6. *Do you support the election of regional leaders?*
7. *Do you approve of funding for state institutions directly from the budget?*

Once again a referendum was being used to establish policy direction as well as to consolidate power. This is clearly the case in questions 1, 3 and 4.

As an important note question number 2 did not seek to make presidential terms seven years, but was rather a 're-starting' of the current presidency. Lukashenko had clearly been unable to implement almost all of his policies and ideas in the first two years, and it was hoped that the new constitution would enable him to do so. As well as granting the president expanded powers, for example to set regional election dates and appoint senior ministers, the new constitution also reorganised the government bodies.

The proposed new legislature was to consist of two chambers, the House of Representatives, and the Council of the Republic. The first of these was to be made up of 110 deputies elected nationally by the people. The Council of the Republic was to be regional in representation, with eight members elected from each region (Oblast) of the country, as well as eight from the city of Minsk. An additional eight members were to be selected by the president. The two chambers meet separately and each has their own chairperson.

The new constitution however was not aimed at establishing a dictatorship. The President's appointed deputies were still very much a minority, and could easily be outvoted if need be. Also the House of Representatives, was to be granted the power to pass a vote of no confidence in the government, and even to set the date for the presidential elections. The Council of the Republic acts as a watchdog on local government and ensures that legislation is carried out. The Council also approves bills debated in the House of Representatives, and acts as an 'upper chamber'. Again the Council of the Republic acts as a safeguard to presidential power, with the majority of its deputies elected, and it also has the power to approve, or not, presidential decrees on declaring of a state of emergency, martial law, and military mobilisation. The new constitution also allowed for the parliament to be empowered to impeach the president, should the need arise. The Council of Ministers was to remain as the central body of state administration. It is officially *"accountable to the President and responsible to the Parliament"*.[7] The Council of Ministers also includes the Prime Minister, and the heads of the various ministries. It acts in a very similar way to the 'cabinet' in British politics, but with much stricter regulation in form and role.

The new constitution was to clarify, and actually allow the governing of Belarus, and came about in part because of the shortcomings of the 1994 constitution, and also was born of the fact that Lukashenko had not come to the presidency on the back of a political party. The new constitution certainly enhanced the role of the president, but was not a granting of absolute power. Safeguards were in place, and a BBC report of the new parliament being *"handpicked"*[8] by Lukashenko simply was not true, or in fact possible.

The actual referendum resulted in a clear victory for Lukashenko.

Final voter turnout was 84% and of these 70.5% supported the new draft constitution. The proposed change in national holiday was supported by 88.5% of voters. This being a clear indication of the relevance of the Soviet experience in Belarus. The abolition of the death penalty was rejected, although Lukashenko believes that it is something that must eventually happen.

The people of Belarus craved stability and order, which was what Lukashenko was promising them, and the new constitution, it was hoped would be the way to enable him to deliver.

After the referendum the new parliamentary system was put into practice, and 110 of the elected deputies took their place in the new House of Representatives. Talk of impeaching the president disappeared as once again the parliament had failed to secure popular support. With power consolidated (power that most elected leaders take for granted e.g. the ability to direct fiscal and foreign policy), Lukashenko was now able to begin turning his promises into reality.

Chapter 11. The Belarusian Economy under Lukashenko.

"The economic course of Belarus is towards a socially orientated market economy".[1] A.G. Lukashenko.

When the Soviet Union passed into history in 1991, its constituent nations found themselves suddenly economically 'free' however in no position to enjoy this. By this it is meant that each republic could choose the type of economy it wished to pursue in the future, be it market, planned or mixed. Unfortunately the Soviet system was built around each republic serving as a building block in the larger whole. This meant that as stated earlier, raw materials and fuel may be located in different republics to the manufacturing plant requiring them. An example in Belarus being that it has very little oil, but does have refineries.

The Soviet Union guaranteed work and employment for all of its citizens. One way of achieving this had been to build enterprises in large populated areas with less regard to cost saving measures in terms of transportation costs. This was because of the guaranteed work, which was provided by the railways, canals, merchant navy etc. in getting materials and completed goods from one part of the union to another.

In this regard former Soviet enterprises were poorly prepared for the profit centred market economy, and the first savings made by new private owners tended to be by using more profitable imports, and by making wage cuts. For example the lucrative Russian oil industry would no longer subsidise a small loss making enamel plant in Kazakhstan, simply to preserve jobs.

The first changes in Belarus had not been as dramatic as those undertaken in other republics, but corruption and profiteering had begun to take hold. The Belarusian economy had been healthy in the Soviet Union and the opportunity for successful private enterprises certainly existed. Lukashenko was elected as president at a time of high inflation, the new Belarusian Rouble had been re-valued several times, and inflation was almost out of control. The Belarusian people had also shown their scepticism of market reforms, and certainly events abroad seemed to confirm their fears. In Russia it was well known that pensions were no longer being paid on time, if at all, and the social security system was starved of funds. For example by 2001 it was found that some ten million Russian children had never been to school.[2] A number equal to the total population of Belarus, and particularly shocking given the Soviet Union's pride in educational achievements.

The situation in Belarus could have potentially been exactly the same. The Belarusian economy was geared towards heavy industry and large-scale collective farming. Consumer goods were becoming scarce, and available energy supplies were being sold to the highest bidder. Coupled to the problem of the shrinking Belarusian economy was the problem that Lukashenko faced in the parliament and national bank. This was summarised well by the Belarusian economist, Professor Leonid Zlotnikov: *"Having assumed power, Alexander Lukashenko was in no position to immediately change the flow of economic processes to suit the requirements of grass roots, because he had to rely on the former state bureaucracy and reckon with its understanding of the situation"*.[3] It wasn't until the 1996 referendum that Lukashenko was truly able to put his economic policy into effect.

Lukashenko is not averse to the introduction of market reforms. He is practical enough to realise that in a country dependent on fuel and raw materials from the outside world, he cannot create a 21st century version of Enver Hoxha's self sufficient Peoples Republic of Albania. Indeed Lukashenko has called his economic and social policy *"Market Socialism"*.[4]

The focus of his economic policy is the preservation of social guarantees, and the removal of unemployment. Unlike in a classic market economy where profit is the prime motivator for the owner or owners of a business, Lukashenko wants to ensure that society prospers too. Thus there are still incentives for entrepreneurs, but also guarantees for those they employ. Lukashenko summarises the concept thus: *"Planning and market, private, state and public forms of property, financial activity and social guarantees are not mutually excluding but complimentary parameters"*.[5] From this we can see that Lukashenko does not wish to keep a 'dictatorial stranglehold' on the economy as often portrayed in Western media. The reality is that Lukashenko proposes a viable system where public and private business work together to provide development and ensure protection for society. Belarus will have few millionaires, but just as few destitute.

This is where one of the main points of argument between the USA and Belarus arises. For example Lukashenko insists that nothing should be imported if it is available within the country. The USA has similar protectionist trade laws, but reacts badly when such laws effect its interests abroad. One example in Belarus being that McDonalds was asked to stop importing cheaper straws etc. from neighbouring Poland. Another action was that Lukashenko ended the usually taken for granted tax and customs exemptions on McDonalds. As will be discussed later the antagonisms between Belarus and the USA stem more from differences in economic policy than from genuine concern over human rights or democracy. Indeed Professor Chomsky summarised the US definition of democracy as being:

"*Domination of the economy and social and political elements by domestic elements that are properly sensitive to the needs of the corporations and the US government*".[6]

Part of Lukashenko's socially oriented economic policy is also the protection of the environment. Belarus suffered heavily by the man made disaster of Chernobyl, and as such Lukashenko does not consider long term harm to be worth any short term profit. Belarus has signed up to the Kyoto protocol on climate change, and the environment and economy are to Lukashenko not mutually exclusive. In 1998 he stated, "*the major systems of energy, transport and communications and the branches consuming the natural resources should normally be under state control or public management*".[7] The Kyoto protocol requires countries to drastically change their production methods to reduce pollution. This will be very expensive for countries such as Belarus, but is ultimately an essential measure. It is notable that the worlds biggest polluting country, the USA, (also the richest) has thus far refused to sign the agreement.

After 1996 Lukashenko practically halted privatisation. His aim was to regulate what value enterprises had, their suitability for privatisation, and who should be deemed responsible enough to own them. 1994-96 had seen widespread discontent in Belarus at the deadlock between government and president, and also at the continued erosion of the Soviet economy with its replacement by the unpredictable 'free market'.

Shushkevich and Bahdankevich had actually ended price controls on bread and milk, as well as removing subsidies on housing. These measures were primarily aimed at meeting the IMF's requirements, and certainly not those of the people of Belarus. In January 1995 a protest was organised by trade unions in Minsk, and was attended by over 20,000 citizens. The protesters demanded higher wages to simply cover the price rises. However inflation practically rendered most wage increases ineffective. In the words of historian David Marples, *"the workforce of Belarus was being reduced to impoverishment"*.[8] To make matters worse when the government allocated subsidies to the ailing agricultural sector the IMF suspended all credits, as this violated the principle of 'free trade'. Under such circumstances it is easy to see why the people put their trust in Lukashenko, who promised to halt wholesale privatisation. Also his proposed union with Russia would certainly bring economic benefits for Belarus, particularly in terms of fuel imports.

In 1996 Lukashenko began to take hold of the economy. The Inter-Bank Accounting Centre was returned to government control, which allowed better regulation of financial affairs. Secondly Lukashenko promised to stop inflation by using state reserves to prop up the value of the currency. Such practice is risky, and ultimately unsustainable. However as a short term measure it achieved its goal of maintaining wages that could meet prices. In 1996 the hard currency reserves of the Belarusian National Bank were only 10 million US dollars. This in a socially orientated economy of course equated to a spending power of a mere one dollar per person. That the Belarusian economy could recover from this, and still cover the costs of health, education, and the social welfare system is truly an impressive achievement.

By controlling the rate of market reforms Lukashenko ensured jobs, and also was able to encourage the growth of industry and enterprise. Under the principles of free trade, industries are able to absorb rivals, and appropriate their assets with scant regard for any other consequence but profit. The collapse of the Soviet Union opened up a market the likes of which had never been seen before, with many opportunities for easy exploitation by foreign buyers, and corrupt officials 'at home'. Roman Abramovich being typical of the post Soviet 'oligarchs' who were able to make vast personal fortunes at the expense of their country. Abramovich and a close associate Boris Berezovsky were able to take ownership of the Siberian oil industry through their political connections, in particular with President Yeltsin. When the Sibneft oil company shares were made available, only Abramovich and Berezovsky owned companies were allowed to bid for them. Buying up the industry for less than 200 million US dollars;

Abramovich later sold just over 70% of his shares in this business back to the Russian state at a cost of over 13 billion US dollars.

It is this kind of business practice that Lukashenko has committed himself to barring from the Belarusian economy. Professor Zlotnikov however predicts that *"In case the [Lukashenko] regime falls, Belarus will most probably follow the oligarchic capitalism model"*.[9] The reason for this is the large degree of state control that remains over branches of the economy. As of 2005 approximately 80% of all industry remained under state ownership.[10] Should the government in Belarus change, particularly to a more 'Western looking' one, then this 80% of industry working toward the fulfilment of social guarantees, would likely be 'auctioned' in the manner of Sibneft.

One of the biggest criticisms levelled at the command economy, and state run industry is that of inefficiency. However Belarus has proven that it can 'go its own way' and still perform well in economic terms. Of all the countries of the CIS, only Belarus has thus far equalled the pre 1991 Soviet level of GDP physical volume, this was achieved in 2002.[11] Also Belarus has managed to regain control over inflation. Levels of inflation actually decreased more than twenty times following Lukashenko's election. At the height of capitalism in Belarus in 1992, inflation stood at 971%, but by 2003 this had been reduced to 34.8%.[12]

Unemployment, which had been unheard of in the Soviet Union for over sixty years, reappeared in the late 1980's. Following the events of 1991 unemployment became common, and all work was taken on a day to day basis. Many people simply went to work out of faith or habit, with no guarantee of being paid. Many enterprises had to pay their staff with the products they made which could then be bartered with other workers.

By the end of 1996, around 4% of the total labour force in Belarus was officially unemployed[13] (although underemployment and 'casual work' dramatically reduced this figure).

Lukashenko took direct action to resolve this problem, and in early 1997 issued a decree that enterprises and industry must not simply lay off workers, but rather redirect them into other jobs. Thus employers took on a greater responsibility for their workers, and also were able to improve efficiency in some areas by reducing waste in others. This policy of course is greatly assisted by the nature of large state control in the economy, whereby production can be linked to the availability of labour, and production quotas. The aim being to reduce waste and protect jobs and livelihoods. Lukashenko regards the role of state regulation not to be a form of bureaucratic exploitation, or interference but rather it serves to *"favour the interests of the country and of the society as a whole"*.[14] To this end Belarus has manage to achieve one of the lowest unemployment levels in Europe from 3% in 2004,[15] to 1.6% in June 2005, and by late 2006 this was down to 1.3%.[16] This is actually one of the lowest rates in the world coming after small islands and principalities such as Jersey and Andorra. Significantly the reduction in unemployment was not made at the sacrifice of productivity. Industrial output between 2004 and 2005 increased by 9.7%.[17] Throughout 2006 both industrial and agricultural production continued to increase, as did the production of consumer goods.

The Socially orientated economy also managed to increase real pensions and spending in health and education. Belarus has achieved this not from loans or by selling off state assets for short term benefits, but by careful planning. Living standards for the whole of the population have risen since 1995. Real wages and salaries have year on year increased by over 100% of the previous years value.[18] Even with the low level of real wages in 1995 this is still an impressive rise, particularly with the decline in inflation taken into account. Such statistics are also confirmed by primary sources. Prior to the 2006 presidential election Russian journalists travelled to one of Belarus' agricultural towns, Krynichny, some 280 kilometres south east of Minsk. There, far from the political spotlight, they found well-stocked stores, with goods at affordable prices. A local man was quoted as *saying, "there used to be no bread. Now there is everything: bread, wine, vodka."* He also added that before Lukashenko took power *"we were going around without underpants!"*[19]

These simple things show that planning in an economy does not have to lead to shortages in basic goods. The market guarantees choice, but Lukashenko's methods mean that necessities are not sacrificed for the manufacture of lucrative luxuries.

Conversion processes have been undertaken, directing centres of production to fill gaps in the economy. Also essential to the economic growth of Belarus has been the production of high value goods for export.

In the first years of Lukashenko's rule trade was predominantly with Russia. The proposed Belarusian/ Russian union also granted Belarus favourable terms in dealing with its eastern neighbour. Belarus profited from this directly in terms of lower fuel prices, and the ending of customs fees between the two states. This key policy of Lukashenko's has meant that Belarus has been able to apply its own methods and social safeguards. Before Lukashenko began the process of seriously negotiating a formal economic union with Russia, Belarus had been threatened with a fuel crisis, as it was unable to pay the Russians as much as the West could for gas and oil.

Belarus is not entirely dependent on Russian trade, Lukashenko has been finding new trading partners, vital to continued economic growth. This sound economic policy also serves to preserve Belarusian independence in policy making. The fears of the BPF that Belarus would lose its sovereignty under any union with Russia remain unfounded so long as Lukashenko continues to trade with the rest of the world.

It is estimated that in the late 1990's around 70% of Belarusian exports went to Russia.[20] By 2004 this figure had been reduced to 47%, with EU, African, Asian, Middle Eastern and American countries buying the rest. Despite its anti-Lukashenko official line the USA has also been happy to trade with Belarus. Belarusian exports to the US growing by 76% between January and June 2004 in comparison to 2003.[21]

This shift in trade was not at the cost of productivity, with the overall export of goods and services growing by 19.5% throughout 2004.[22] This all being achieved in less than ten years, from hard currency reserves of only 10 million US Dollars. Belarus was able to boast a surplus in foreign trade in 2005 of some 294.4 million US Dollars.[23]

Even the World Bank, and IMF, who had previously condemned Belarus for its 'non-market' methods began to acknowledge the economic growth. The reason for their interest being that a growing economy offers foreign investors a favourable business environment. Indeed the World Bank's report in June 2005, was actually titled: 'Belarus: Window of Opportunity'. This report highlighted the fact that economic growth in Belarus was genuine, and broadly benefited the population.[24] The IMF survey of August 2005 also confirmed that inflation was falling, and real wages rising. The IMF noted low government debt in Belarus. There is some irony in this observation, as it was by *not* meeting the criteria for IMF loans that Belarus was able to be in this position. Lukashenko speaking to the Russian Duma in 1999 declared the IMF to be *a "pack of swindlers"*.[25] He received rapturous applause, as at the time the Russian government was attempting to borrow 600 million US Dollars to carry through market reforms.

This hostile attitude to the IMF has helped to generate criticism that Belarus is adverse to foreign investment. Certainly in the case of McDonalds, as mentioned earlier there have been difficulties; and also Lukashenko actually closed one McDonalds in Minsk in 2002 demanding that healthy food be sold instead. However the reality is that foreign companies are welcome to expand to Belarus, but only if they are prepared to follow the same laws and legislation as applies to Belarusian enterprises. The only concessions granted are in the six 'Free Economic Zones'. The aim of these zones is to attract both foreign and domestic investment, and provide jobs. The enterprises in these zones pay half of the normal rate of income and profit taxes, and for the first five years of business their taxes are suspended. The aim is essentially to reduce set up costs for new industries, and unlike similar enterprises in the developing world are not used to establish 'sweat shops'. Indeed the Free Economic Zones in Belarus have served to fill 'gaps' in the Belarusian economy, reducing imports, and raising exports.

The Belarusian budgetary and taxation system is strictly controlled, as the state makes many guarantees to its citizens it has to ensure it is able to pay for them. As well as income and value added tax, Belarus also levies a profit tax. This is certainly off putting to foreign investors used to using poorer nations as a source of cheap labour and resources. Also Belarus pursues an environmentally sound economic policy; and puts its words into action in the form of ecological taxation on oil refineries, and petrochemical processing. Again this can lead to greater costs in running a potentially polluting enterprise in Belarus. Lukashenko is following a sensible approach to the environment, by taxing polluters he is forcing them to change their practices, and hopes to meet the terms of the Kyoto Protocol on climate change. Perhaps Lukashenko's background as a farm manager, and not an oil company director, has made the making of environmentally ethical decisions easier.

The advantages of Belarusian economic policies are clear. Lukashenko has not sold out his workforce to the highest bidder, and by protecting jobs and social security Belarus has not seen a 'brain drain' of skilled workers. Notably in contrast to Poland, where the free market has created alarming unemployment (almost 20% of the population in 2002) and a near exodus of young people to Western Europe.[26]

'Experts' have warned that Belarusian economic growth cannot continue unless greater market reform takes place. These apparent experts have been saying this since 1996, however the statistics prove them wrong. Even their own statistics when it suits their interests, such as the World Bank and IMF reports. Lukashenko lived through the Brezhnev era, and is more than aware of what stagnation does to a society and its economy.

2006 saw further increases in the Belarusian GDP as well as industrial and agricultural production. Even the IMF acknowledges that Belarusian economic policy has resulted in continued economic growth and a decrease in inflation. The IMF conceded that the inflation rate in Belarus was the lowest throughout the CIS in 2006. Furthermore this economic success was due to the "*dominant role of government in economic activity, while the private sector, subject to pervasive controls and government interference, contributed only one fourth to the GDP*".[27] Despite this, the IMF's recommendation to Belarus was to cut government spending and subsidies, eliminate wage targets and to increase privatisation, particularly in regard to foreign investment.

Lukashenko believes that progress in the economy and achievements in the social field are inextricably linked, and somewhat reliant on each other. Talking of the privatisation in Belarus he said it was "*of a targeted nature. There were no sweeping privatisation of enterprises. The state refused to manage only those enterprises with which it could not cope. We treated every enterprise we wanted to sell as an individual entity. The main condition for would be investors was to preserve the work collective and the social privileges that were available when the enterprise was a state owned one*".[28] It is just these elements of social protection that the IMF calls 'interference' and is targeting because of their lack of 'profitability'. Fortunately for the working people of Belarus, investors have to follow the Belarusian government's policies and not the recommendations of the IMF. In light of this, Lukashenko takes a personal interest in promoting Belarusian interests abroad, and is attempting to reduce Belarusian reliance on Russia, without distancing himself from the Russian people themselves. Here is perhaps one of the biggest paradoxes for Lukashenko, his belief in Pan-Slavic unity, and the natural brotherhood of Belarusians, and Russians. Despite the huge gulf between the actions of the Russian government in its economic and social spheres, in comparison with those of Belarus.

In 2005 Lukashenko visited the Peoples Republic of China for the third time. Lukashenko met the Chinese President Hu Jintao, and amongst other achievements he secured a 500 million US Dollar[29] 'up front' payment for Belarusian goods and services to be provided to China. Speaking to a correspondent of the Chinese Xinhua news agency, Lukashenko alluded to what Belarus offered China in return for the huge investment: "*We have highest technologies, nano-technologies, highest research facilities, and we are able to offer this to China. In this way, China, Like an enormous bulldozer, is able to 'grapple' our economy and move it forward together with us. It will give rise to colossal development inside Belarus, it will also be beneficial for China*".[30]

Steady economic growth, coupled with expanding markets mean that Belarus is certainly well prepared for the difficulties it may face. Lukashenko's economic policy is certainly unpopular with the West, but for Belarusians it has led not only to stability but also improvement. And it is this real qualitative result that is as important as any statistics on paper. A German election observer in 2000, following his experiences of Moscow, Sofia and Bucharest asked Belarusians in Minsk if there was hunger there, "*they laughed out loud that he could even suggest it*".[31]

Chapter 12. Social Policy in Lukashenko's Belarus

"The fundamental values of the society of the Republic of Belarus are freedom, social justice, labour, solidarity and peace".[1] *A.G. Lukashenko.*

In 1998 the Wall Street Journal reported on the state of Russian society, with the intriguing headline of *"Russia is Looking West"*.[2] However the article went on to explain that Russians both young and old were not looking at *the* West, but rather to their western neighbour, Belarus. One Moscow resident was quoted as saying, *"they have shown us the way forward"*.[3]

What is this direction that could have attracted the attention and support of those living in the capital city of the 'new' Russia? The answer lies largely in the social policy of Belarus. Lukashenko's socially orientated economy generates significant revenue for the state, and the key to the Belarusian system is that this revenue is redistributed to the society that created it. This is the fundamental core of social justice. However Lukashenko is no utopian dreamer, he appreciates that there are more complicated forces at work in the economic and social spheres. Lukashenko has referenced Japan, Malaysia and Singapore as countries that have had rapid economic growth without creating a huge disparity in incomes. Thus discrediting the popular free market myth that a wage level distribution of profits undermines intensive efforts in enterprise and industry. Lukashenko follows closely the Leninist position *of "From each according to his abilities to each according to his needs"*.[4] Although he words it differently it is clear that the underlying principle is the same: *"social justice is first of all a citizen's possibility of consumption of public products that depends on their input into its manufacturing. Although the minimum of the major personal needs must be provided for all"*.[5]

As in the case of the USSR, Belarus places a high value on labour. Unemployment is viewed as being not simply unfortunate for the individual, but corrosive to society as a whole. Therefore Belarusian social policy is closely tied to that of the economy. In free market economies labour is often carried out by the lowest bidder. Thus if a U.S or European firm finds cheaper labour or services abroad, it evaluates the cost of redundancies against the profit from using foreign contractors, and largely on costs alone is the decision made*. In Belarus the situation is reversed. Lukashenko regards labour as "*a man's ability to create material and intellectual values*" and to be "*the basic characteristic of any society*".[6]

Belarus needn't look too far to see the damage inflicted on society by unemployment and the closing of industry. In rural Russia just across the border, following the end of communism life expectancy has dropped from the Soviet average of around seventy, down to fifty-eight years.[7]

A Chicago Tribune news report described the Russian situation thus: "*Fifteen years of post-Soviet capitalism has left rural Russia straggling far behind. Russians in collective farms across the country's eleven time zones could count on a safety net of free housing and health care and on regular paychecks during the Soviet era. In today's Russia, those same villagers live day-to-day, shivering through stretches of winter without heat, cringing at the sight of their children in tattered school clothes*".[8]

Such problems are not limited to eastern Europe. Studies into the consequences of Margaret Thatcher's policy of closing Britain's coal mines, in order to import cheaper coal has found similar alarming results. Research from Durham and Cardiff Universities reported that "*the coalfields remain blighted by severe socio-economic problems, relating to unemployment, long-term sickness and poverty. Poverty affects some of those in employment because new jobs tend to be low paid*".[9] The importance of this comparison is that it shows that the closing of industry causes problems that recognise no national boundaries.

Lukashenko built his election campaign on social security, and prosperity for all in Belarus, and he summarises the importance of employment in achieving this: "*Only labour can provide a high level of life for everybody and an advanced degree of social development as a whole*".[10]

As covered Belarusian unemployment is exceptionally low, and the economic policy protects Belarusian manufacturers. If goods or services can be obtained from Belarusian sources then they must be! This provides the employment vital to society, as well as the taxes needed for social projects. The economy is tied to social policy, and this can be seen by the keen interest that Lukashenko has in all aspects of production. As an example, at a meeting held by Lukashenko on the procurement of brewer's barley he said: "*If even a small quantity of barley is*

---

* This is the essence of 'Globalisation'.

imported from abroad I will regard this case as corruption, as a detriment inflicted upon our peasantry. We cannot today, once we have reached normal production volumes of brewer's barley, import this product from outside the home country. First of all, we need to support our domestic manufacturers".[11] What is significant in this statement is that Belarusian 'protectionist' policy, is not aimed at protecting the profits of a corporation or a financial supporter, but rather the Belarusian workers, and their social welfare. Here can be truly seen the legacy of recent Belarusian history as part of the Soviet Union.

Indeed ideology plays its part in Belarusian social policy. Few nations have a 'state ideology' but rather a dominant system. In the Soviet Union there was a centralised economy and the attempt to establish communism, whilst in the West there is capitalism, with varying degrees of market and mixed economies. The prevailing purpose of capitalism is to create wealth through investment, the control of resources and the lowering of costs. Social welfare however, is very expensive. For example pension increases being kept below the level of inflation does not represent what a government can afford, or indeed what the pensioner contributed whist working, but is rather a reflection of what the government considers to be tolerable by 'the market'.

Again this is where Belarus differs from the accepted practice. Belarus since 1994 has re-evaluated the importance of ideology. Capitalism promotes the individual 'who can', at the expense of those who can't. Hence the staggered quality of healthcare available in the USA dependent on which health insurance is affordable.

Lukashenko's 'market socialism' is an attempt to use the benefits and mechanisms of the market not to divide, but to benefit society. To this end the Belarusian economy continues to grow, whilst income disparity remains one of the lowest in the world.

Income disparity is measured by a calculation known as the GINI co-efficient. The scale goes from 0 (no income disparity) to 1 (complete disparity). In 2005 the GINI co-efficient of 113 countries were tabled, and Belarus had the lowest at 0.217.[12] (Meaning that the highest income is only about five times more than the lowest).

The Belarusian Social and Labour Policy mission statement reaffirms the commitment of the state to economically protect and improve the standard of living for all Belarusian citizens. To this end a nine point programme is outlined, which is backed and financed by the state, and is not reliant on investors, or the workings of the 'market'. The state makes good on its promises through policy and regulation. Contracts are not simply given out to the lowest bidder, no Belarusian state hospital or prison is run by a profit orientated company.

The nine point programme aims:

1. To ensure growth of real monetary incomes of the population as a condition for improving the standard of living and increasing demand and readiness to pay of the people;
2. To increase real wages as the main source of people's incomes and an important incentive for labour among employees;
3. To increase minimum social guarantees provided by the state;
4. To increase efficacy of employment of population and labour competition in the labour market;
5. To increase the level of pension support;
6. To decrease the share of low-income population;
7. To provide social support to all who need it through better targeted support, improvement of social services, etc.;
8. To provide access to broad sectors of population to medical aid and improve quality of medical services;
9. To increase quality of education meeting the needs of the reformed economy and requirements of international educational standards.[13]

Belarus protects the minimum wage that essentially became void across the former Soviet Union in 1991. The minimum wage is constantly monitored and re-valued to maintain at the very least, sustenance level. Indeed the first act of Lukashenko on being elected President was to double the minimum wage. Wages play a vital part in the Belarusian social planning. As so much major industry, agriculture and enterprise is still run by the state, wages can be set to guarantee a more even balance in earnings. To this end resources are used to set wages in all sectors, to represent the labour used, and not merely the end product's market value. Such an approach is an investment in society as well as the economy. The Belarusian economic and social systems are intertwined. Companies can, and do make profits, but as a result so does the nation as a whole*.

---

* As an example of the converse situation; US finance company, American International Group

The prime reason the IMF withdrew loans from Belarus was that the Belarusian government granted subsidies to agriculture to prevent the very real threat of starvation and the complete destruction of the Belarusian rural economy. Other eastern European and former Soviet countries took the IMF loans and followed the terms that came with them, including no subsidies, and strict adherence to the 'market'. The result in Russia has already been mentioned, but also in Poland the rural population faces extreme hardships, and cannot compete with imported produce from Germany, which *does* subsidise its farmers, and therefore artificially lowers prices. Thus western Europe has protected its farmers at the expense of those in the east, all in the name of 'free trade'.

Belarus, in protecting the interests of the agrarian sector has actually seen improved output in foodstuffs. The Food and Agriculture Organisation of the UN (FAO) noted in 2005 that in contrast to decreases of per-capita agricultural production in western Europe and the CIS, Belarus maintains a stable increase.[15]

Belarus has maintained its agricultural sector, and rural towns and villages do not merely represent expensive property for commuters. The contraction of agricultural per capita output in the free market countries simply reflects a concentration of capital, and reliance on cheap imports. According to the FAO Belarus stands on an equal footing with the most developed nations in maintaining the share of the population considered to be undernourished at less than 2.5%.[16]

This development of the countryside is no accident, it is policy. The USSR in its last years began to see a concentration of resources and privilege in the towns at the expense of the countryside. This was in part the fault of Brezhnev era stagnation and 'beurocratisation', and partly, Gorbachev's introduction of market elements into the economy with perestroika. In Belarus the development of Minsk was almost at the expense of the rest of the entire Republic. In Russia and Ukraine the situation was, and remains this way, with Moscow, St. Petersburg and Kiev having hypertrophied development and wages, at the expense of their other cities and districts.

---

in April 2006 paid almost 99million dollars to have 'AIG' printed on Manchester United football shirts for four years (14). This shows the enormous waste prevalent in Western economies. In a state owned enterprise this money could have been used to improve the quality of healthcare, education etc.

Lukashenko regards the basics of urban and rural life to be essentially different, and as such does not advocate applying an urban model to the countryside. He also does not consider one way of life as being superior to the other. This is a key point from Lenin, that whilst the urban working class are considered to be the 'vanguard of the revolution' the peasantry are no less important in the fight against those who live off the labour of others.

Lukashenko's solution to the 'revival of the villages' is twofold. The first is the 'easing of rural life' which is to be done by *"increased mechanisation, electrification and application of new computer and information technologies to the whole rural population"*.[17] The second part of the scheme is 'de-urbanisation'. This process is to be achieved by stopping the 'spread' of towns and cities. To this end Lukashenko envisages keeping industrial development focused, and encouraging the building of low level and individual structures. Essentially creating the appearance of small towns or large villages, as opposed to the Soviet era's concrete sprawl. Lukashenko wants this policy to nourish the Belarusian culture, and the traditional 'attachment to the land'. By supporting the building of communities, Belarusian social policy hopes to strengthen the family unit, as well as the sense of social belonging and togetherness. Ultimately this should reduce the number of economic migrants within Belarus. Lukashenko has expressed concern over the potential psychology of a person who is 'rootless'. He believes this to be the breeding ground for the consumerist mentality that leads to a decline in moral standards, and the young being drawn into gangs and crime. The Belarusian state follows a policy whereby the individuals life opportunities and access to services are not dictated by the accident of fate of their birthplace, or as has been seen in the UK, by a so called 'postcode lottery'. According to Lukashenko, *"it is not to a person to move around in search of the adequate living conditions (education, job, information and cultural values) but the very living and activity conditions should be made available to everyone regardless of where they are"*.[18] One way this policy is put into practice is by the use of 'specialists'. Higher education is free, but does come with a condition. Students gaining vocational qualifications may be sent on placement to a part of the country where their skills are in demand. This work period can last up to five years. The principle is clear, and is aimed at preventing a saturation of the skilled workforce in Minsk. Such work placements are not punitive, or permanent, but are consistent with the policy of maintaining sustained progress across the whole country.

One of the greatest achievements of the Soviet Union was in the field of education. No matter where they lived, Soviet children were guaranteed access to free education and the chance of scholarships to prestigious universities. Communist and socialist governments the world over have always had literacy and education programmes as core principles.

Belarus has continued in this tradition. This is in stark contrast to the decline in public service spending in the other former Soviet republics. Russia's headlong dive into the free market has kept funds away from the social sector with the result of annual GDP spending on education falling from 7% in 1970 to just over 3% in 1994.[19] In available public expenditure on education, Belarus surpasses all the CIS countries plus the USA, and most European countries including Germany, France, Great Britain, Ireland, Belgium and Holland. Belarus spends 6% of its GDP on education with a draft law aiming to increase this to 10% by the end of 2006. Notably the country who spends the most on education is communist Cuba with a staggering 18.7% of its GDP.[20]

The result being that according to the United Nations human development report of 2004 Belarus leads the CIS nations in adult literacy at 99.7%. The Belarusian education system aims to provide a standard quality across the nation by the equal allocation of resources, and a set curriculum. The aim is to gain the maximum return in terms of quality of education, for the state investment. This is in contrast to the de-regulation spreading across most Western countries. For example the introduction of 'market values' into British education began with league tables, but has resulted in a steady decline in confidence in the system. Teachers warn that they are no longer 'teaching' but instead giving instructions in exam techniques. A further problem is what teaching unions have called the 'ghettoisation of education'. UK delegates to the National Union of Teachers 2006 conference criticised New Labour's educational 'reforms' as leading to an *"increasingly divisive, segregated two tier system"*.[21]

The 'reforms' in question would further lower the amount of GDP that the British government would spend on education as the private sector takes over. The results for poorer families would quite simply be that their access to quality education would be severely restricted.

Under-performing schools would not attract investors, as any profit margin would be presumably lower. NUT delegate Mary Compton summarised the importance of opposition to this bill thus: "*In fighting this bill, we are part of a international struggle to wrest education from the privateers and the profiteers worldwide*".[22]

In Belarus it is not the marketplace that dictates educational policy, but the educators themselves. Amongst the major priorities of the policy are; " [the] *restoration of the national and cultural foundation of education; orientation of the education to educating a free and creative and moral personality; strengthening of physical and mental health of the nation and individual*".[23]

The key point of these priorities is to educate in a holistic way that serves the nation by creating a highly skilled and socially conscious workforce. To this end Belarusian educational institutions offer a wide range of academic and vocational courses. Belarus has over 150 vocational institutions teaching technical and professional skills and qualifications. Added to this are 39 vocational schools for students with disabilities.[24] Belarusian social policy is fundamentally an insurance of social inclusion. Belarus is also committed to state sponsored lifelong learning. Lukashenko commented in 1998 that: "*We must realise that nowadays it is impossible to train a person 'once and forever'. Technologies and correspondingly, qualification requirements in the large majority of the scientific production activities change drastically each 5 to 10 years*".[25] Between 1990 and 2004 the number of citizens in higher education almost doubled.[26] Scientific research is also actively supported by the state. Grants and scientific journals are dedicated to the constant development of ethical and honest research practice. By maintaining an effective grant system and means of publication Belarusian scientific research is not at the mercy of the goals and whims of independent business. One example of the latter case is that when it was discovered that a genetically modified milk producing hormone caused cows to leak puss into milk buckets, the US firm responsible had the test data "*buried*".[27] A lack of government regulation does not break up a monopoly on truth, it simply allows the highest bidder to redefine the truth, and decide what *it* considers to be in the public's best interest.

By investing in education the Belarusian system is rewarded by the workforce it produces. Courses are geared toward careers, and no tuition fees are charged. Furthermore some 70% of full time students qualify for grants or stipends which cover rent and living expenditure. Higher stipends are paid in research work, and the science and technology field. Notably the stipend is increased the better the student performs.

Belarusian inclusive social policy also guarantees maternity stipend rights for students, and provides for childcare to allow continuing education for those with families.[28] Further to this, much like in the Soviet Union or Cuba, foreign students are invited to study in Belarus on an equal footing with Belarusian citizens.

Despite claims made by Belarusian nationalists that the Belarusian language is being made extinct by Lukashenko, many schools still teach in Belarusian. The joint status of Russian and Belarusian protects the Belarusian language from such a fate. Entry into Belarusian higher education is granted depending on the results of a national test that may be taken in either language, which one is entirely up to the student.

Another criticism levelled at Lukashenko is that he has not reformed education, but simply carried on the Soviet model in style and content. Again this is not the case, although classes in Belarus certainly follow a social agenda. With the aim being to educate the future generations as responsible citizens, with a strong work ethic. Over the years since Lukashenko's election almost 4000 new educational texts have been published, as well as frequently updated wall maps and charts. The myth of Belarusian schools teaching from 1960's Soviet texts, is again manufactured, Lukashenko is more than aware of the ever changing world and does not want his nation to be left behind, or seen as merely some kind of 'museum of the USSR'.

This does not mean that Soviet history is being ignored, or 'revised'. An optional course to supplement general history, 'The Great Patriotic War of the Soviet People' has been introduced across the education system since 2004. The aim of this course is to teach the younger generations the scale of sacrifice made to preserve Belarus, and indeed the importance of the victory over fascism. Key issues in the course are international solidarity, respect for the older generations, and the sacrifice paid by Belarusians for their independence. As covered in chapter five, it is impossible to play down the importance of the Second World War in forging the Belarusian nation, and culture.

In Belarusian schools there are weekly discussion groups, where pupils are encouraged to debate domestic and international affairs.

These fifteen-minute sessions are also bolstered by a monthly talk. Where children are informed of world news as well as political and social issues. These talks and sessions certainly favour the state ideology, and are meant to instil patriotism and values into young Belarusians. Much like swearing allegiance to the flag in US schools, but perhaps with more discussion.

Alexander Segodnik, the head of a local education department in Grodno summarised the role education plays in political and social development of the young: "*School is an ideological tool of the state. It indicates what the state wants, what its goals are and what the means of achieving them are. We are creating future citizens and patriots!* "[29] Beyond its education policy, Belarus also pursues an active programme in regard to the youth of the country. Lukashenko has commented that with young people being such a 'mobile' part of the population, the discrediting or ending of moral and cultural values effects the young first. Lukashenko regarded the collapse of the Soviet Union, and indeed a broader rejection of ideology or morals to have "*brought about rising juvenile delinquency and an increase in violent behaviour*". Further to this he added, "*the stratification of society also favoured the increasing number of juvenile delinquents*".[30]

His reasoning is that when Soviet institutions such as theatrical and sports groups, as well as public libraries and youth centres had their budgets cut or stopped after 1991, the privateers moved in, bought the properties and made a profit by converting them into luxury apartments, nightclubs etc. The result was the young being 'ousted onto the streets'. This led to a corresponding rise in crime and antisocial behaviour.

Lukashenko's analysis seems indeed to be accurate, particularly when we look at the problems in western Europe and North America caused by youths lacking a direction for their energies. As for his comments about social stratification adding to the problem this can be crudely but effectively seen to be the case in the UK, where working class youths are labelled 'Chavs' by their more affluent peers, and unfortunately also by the media. This derogatory term is another example that Tony Blair's claim that Britains "*class war is over*" is either completely untrue, or a declaration of total defeat for the working class.

By investing in education and genuinely constructive youth projects, Belarus has seen a considerable fall in crime, and other anti-social behaviour. The backbone of this achievement is genuine investment, and vitally a moral base on which to build. Lukashenko does not believe in 'managing the symptoms' of a problem, but in curing the cause. Teaching respect and the principles of social justice aim to create a more cohesive society than one based on consumerism, and the culture of want, which has been so corrosive elsewhere.

When Lukashenko worked for the Soviet youth organisation 'Komsomol' he was clearly impressed by the constructive and creative outlets it offered. In 2002 several existing youth groups were combined into the state supported Belarusian Republican Youth Union. Known by its Cyrillic initials of BRSM. Though it is the largest youth group, it is not the only one, indeed other non partisan youth groups also receive state funding. The BRSM is considered to be the legal successor to the Komsomol, and as such displays the emblems of the Orders of Lenin and the Red Banner awarded during the Soviet era. The State Committee for Youth Affairs ensures that constructive and progressive activities are available and funded for Belarusian youth. They provide the funding for the BRSM, and also maintain close links with other state committees and ministries. The BRSM also offers references for young Belarusians when seeking employment, and provides certificates of recommendation for its members. Belarusian youth groups take part in active labour and work experience placements. The BRSM has also been credited by the United Nations as taking an active role in reducing infection rates of HIV and AIDS in Belarus. The BRSM raises awareness of the diseases and their prevention. Further to the moral guidance passed on to the members by the organisation itself. The BRSM officially is not a political organisation, although its patriotic and socialistic outlook and emblems has led it to be nicknamed the 'Lukamol' by opposition activists. For the most part the BRSM involves itself in arranging sporting events including regional and international competitions. As well as involving Belarusian youth in public events and anniversaries. For many young Belarusians, the Soviet Union is not a living memory. Thus if Belarus is to maintain its independent development model, and 'socially orientated economy' young people need to be involved, and educated to the goals and benefits.

Lukashenko summarised his vision for, and the purpose of the BRSM thus: *"The youth - our major pillar - is at the heart of our plans and targets. We have hardly used its powerful potential yet. We often 'brush aside' youth's initiatives. Many managers avoid direct contact with the youth, they are afraid of acute questions. They are incapable of involving young people into useful public activities. We should work in this direction. It will help avoid a number of negative phenomena in the youth environment. This situation calls for a greater role of the Belarusian Republican Youth Union. It should demonstrate its abilities as an organiser, a leader of the national youth movement".*[31]

Belarusian education and youth policy are planned and consistent with the aims of social policy as a whole. The education system aims to produce a broadly educated and skilled workforce. Whilst a wider youth policy maintains a sense of social inclusion for the young, as well as focus for their energies and ideas. The Belarusian system could not function for long without such a positive strategy for young people. Anti-social behaviour fuelled by the consumerist values of 'want' is unfortunately prevalent in Western society. The capitalist ethos is individualist, and the dictates of the market in the social sphere has often served to fragment the family unit (and consequently society) by charging high prices for childcare, and withdrawing funds from non-profit social organisations and youth groups.

Belarusian state ideology is inclusive, and collective. Thus social stability is as vital as economic growth. Disenfranchisement and inequality of opportunity are not permissible. Belarus does not allow the market to dictate where money should be spent, and who should benefit; everyone plays their role in society, and as such receives their fair share of the profit. Lukashenko's goal of a *"strong and prosperous Belarus"*, is not to be achieved for a minority or an elite, but for the whole nation, hence the motto adopted in 2006 *"the state for the people!"*

This investment in young people is vital for the continuation of the economic and social progress made in Belarus, but it is not done at the expense of the older generations. In fact Lukashenko receives almost universal support from pensioners and particularly war veterans. The reasons for this go further than merely the level of pensions, or free public transport. The economic growth and relative success of the 'Masherov years' came from the hard work and dedication of these citizens of the BSSR.

Lukashenko's positive opinion of the USSR, as well as the preservation of Soviet national holidays, and a rejection of nationalism have all found favour with the older generation.

These Belarusian people have righteous pride in their history. They have known what it is to see everything they have worked for destroyed, and what shortages really mean. Thus when young people returning from visits to the West made comments about 'needing' designer clothes or computer games, Lukashenko's subsequent comments of concern about such *"consumerist values"* being out of place in Belarus were well received by this demographic.

Maxim Medvedev a young Belarusian opposition activist interviewed citizens of Pinsk in south-west Belarus trying to gain qualitative data on genuine public opinion on Lukashenko. He found the President had support from all ages and groups. Of the pensioners there was strong ideological support as well as the more practical. Retired collective farm workers were concerned at what would happen to their communities if the land was simply sold off, whilst all commented on their regular pension payments which are so rare in Eastern Europe. One pensioner commented, *"Who will take care of us in case Lukashenko leaves his post?"*[32]

It has been frequently reported that in Russia, pension payments almost ceased after the collapse of the USSR, and that the current situation, although better, is still not comprehensive, or of subsistence level. This plight is not unique to Russia, most of the former socialist nations of eastern Europe have let their social security decline, many at the behest of the IMF, to create 'favourable investment conditions'.

The current Belarusian pension law is based on the 1956 Soviet one amended in 1993 and again by the Lukashenko government in 1999. The continuation of the Soviet law is important, as it does not simply start 'afresh' from 1991.

The worker contributes one percent of their earnings, whilst the employer is responsible for between 10 to 35% of the payroll. The government provides the rest of the money. This same 'social insurance system' is also used to fund sickness and maternity pay, as well as family allowances to employees.

Belarusian workers are entitled to a state pension when they reach 60 (men) or 55 (women), with 25 and 20 years of insurance coverage respectively. The money paid into pension funds by these workers is used solely for their pension. Social insurance is not money for the government to speculate with.

The Belarusian system is aimed at allowing people to have a retirement, and not simply work until they drop. In 2005 British workers were told that to qualify for a pension men would now have to work until 70. The bitter irony being that in poor areas, British male life expectancy has actually fallen below 70 years.[33]

In Belarus the qualifying conditions for pensions are reduced for workers in hazardous work, as well as the following groups: War veterans, parents of disabled children, disabled people, mothers of five or more children, as well as mothers of military personnel killed in service.

The Belarusian pension is closely monitored to ensure that inflation does not de-value the benefit received. There *is* a link between pensions and earnings. In April 2006 Lukashenko raised the pension by seven percent, to better represent the rise in real wages of Belarusian workers. Pensions and benefits are not used as political tools in Belarus to be raised before elections and stealthily reduced when funds are required elsewhere. The Belarusian pension and benefit system is based on a legal framework established in 1999 that ensures that all payments must at least meet actual living costs.

This social insurance system also provides for maternity benefits. Belarusian women, including students, and the unemployed are guaranteed state support in the form of maternity payments of parity with their existing wage, grant, or benefits. This maternity pay is available for up to 140 calendar days. As of 2006, in Britain maternity pay is available at 90% of earnings for the first 6 weeks only, before a lower rate is introduced. In the USA maternity pay is entirely at the whim of the employer, but by law women are allowed unpaid leave to have a baby, provided they have worked full time at the same place for over a year (this only applies if the workplace has over 50 employees).[34]

Maternity leave in Belarus is also extended to those who adopt babies. Belarus has a positive and progressive outlook on the family. Support is available for those who have children, including the provision of childcare for those who work.

The Social insurance system provides a 'safety net' to protect all social groups. A common criticism of Belarusian social policy is that it has resulted in a low standard of living. This is true only in comparison to the more affluent citizens of other nations, but does not take into account the 'unseen' advantages of a comprehensive social policy.

Thus social policy in Belarus, particularly in terms of pensions and benefits provides a guaranteed level of support for survival. Few Belarusian pensioners will have luxury cars or the latest computers, but they will be able to afford food, fuel and the essentials that allow them to enjoy a peaceful retirement. Belarusian life expectancy is higher than all former Soviet states with the exception of Georgia, this is particularly impressive in light of the impact of the Chernobyl accident on Belarus.

A significant factor in assessing quality of life is the availability of, access to and quality of health care. Along with education, healthcare provision is a staple of socialist and communist systems. The logic is simple. The citizens contribute to society, and thus society cares for them in return. (A healthy worker, can work harder, is a more cynical approach to the same issue).

Lukashenko does not have a narrow view of what constitutes 'public health' or what it should achieve. He believes that the health care system should *"encompass not only the purely medical activity and institutions, but it should also supervise the organisation of a wide range of physical, sporting, ecological, educational and physiological activities"*.[35]

This policy is as pragmatic as it is ideological. It is a recognition of the social and economic benefits of prevention over cure. In a society where health care is free more emphasis for example will be placed on healthy eating or smoking cessation campaigns. In countries with private medical care, the less healthy the lifestyle, the more profit can be made out of those who pay for their operations and treatment.

The Belarusian system as envisioned by Lukashenko is wide ranging, but with the ultimate goal of *"preserving and improving health conditions of each individual citizen. Everybody's health is the public wealth"*.[36]

This is no idle boast, or temporary state of affairs, but is guaranteed by the Belarusian constitution. Article 45 of which states that: *"Citizens of the Republic of Belarus shall be guaranteed the right to health care, including free treatment at state health-care establishments. The State shall make health care facilities accessible to all of its citizens. The right of citizens of the Republic of Belarus to health care shall also be secured by the development of physical training and sport, measures to improve the environment, the opportunity to use fitness establishments and improvements in occupational safety"*.[37]

The Belarusian economy diverts large amounts of resources to this end. Particularly in regard to the overlap between health policy and its relation to education, pensions, and recreation.

Public health expenditure in 2001 represented 4.8% of the GDP.[38] This figure is good for the region, and for what the UN term a 'medium human development nation' (In fact Belarusian commitment to health resources ranked 7th in this category). According to the World Health Organisation in 2005 this percentage had increased to 6.4%.

Lukashenko's government acknowledges that this figure can be improved in accordance with Belarusian economic growth. Thus the target for health spending as a percentage of GDP is 7.5% in 2007. The target here as in education, is not only to maintain a standard of service ahead of the CIS countries but also to challenge and surpass the EU and USA in terms of spending of available resources.

Belarus faces a unique challenge in health care provision as a result of the Chernobyl accident. With the majority of the fallout hitting Belarus, the medical aftermath has been particularly acute. Cancers are worryingly common and have notably effected children. Chernobyl's legacy in Belarus is that of mortality and morbidity.

The overall health policy of prevention over cure is not applicable to this unique tragedy. This is what Lukashenko has referred to as generations of Belarusians having *"to carry the cross of Chernobyl"*.[39]

The Belarusian system is directing funds and resources into health care provision. Although it is true that in comparison to their Western counterparts Belarusian Doctors are not very well paid, there has not been a shortage of people wanting to practice medicine. Indeed in a country that places such a high value on the social sphere, the role of the doctor is a particularly valued and respected profession*. In Belarus, state prizes are conferred upon health workers, and the importance and honour of working in the health service is emphasised in Belarusian media. There is also the honorary title of 'Merited Doctor of the Republic of Belarus' which can be conferred by Presidential Decree. This title certainly is a Soviet sounding and inspired award. Such awards follow the socialist principle that human beings do not work or endeavour purely for financial reward, and that the nation as a whole recognises and appreciates their labour. This belief is proven by the fact that in Belarus during the period of 2001-2003 there were 450 medical doctors per 100,000 of the population.[40] This figure is ahead of its neighbours Russia, Poland and Ukraine. Also, significantly, Belarus has more Doctors per 100,000 people than does the USA, UK, and most of western Europe, despite the huge gulf in the financial incentives to enter the profession.

---

* Karl Marx stated that under capitalism, the most respected of professions such as the doctor or priest were reduced to the same level as every other, simply being measured in terms of salary, and becoming 'wage slaves'.

It is not only in terms of doctors that Belarus performs well. A qualified midwife supervises every birth where possible. In fact Belarus is one of only 30 countries in the world to be able to claim this. As of 2005, even the USA is not one of these nations.[41] Belarus also maintains one of the most comprehensive child immunisation programmes in the world. The percentage of one-year-olds immunised against measles and tuberculosis in Belarus is officially 99% (no nation has any higher), and many Western countries are significantly lower.[42]

The UN body UNAIDS (charged with combating HIV and AIDS) has also noted the success of Belarusian social and health policies in dealing with these problems. Increased resources are being used to provide antiretroviral treatments, and also methadone programmes for IV drug abusers. The current trend in Belarusian HIV/AIDS awareness and treatment means that Belarus may become the first eastern European country to stop the increase in these diseases. If this trend continues, incidences of HIV and AIDS ought to be actually declining in Belarus by 2010.[43]

The Belarusian system allocates resources as an investment in society. This results in a correlation between economic growth and improvements in quality of life and access to services. According to UN Human Development Reports, Belarus is climbing year on year in terms of its human development index. An important factor in United Nations reports is that independent figures are used and reflect what is really happening within a country, not official statistics as put out by a government or their opponents.

In 2004 the World Bank compiled a report on Belarus entitled: 'Belarus: Poverty Assessment. Can Poverty Reduction and Access to Services be Sustained?' This report is enlightening, as it comes from a source that is far from supportive of Lukashenko. The social policy of Belarus is explored and evaluated constructively, and the conclusion is highly positive. As stated earlier the World Bank and IMF compile reports on nations in order to assess them for their financial investment stability. The theory being that healthy citizens in stable countries make good consumers. Also in a country with low unemployment there ought to be more disposable income, particularly when combined with decent life expectancy and pensions. Hence the World Bank's interest in Belarusian social policy.

According to the report, "*The poverty reduction and inequality performance of Belarus is impressive*".[44] Also "*Belarus can be justly proud of the elaborate system of social services it provides to its population. The ability of households to access quality education, health and social protection services makes a large difference to their living standards in the present, and their prospects for the future*".[45]

The World Bank noted that poverty had fallen most substantially in the period of 1997-2002. This period being immediately after Lukashenko's 1996 referendum and the consolidation of the presidency. On social protection the report concluded that, "*Pensions are found to be the most adequate benefit, in part as a result of the policy of indexing pensions to real wages. Child allowances are also found to provide adequate protection*".[46] Furthermore health and education was praised. The report also made special attention to the number of students in Belarus who were learning foreign languages, and the technical quality of education. On health, the World Bank noted that "*overall health expenditures are progressive, in the sense that the poor benefit relatively more than the better off*".[47]

The social policy of Belarus is vast and ambitious. However its goals are being achieved, and as seen it is not only Lukashenko who thinks so. The UN and even the World Bank note the success of the Belarusian system, and its proportionally high spending on social projects. Nor is it simply a case of the right balance on paper. Facts and figures translate into a positive experience for the majority of Belarusians, as witnessed by those who work or travel in the region.

A good example is that of US lawyer and writer Chad Nagle. He described Belarus in the year 2000 as an 'oasis in the heart of Europe'. In this article he said "*speaking from experience, Belarus is a refreshing change for someone who's travelled extensively in the old Evil Empire*".[48] Nagle as others, comments on the graffiti and litter free streets of Belarusian towns, as well as the visible sense of purpose and dignity in the people as they have jobs to go to, and shops they can afford to use. Ultimately Belarusian social policy is tied to the economy as in all nations, but the difference is Lukashenko makes the economy work for the people instead of the other way around.

Chapter 13. Human Rights in Belarus.

"If there are no pre-texts for intervention – imaginary ones are created. To this end a very convenient banner was chosen, democracy and human rights. And not in their original sense of the rule of people and personal dignity, but solely and exclusively in the interpretation of the US leadership".[1] A.G. Lukashenko.

The prime justification for US and European opposition to Lukashenko is that of human rights abuses in Belarus. As in Iraq the West needs to claim a higher moral position to excuse the questionable morality of its actions. However the situation in Belarus under Lukashenko is hugely different to that of Saddam Hussein's Iraq. Lukashenko has not used chemical weapons on an ethnic minority, and nor has he banned opposition parties. Human rights are specifically protected by the Constitution of Belarus, and the reality of 'Europe's last dictatorship' is very different from the widely propagated myth. The majority of human rights concerns in Belarus are the result of accusations from abroad, and as such there will be some crossover with the next chapter. This chapter will focus on inter-ethnic relations within Belarus, religious freedoms and the rights of women. As such it is very closely tied to the previous chapter on social policy. Also political freedoms will be examined, but elections and political parties are specifically discussed in chapter 15.

Human rights are a very sensitive issue, and objectivity is often clouded by differing interpretations of ethics and moral philosophy. Indeed for any one nation to criticise human rights practice in another, it ideally should (at least) set a better example itself. Different political or theological ideologies place differing levels of importance on certain rights. For example the Nazis strict racial theories meant that certain people were exempt from any legal protection based purely on their ethnicity.

The Belarusian system is an open and inclusive one. In his book 'Belarus Tomorrow' Lukashenko sets out his approach to, and interpretation of, human rights. The key basis for the Belarusian legal framework is the UN declaration of human rights adopted in 1948. Lukashenko specifies the link between rights and responsibilities. The duty to ensure that expressing your own freedom does not result in the infringement of someone else's. Lukashenko wrote that, *"the politi-*

cal and human rights and freedoms remain senseless if they are not confirmed by social and economic rights".[2] Essentially meaning that freedoms are no use if they exist solely on paper. This is also a direct link to Belarusian social policy, and Lukashenko's belief in the value of labour to both the individual and society. Amongst the human rights expected, such as freedom of movement, and expression, Lukashenko also considers employment, education and healthcare as human rights.

Despite the frequent accusations of fascism in Belarus, and alleged anti-Semitism within the government, the reality is that Belarus is a remarkably tolerant society. The historical reasons for this have been explained, but Lukashenko's social policy has also been a significant factor in creating unity in Belarus. Very few states would consider persecution of ethnic minorities as acceptable, however many nations without ideological leadership are prone to reactionary scapegoating legislation when faced with a 'majority outcry' sparked by 'independent media'. Of course how independent the media truly is in Western societies is debatable. Any privately owned newspaper can be used as a platform for the owner's opinions and beliefs.

Belarusian policy in regard to ethnic minorities is very clear, and also quite inflexible. Lukashenko's threat to *"tear the arms off any fascist I find"*[3] is typical. When reading any official Belarusian publications about the country, and indeed in correspondence with diplomatic staff of the country, the theme of social and ethnic harmony is frequently encountered. Belarusians are proud of the stability in their country that has historical roots in various nations and of course the Soviet Union. Distinctly the anti-Semitism widespread in eastern Europe is notably rare in Belarus. In fact anti-Semitism in eastern Europe is worryingly commonplace, and most surprising given the first hand experience of most of these nations of the holocaust. 'Skinhead' and neo-nazi groups exist across eastern Europe, including in Belarus. However in Belarus they are actively fought by the state, which has little time for nationalism.

Viktor Gaisenak headed the Belarusian delegation to the 2004 Organisation for Security and Co-operation in Europe (OSCE) conference on anti-Semitism. In his statement to the chairman he praised the deep history of Jewish life in Belarus, and the importance of the role played by Jews in forming the Belarusian nation and culture. He said *"Jews have been living on the territory of Belarus for more than six centuries, they are an integral part of the ethnic composition of Belarusian society and have been fully integrated into the life of that society*".[4] He expanded on this by acknowledging the threat posed by the increase in right wing groups, and the influence of nationalist elements. He added, "*although few in number, cases of anti-Semitism are a source of deep concern and disquiet to us*" and "*the laws of the Republic of Belarus make it possible and necessary to wage an uncompromising fight against all manifestations of anti-Semitism*".[5] The historical role of Jews in Belarus was noted here, as was the problem of the spread of anti-Semitism across Europe resulting from an increasing acceptability of xenophobia and aggressive nationalism. Gaisenak warned how open borders and the Internet could allow such phenomena to spread "*like a cancerous growth throughout all of Europe*".[6]

Belarus also supports its claims of inter-ethnic equality and understanding with action. At the 60th meeting of the UN Commission on Human Rights, Belarus and Russia tabled a joint resolution intended to draw the international community's attention to the dangers of the 'resurgence and spread of neo-Nazism, neo-fascism and aggressive nationalism'. This Belarusian/Russian resolution was adopted by majority vote, but was not supported unanimously. At the OSCE conference, Gaisenak raised this issue declaring: "*To our surprise, European Union countries, The United States of America and Japan voted against the resolution. What is the conclusion to be drawn from this by neo-Nazi and neo-fascist elements and the other such scum against whom this resolution was directed?*"[7]

According to an independent study undertaken by the Stephen Roth Institute at the University of Tel Aviv, anti-Semitism in Belarus has declined since Lukashenko was elected president. The report of 2000-2001 followed the usual Western approach of presuming Lukashenko to be a dictator, but did declare that he was "*supportive of the Jewish Community*".[8] The report notes that the authorities in Belarus repeatedly express support for the Jewish population. Added to this, official warnings had been sent to three Belarusian newspapers that regularly printed anti-Semitic articles. One of these publications was 'Nasha Niva' (Our Wheatfield). This newspaper was eventually closed down by the Belarusian government in 2006, to much international criticism for stifling independent media. This was also the case in 2005 when the racist 'Narodnaia Volia' (Peoples Freedom) newspaper was banned.

Both of these cases are cited as examples of human right abuse in Belarus. Namely that the government is not allowing independent media. This is patently untrue and serves as a crudely opportunist tool with which to attack Lukashenko. The newspapers in question were independently acknowledged to be frequently publishing anti-Semitic articles, with little regard for the human rights of the Belarusian Jewish community. In 1998 Lukashenko wrote: *"The only restriction to freedom – and the most significant one – is the freedom of others. We are in favour of a strict observance of this interlink"*.[9]

In any nation that has undergone dramatic economic and social upheaval the danger of xenophobia should not be underestimated. Russia has seen a terrible increase in attacks on foreigners. In late 2005 there were four fatal stabbings of African students in St. Petersburg alone, with a further 800 reported 'hate crimes'.[10] Simon Samba Samba of the Cameroonian embassy in Russia commented *"when people came to study here in communist times, it was not like this"*.[11]

Indeed the dangers of racist and anti-Semitic publications and media are all too real. In December 2000 a synagogue in Minsk was firebombed. A furious Lukashenko visited the site and was quoted as saying, *"we won't let anyone harm our Jews"*.[12] This statement is enlightening, not only for it clearly rendering false any assertions that Lukashenko is a fascist or anti-Semite, but also because of the use of the word 'our'. The Soviet Union was often referred to as being a 'communal apartment block of nations', all working and living together. Lukashenko views Belarus and its people in the same way. He does not differentiate between a Russian, Belarusian, Jew or Pole, they have a different ethnicity and culture, but they are all Belarusian citizens. Such is the importance of the social system; everyone works for the benefit of the state, and are thus protected by the state.

Herein lies the reason why divisive articles are deemed unsuitable for publication in Belarus, and why the newspapers that publish them were closed down. Nor is this a happy coincidence for Lukashenko. Independent media does exist in Belarus, and in fact outnumbers official publications. Of the 776 Newspapers available in Belarus in 2005, 221 were state owned as opposed to 555 independent. This trend continues in magazines (146 state to 303 independent). In Radio and TV broadcasting there are 45 state owned companies and institutions with 47 independent.[13] Added to this is the fact that out of all the CIS countries Belarus has the highest rate of individual access to the Internet.[14] Opinion and information are certainly not monopolised in Belarus.

In 2005 a new law was passed in Belarus which according to foreign media including the respected British 'Sunday Times' newspaper, made criticising Lukashenko illegal.[15] This certainly fits the profile of a dictator, if true. Fortunately for the people of Belarus, it isn't. The reality of the law is more complicated, being an addition to an existing one regarding the culpability of acts against an individual or the State. Essentially the law was amended to establish greater personal responsibility for criminal behaviour in regard to slander and defamation.

The part of the law which caused an international media outcry over the claim that criticising Lukashenko was now somehow illegal, was article 369-1 of the criminal code. This article regards defamation of the Republic of Belarus, and is no equivalent of the Nazi enabling act of 1933, or even the US patriot act of 2001. The article establishes responsibility to those who provide a foreign state or international organisation with deliberately false information regarding the political, economic, social, or military, situation in Belarus and the legal standing of citizens. The key issues here are the words 'deliberately' and 'false'. Criticism is not prohibited, but if the criticism is knowingly untrue, and (most importantly) then supplied to a foreign power as a fact, then a crime has been committed. Significantly the legislation makes a distinction between factual information and opinion. Thus no Belarusian citizen can be held to account for expressing his or her opinion. The legal commentary on this article concludes with the statement: *"Providing a foreign state, a foreign or international organisation with one's personal opinions, views or judgements of the situation in Belarus or legal standing of Belarusian citizens without adduction of knowingly false data does not constitute a crime"*.[16] As can be seen this does not make personal criticism of the President a crime, and in fact protects that right by law. As will be seen in a later chapter on presidential elections in Belarus, criticism of Lukashenko has certainly been permitted both in the media, and on the streets.

Such was the international reaction to this new law that the Belarusian diplomatic service issued a press release/commentary in which the law was explained and also how it compared to the laws of other nations was also discussed. Two examples in particular were used. The first was the Polish law that establishes criminal responsibility for the *"insult of the Nation or the Republic of Poland"*.[17] The second example was that of the Netherlands, which prosecutes for defamation. Thus it can be seen that article 369-1 falls closer to libel law than it does to the Orwellian thought control that it was reported to be. The fact that in explaining the new law, Belarus cited international comparisons is not unique, and as will be seen in the next chapter this is part of a trend in responding to external criticism. Indeed the first open complaints of human rights violations appeared in 1997. Voiced not by Belarusian activists, but in the decidedly partisan 'New Europe' magazine. So concerned was the writer in question that she suggested Russia "*should take over*"[18] in an attempt to show Belarus how democracy was supposed to work. The ironies were conveniently ignored. Russia's human rights record was already a major cause for concern, but Russian economic policies were decidedly Western looking. Thus the human rights concern was the 'convenient banner' used by the West to conceal its real intentions and specifically its economic goals.

The USA and UK justified military intervention in Afghanistan not only because of the established link between Al Qaeda and the Taliban, but also because of the appalling human rights actions within the country; particularly abuses against women. Incidentally the existence of discrimination against women in Afghanistan had also been used as a moral justification for the Soviet intervention in 1979. The USA at the time took a different position and at first discreetly, and then overtly armed and trained the Mujahideen rebels who were to become the Taliban. The propagandised and protected place of women in the USSR did not survive its dissolution. In Belarus women made up an unequal share of the unemployed in the years 1991 –1996, averaging around 65%.[19] Further to this women were largely separated from the political apparatus and influential jobs. Social circumstances in transitional Belarus also acutely effected women, as alcoholism and domestic violence increased across former Soviet states. Lukashenko's belief was that such social problems grew out of unemployment and the resulting lack of purpose and self worth. Thus his policies aimed at full employment and the state ideology strive to minimise such social problems as well as serving the national economy.

Lukashenko himself does not drink alcohol, and many women in Belarus comment on this fact. Vera Mayuk, a 45 year old worker commented in 2001 (to opposition activists), "*I like Lukashenko very much. He is handsome, clever and a good speaker. He doesn't drink and smoke, he goes in for sports. He can ski and play hockey. It is impossible to compare him with our husbands*".[20] Belarusian women are also protected by the constitution of the Republic of Belarus. Article 22 states that *"All shall be equal before the law and entitled without discrimination to equal protection of their rights and legitimate interests"*.[21] This article is backed up not only by prosecuting discriminatory employment practices, but also by protecting the rights and financially safeguarding women who choose to raise a family. Such issues as maternity pay and access to a state pension were discussed in the previous chapter.

Further to this overall guarantee of equality before the law article 32 of the constitution states that *"A husband and wife shall be equal in family relationships"*. It continues with; *"women shall be guaranteed equal rights with men in their opportunities to receive education, vocational training, promotion in labour, socio-political, cultural and other spheres of activity, as well as in creating conditions safeguarding their labour and health"*.[22] In addition to this is article 39 which guarantees equal pay for those of equal ability. This is hugely important in maintaining gender equality in salaries, and of course in a largely state run economy this can be easily and effectively applied across different occupations and industries. It is also worth mentioning that these articles were reinforced by the Constitutional amendments made in 1996, which were widely condemned by the USA and EU countries. Such legislation is slowly proving its worth, as women are becoming well represented across all spheres in Belarus. Following the 2001 parliamentary elections, female representation in the National Soviet increased to 28.1%. Local elections in 2003 and again in 2007 saw over 44% of deputies elected female. Added to this political representation, women are also notable in the legal framework of the country, as of 2003 some 46% of judges and 62% of lawyers were women.[23] This has led to a co-ordinated response to social problems effecting women. Particularly in regard to issues such as domestic violence, whilst Belarusian railways even offer separate carriages for women if required.

The Belarusian government has also been particularly vocal about the issue of human trafficking. Many eastern European women seeking a higher quality of life have been 'shipped west' and pushed into prostitution. Journalist Victor Malarek estimates the actual numbers to be in the hundreds of thousands.[24] Lukashenko has raised the issue several times, including at the UN, but the international 'response' to the problem has been lacklustre at best. An Associated Press article in 2005 actually criticised Lukashenko for legislating against human trafficking under the headline *"Belarus Moves to Limit Online Dating"*.[25] The article again cited human rights as the issue in question. Belarusian interior minister Alexander Shurko stated that the *"measures are directed at improving the mechanisms guaranteeing effective counteraction to human trafficking - one of the most dangerous phenomena modern society faces in its development"*.[26] This 'online dating' that the Associated Press would have us believe is the innocent victim are actually websites promoting eastern European 'escorts' and 'mail order brides' where at a click of the mouse women can be added to the browsers 'shopping cart'. For opposing the treatment of women as commodities Lukashenko has once more been pilloried as a human rights abuser.

An interesting example of the way Western media misleads public opinion to serve its own agenda is illustrated by an article in the British 'New Statesman' magazine. This article claims that the Belarusian government is actually involved in *"trafficking women, often country girls who believe they will be nannying abroad but find themselves locked in prostitution"*.[27] This runs contrary to every other piece of information regarding the issue, and unsurprisingly cites no source for this 'fact'. A far more reliable body, the International Office for Migration (IOM) working with the UN declared that *"Belarus has been globally recognised as one of the world's most resolute fighters against the slave trade"*.[28]

Women in Belarus are pivotal to Lukashenko's belief in the importance of the family as a social unit. As such, maternity and child support payments are available, as well as childcare facilities at places of work. Lukashenko has also continued the Soviet practice of conferring state awards on mothers, and also granting a fully paid extra days leave from work per week for mothers of three or more children, as well as to single mothers, divorcees and widows.

The balance in Belarus is precarious between the woman's role as a mother, and as a worker or professional. Critics of Belarusian policy regarding women, often point out the emphasis placed on the importance of women as mothers, and their role in the family. However as seen earlier, the women who do enter professional occupations or politics statistically achieve as well as their male counterparts. The Belarusian system effectively enables and supports women to make the choice to be a 'housewife and mother' or to pursue a career.

An essential human right in any democracy is that of opinion, and political activity. In Belarus there exists a staggering array of political parties and non-government organisations (NGO's). Indeed it is primarily through NGO's that foreign influence is brought to bear in Belarus. The USA, as will be seen in the next chapter, has a particularly keen interest in Belarus, one factor is the market for US business, and access to its educated and highly skilled, but relatively low paid workers (in dollar terms). Human rights issues are created to help achieve this goal. Hypocrisy is almost a guiding principle of such a policy, human rights abusers are tolerated, and even supported, provided they carry out policies that fall in line with US interests. Examples abound, notably the complicated relationship the USA had with Saddam Hussein's Iraq. Added to this is financial and military support for dictators such as General Pinochet in Chile, and Suharto in Indonesia.

This position is hugely aided by a corporate media who are no more likely to undermine their own position than is the government itself. Media magnates such as Rupert Murdoch are exceptionally unlikely to report any positive achievements of a system that advocates egalitarian distribution of incomes, and public ownership of industry. Professor Noam Chomsky has explored the role of the media in Western democracies, and concludes that seldom does the media stray too far from the 'official line'. The government's definition or actual practice of democracy is seldom called into question, but far more disturbing is when 'independent' media propagates a lie.

The citing of sources is not particularly common in journalism, and often it is enough for media outlets to simply quote each other. The major news agencies of the BBC, Reuters and the Associated Press being fine examples. There are several instances of media distortion relating to Belarus and Lukashenko, but the most important is the alleged 'praising of Hitler', by the Belarusian President. This stems from an interview given by Lukashenko to German newspaper 'Handelsblatt' in 1995. The actual interview was on the subject of the Belarusian economy, and significantly actually contained no reference at all to Hitler. Handelsblatt however is cited as the printed source of Lukashenko's pro-Nazi sentiments. The correspondent who carried out the interview, Dr. Markus Zeiner told the British Helsinki Human Rights Group (BHHRG) that *"a tape of the interview had been quoted out of context and with the sequence of comments altered by the Russian media"*.[29] Further Dr. Zeiner actually wrote to the Russian media publications and broadcasters who had used these 'quotes' to inform them of their non-factual base, but never received a reply. Indeed in the spread of this misinformation the actual source is now often ascribed to an interview with Russian television network NTV. The purpose being to divert attention away from a non-existent comment in the Handelsblatt, to its erroneous reporting in Russia.

Lukashenko himself was justifiably shocked by the nature of the quotes attributed to him. In a nation that suffered so heavily as a direct result of Hitler's policies it would be not only insensitive, but also nonsensical to praise him. However this is also the purpose of the distortion; to discredit a popular post Soviet independent leader, in the eyes of his most ardent supporters. Lukashenko himself commented (to another German newspaper, Der Spiegel): *"If I really had said that, I would have been driven out of my post the next day"*.[30] Thus it can be seen that it is not only state owned media that the individual ought to be sceptical of. Sadly, in order to break the latest news, journalists cannot check every source, and thus news agencies often rely on reputation alone as their 'guarantee' of accuracy. Diversity of sources and information is essential in order to establish truth, and this is particularly the case in examining human rights issues in Belarus.

Political freedoms are basic human rights, and expressing these freedoms takes the form of political activity. Such activity is usually the formation of political parties, as well as public meetings, and the expression of opinion through media and protest. As seen earlier, the Belarusian media is in reality diverse, and opposition parties print their own materials and distribute them openly. Although it must be acknowledged that inflammatory publications have had their publishing licences revoked. This is not the stifling of criticism, but is a strong stand on principle.

The Belarusian opposition still has its newspapers, and the more extreme publications are now printed abroad, and mailed back to Belarus, particularly from Lithuania and Poland. Of course the Internet is also a widely accessible resource, and the notion that Lukashenko can somehow stifle all political argument or dissent is naïve. In fact there are three openly anti-government newspapers on general sale in Belarus, as well as 'hostile' Russian ones.[31] This polarisation is something that is rarely encountered in Western countries, where the media is as flexible as the government, with ideology no longer deemed necessary. In fact in considering whether a British newspaper is 'Labour or Tory' or a US one is 'liberal or conservative' is of no significance to the established status quo. In Belarus with such strong ideological policy, anti-government publications are of increased importance. The opposition parties in the West are not calling for a complete overthrow of the existing national system. This is why the open sale (and often free distribution) of opposition newspapers in Belarus is of key importance in exposing the myth of Lukashenko as a dictator.

Amnesty international is probably the most well known of the 'human rights organisations' and have been campaigning for ethical government and an end to brutality since 1961. Amnesty reports on Belarus have made interesting reading during the Lukashenko era. They have showed a remarkable inconsistency. The reason for this is again, the use of sources. Amnesty field reports from within Belarus contrast sharply with statements based on opposition or media sources. For example the Amnesty International report of 2002 is relatively short, and under the heading of 'torture and ill treatment' the example/evidence cited is that of a 26 year old punk musician who was punched by a policeman after being arrested.[32] It has to be acknowledged that this is indeed an abuse of power if true, and certainly the officer should be held accountable. In fact in Belarus police officers and security service personnel found to have abused their position and power are particularly severely dealt with. In comparison with the same year's reports on the UK and USA this alleged abuse of power is notably vague and is hardly evidence of a wider problem. The UK report cites several deaths in custody, and a police shooting of an unarmed man.[33] Whilst the scathing report on the USA, as well as discussing the abuse of human rights occurring at the Guantanamo Naval Base, also lists various acts of police brutality including fatal shootings. Sadly a racial theme is also noted, and there is even a Federal acknowledgement of an alleged "*pattern and practice*" of brutality within one US police department.[34]

It is important to note the comparisons between these countries from a largely non-partisan organisation such as Amnesty International. After all human rights form the basis for so much criticism of Belarus from the US and UK governments and media.

The 2005 Amnesty International report unfortunately uses an OSCE representative as one of its prime sources, as well as comments from the nationalist Zubr youth movement. Showing that though Amnesty International cannot be controlled, it certainly can be manipulated. The focus of this report leading up to an election year is on political freedoms, or the lack thereof. The objectivity and neutrality of the OSCE will be further discussed and examined in chapters 14 and 15.

Political leaders in the USA, and EU nations seeking a pro-Western, pro-capitalist president in Minsk use their media to spread the myth of a lack of freedoms in Belarus. In turn this justifies any action that must be taken in regard to influencing the electoral process, or measures taken after it. This was seen in Georgia and Ukraine, with 'velvet revolutions' toppling the pro-Moscow or independent candidates if the vote was close enough to allow such a show of force to be influential.

In Belarus however the opposition to Lukashenko is far less organised or united. Western analysts frequently comment that "*even if he doesn't rig the vote, he'll probably win*". Thus if the Belarusians cannot be relied upon to vote 'the right way', then the West must make the whole process suspect in order to justify isolation and sanctions. These being the economic weapons used to cripple Serbia and Iraq before the troops moved in to restore order, and help 'construct democracy'.

This issue will be further examined further in the following two chapters. Of note is that the Western sponsored candidate in the 2006 Presidential elections, Alexander Milinkevich stood on a platform which actually seemed to be designed to lose. However such tactics have not gone entirely unnoticed. British journalist Neil Clark ran a comment in the Guardian that the West's support for human rights and democracy is clearly hollow. The example used was the case of Belarus in 2006. Clark noted that Lukashenko's opponents acknowledge his majority support,[35] and also that the West is yet to threaten sanctions on countries such as Turkmenistan or Egypt, who enjoy good economic relations with the US, but both have a negligible level of genuine democratic development.

The most significant accusation of human rights abuse in Belarus is that of 'missing people'. The opposition, and even the US government, presume that certain missing people have been murdered at the order of Lukashenko. How far they actually believe this, and how far it serves as a useful political lever is open to debate. One of the first high profile cases was that of the former head of the Belarusian National Bank, Tamara Vinnikova. She was charged with embezzlement in 1999, before being reported as missing. The Belarusian United Civil Party website still (2007) considers her to be dead, executed by Lukashenko's police (apparently having been drowned). This is in spite of the frequent interviews she has granted to the press from her new home in London since 2000.[36] In fact Interpol and the Belarusian authorities were aware of her whereabouts and were seeking her extradition to face prosecution for the crime of grand larceny. Despite Vinnikova informing an opposition newspaper in December 1999 that she was alive and well, and determined to continue in politics, she is still used as an example of the use of 'death squads' by Lukashenko. She clearly was of greater use to the opposition as a possibly dead disappeared person, than as a very much alive spokeswoman awaiting trial over corruption charges.

Another of the 'disappeared' is former interior minister Yuri Zakharenko. He had worked in the campaign team of Mikhail Chigir during the previous election campaign, and had gone on to resign from his post over disagreements on policy with Lukashenko. The Zakharenko case is certainly different from that of Vinnikova, as foul play certainly seems to have taken place. On the evening of his disappearance he had telephoned his wife to say he would be home in ten minutes, but never arrived. He also had reportedly spotted people following him in new, foreign cars, prior to his disappearance.[37]

It is important to note the reason for Zakharenko's resignation was not one of moral indignation as has been claimed. Lukashenko had decreed that there was to be an end to special privileges for Ministry of the Interior personnel, that they would have the same access to services and pensions etc. as every other Belarusian citizen. Zakharenko himself was also allegedly involved in a business scam regarding the importation and sale of second hand cars.[38]

The public commission set up to investigate this case reported that Zakharenko had been set upon by "*several civilians who pushed him into a Zhiguli* [Lada] *car with no licence plates, then drove away*".[39] The result of this public commission, and further intelligence was that 'traces' of Zakharenko had been found in Ukraine. The Belarusians also applied to the Ukrainian legal bodies to further investigate this lead.[40] There had also been reports that Zakharenko managed to escape and was alive and living in Berlin.[41] Importantly Zakharenko's family made a successful application for political asylum in Germany in 2000.[42]

What is important in this case is that it is not clear exactly what did happen to Zakharenko, he apparently was kidnapped, but by who and why can only be speculated upon. The case was unquestionably investigated despite opposition claims that it was not, also possible Mafia connections and corruption were investigated. This was much to the displeasure of Zakharenko's family, but certainly was a probable avenue of investigation in light of his widely rumoured involvement in dubious business practices.

The next 'disappearance' occurred only four months after Zakharenko. In this case it was Belarusian MP Viktor Gonchar and his associate Anatoly Krasovsky. The two men went missing following a visit to a sauna in Minsk. Gonchar was an outspoken opponent of Lukashenko, and as a Member of Parliament, he had a high profile. However this profile does not necessarily translate into popularity or influence. As mentioned earlier the parliament in the first years of Lukashenko's presidency had been one that was widely considered in Belarus to be obstructive and even obscurant.

After reporting her husband missing to the Belarusian KGB, Irina Krasovsky proceeded to visit a number of foreign embassies to try and gain assistance in the search.[43] Soon afterwards Viktor Gonchar's wife wrote a letter to the OSCE commission accusing the government of complicity in her husband's disappearance. This case was certainly of concern to Lukashenko, and potentially embarrassing for him and the government. Belarusian TV reported on the case and Lukashenko had demanded hourly updates on any progres.[44] Despite this, the US ambassador announced that the West was *"carefully following the investigation"* whilst his German counterpart expressed concern over the *"reluctance"* of the authorities to investigate.[45] This interest from the West in ignoring what was actually happening in favour of what may have happened in Belarusian internal affairs was to become typical, as will be discussed in the next chapter.

The police investigation was unable to trace the Jeep Cherokee that the pair had been using, whilst Gonchar's driver reported that some of Gonchar's friends had actually found the jeep, but would not share this information with the authorities.[46] The police investigation, headed by Valentin Potapovich concluded that there were three possible explanations for the disappearances. Firstly that the pair had been the victims of street crime, secondly that they had engineered their own disappearance (this was around the same time as the KGB discovered Vinnikova to be living in London), and finally that the two had been abducted in relation to Krasovsky's financial activities. On the 25th of September it was reported in the Belarusskaya Niva newspaper that Gonchar had actually been seen in Lithuania in conversation with the self-exiled former speaker of the parliament Semyon Sharetski.[47] An International body, the Inter-Parliamentary Union noted in 2006 that there were grounds for suspecting a financial motive behind a possible 'self disappearance'. Reporting Mr. Gonchar to be *"heavily indebted because of his business in the Russian Federation, and Mr. Krasovsky had been summoned to appear in court on a charge of tax evasion"*.[48] It was also noted that Mrs. Krasovsky had apparently refused to cooperate with the Belarusian investigation, and was now living in the USA.[49] Contrary to the claims of the opposition, and indeed the concerns of Western governments, the case has not been ignored or closed. In fact the investigation has been reopened seven times, and the prosecutor general still reports on it to the Belarusian parliament. The timing of these disappearances was also crucial coming as they did at a time of increased external interest and interference in Belarus in the run up to parliamentary elections.

One of Lukashenko's aides, Mikhail Sazonov wrote a letter to the OSCE chief in Belarus, Hans Georg Wieck, expressing frustration at these events. He noted that the disappearances had come at a crucial time in attempts at establishing a government – opposition dialogue. In the letter he wrote that Lukashenko was *"extremely worried about what has happened to Gonchar"* and all necessary steps were being taken to find him. Sazonov continued that *"there are forces that are interested in breaking the emerging dialogue. We believe that whoever organised and carried out Gonchar's disappearance did so with this goal in mind"*.[50]

What is of prime importance in the cases of Gonchar, Krasovsky and Zakharenko, is that not only would their murder or kidnapping by the Belarusian authorities have been counterproductive, but also exceptionally difficult to achieve. Particularly in the case of Zakharenko, who as former head of the Interior Ministry was both popular and familiar with those who would have been charged with such a task. As mentioned earlier Zakharenko resigned over the withdrawal of privileges for his personnel, and even the opposition's United Civic Party admitted that: *"The involvement of the Ministry of Internal Affairs is out of the question. Firstly, it would have been unethical. Secondly, there would have surely* been a leak from them by now. The possibility of KGB involvement is also minimum, as Lukashenko has not yet managed to ruin its apparatus. They still have seasoned staff members there, who know what it might lead to".[51]

Not only then would the security services have been unlikely to carry out the acts, but also would have thoroughly investigated them. As acknowledged above, Lukashenko did not have unconditional support from these forces. The Belarusian MVD (interior ministry) and KGB troops would be the very people most able to overthrow any president, particularly if he attempted to use them to first 'disappear' someone (especially their former head) and then have this covered up. The notion of a death squad formed by the presidential administration that could outsmart the professionals in the MVD and KGB is also particularly implausible.

The other high profile disappearance of note is that of Dimitry Zavadsky. What sets this case apart from the previously mentioned ones, is that the Belarusian authorities have actually charged and imprisoned people over the abduction. Zavadsky was a cameraman and journalist with the Russian ORT network. He had covered the war in Chechnya and had press accreditation with the Belarusian presidential administration.

Zavadsky went missing on July 7th 2000 on his way to Minsk international airport to meet a colleague. The opposition and Western governments were quick to add Zavadsky's name to the list of political disappearances in Belarus, despite there being no obvious reason why Lukashenko may want rid of him. Zavadsky's wife and the colleague he was supposed to meet at the airport, Pavel Sheremet, provided the first clues in the case. They reported that he had been receiving threatening phone calls after he returned to Belarus from reporting in Chechnya. In the documentary film that Zavadsky worked on, it was alleged that former Belarusian military and security personnel hired as advisors by the Russian forces had also been illicitly training the Chechen rebels. According to the investigation, Zavadsky had actually filmed the arrest of one of these men, Valeri Ignatovich.[52] Zavadsky had also gave an interview to a Belarusian newspaper claiming that a small group of Belarusians had even been fighting against Russian forces in Chechnya.[53]

In August 2000 Belarusian police confirmed that Zavadsky's disappearance was being investigated as a premeditated crime, and that there were actually five suspects. The following May at a press conference the deputy prosecutor general and the head of the investigation announced that there was enough evidence to charge two men with Zavadsky's abduction. Ignatovich was one of them, together with another man, Maxim Malik. Both of these men were former members of the elite 'Almaz' (Diamond) Belarusian police unit.

Since leaving Almaz, Ignatovich had established a criminal gang, and had also been involved in the purported military assistance to Chechen rebels. The gang was linked to seventeen crimes, one of which was the abduction of Zavadsky, in reprisal for his newspaper interview. Police found a shovel in Ignatovich's car that had Zavadsky's blood on it, however his body was never found.

Lukashenko took a personal interest in the case, as Zavadsky was considered to be a colleague. In July 2000 he promised to *"wring the necks of those responsible"*[54] for the disappearance. It appears that the abduction was possibly originally intended as a ransom plot as opposed to a simple murder. Lukashenko discussed this with ORT journalists. Saying their bosses had *"a lot to disclose about Zavadsky"*.[55] Lukashenko claimed to have information that ORT had been asked to pay a ransom for Zavadsky's release, this was later confirmed by ORT director Konstantin Ernst.[56]

On March the 14th 2002 Ignatovich and Malik were sentenced to life imprisonment for the abduction of Dimitry Zavadsky as well as one other murder and a series of armed assaults and robberies.

Despite this, and the lack of a credible reason as to why Lukashenko should want Zavadsky murdered, his name was still included in the list of politically motivated disappearances that justified the US Belarus Democracy Act (see next chapter). In fact one of the more common allegations is that there is a connection between Zavadsky's disappearance and a broader repression of independent media in Belarus. Yet as seen earlier independent media proliferates in Belarus, and according to the Committee to Protect Journalists international report of 2006 of the 134 journalists in prison worldwide, not one was Belarusian.[57]

The issue of the 'disappeared' was discussed with Lukashenko in an interview with the Wall Street Journal. It was noted that in Belarus in 2001 around 1,200 people were reported missing (the lowest rate per head in the world) and more than 800 of these had been found.[58] Of the claims of 'death squads' Lukashenko commented that there *"are about 1,500 people in the Belarusian opposition movement. They cannot endanger the present government. Even if there was any dictatorship in our country, it would be clear for a most vehement dictator, that barbarian methods of dealing with the opposition do not make any sense*".[59]

Lukashenko has also questioned the motives and methods of the opposition who highlight the cases of the 'disappeared'. He noted that one man who *has* disappeared, the pro-Lukashenko artist Andrei Bubashkin, is never mentioned during opposition 'vigils for the missing'. However the reverse is true for political scientist Anatoly Maisenya who was killed in a car crash in 1997, and MP Gennady Karpenko who died in hospital the same year following a brain haemorrhage. In 2001 opposition activists were still carrying portraits of these two men as 'disappeared'.[60]

The BHHRG reporting on disappearances noted that when monitoring and assessing the human right situation in a country a useful index is the number of asylum seekers and refugees it creates. "*Belarus figures nowhere in the international league tables despite its media reputation as an unusually repressive state*". The report also points out that the "*British Home Office has no special statistics on Belarusian asylum seekers because there are so few*".[61]

The question of 'disappearances' is certainly an important one, and also represents a serious threat to the credibility of Lukashenko and his government. However in order to establish guilt there usually has to be evidence that puts a case 'beyond all reasonable doubt'. Clearly there is a lack of reliable or overwhelming factual information to say that Lukashenko was involved in any of the above disappearances; if indeed they did disappear at all.

Ultimately, as will be seen in the next chapter, human rights are an issue used as a weapon by the powerful countries against the weak, or at least as a lever to influence policy. Human rights in Belarus are not violated to the extent that they are in many other countries, and indeed the Belarusian system allows a greater deal of social protection than would be seen even in the USA. When the Western powers talk of freedom in Belarus in reality they mean economic freedom, primarily of the business and land owners at the absolute expense of those who rely on them for work, services or homes. Thus it is this freedom of exploitation which does not exist in Belarus, and which most concerns those who see a 'window of opportunity' there.

Chapter 14. International Relations: Belarus and the World.

"Like you, what we need from the world is peace and stability. Nothing more. The rest we shall create ourselves through our own efforts".[1] *A.G. Lukashenko.*

Two issues have primarily dominated Belarusian relations with the rest of the world since Lukashenko's consolidation of power in 1996. The first is that of the union with Russia, a key point of Lukashenko's presidential campaign*. The second issue is that of the relationship between Belarus and the USA. Ultimately when the USA is hostile to Belarus, the EU countries have tended to tow the line of the US position; particularly in the case of Poland.

Lukashenko has been a consistent and vocal opponent of US international policy and hegemony. He has stated his position and always responds fully to accusations made by the US administration regarding Belarus; a courtesy which is seldom returned. This in turn has led to a complicated situation regarding Russia. President Putin likes having a non-EU neighbour in Belarus, but is not often comfortable with what he sees as Lukashenko's direct, and almost confrontational style. In the diplomatic bargaining and bullying of Russian- US relations Belarus is a thorny issue, and in some senses a 'trump card'. The Russian economic and social system is different to that of Belarus, and Lukashenko firmly rejects the Russian system. Thus although he wishes to be a strategic ally of Russia, Lukashenko does not see Belarus as a 'junior partner'.

The USA sees the vast economic potential in Belarus, and it's strategic location in terms of fuel and gas supply from Russia to western Europe. Added to this is the well-educated and disciplined workforce that Belarus has to offer. The potential for cynical capitalist exploitation of Belarus is huge. Russia sees this also, and has oligarchs, and businessmen who would like to make a quick profit from Belarus. However the problem for Moscow, Washington and Brussels is one of influence. A pro-Western free market President is of no use to Russia, and likewise a pro-Moscow free market President is of little interest to the West. Thus, for ten years Belarus has had a president

---

* The Belarus-Russia union is not a union in the sense of either the former Soviet Union, or the European Union, though both are often cited during discussion of the topic.

who fits into neither category, though he is pro-Russian in his world outlook, Lukashenko is no free marketeer. What is remarkable is that throughout this time Lukashenko has been able to successfully pursue an independent policy both at home and abroad, despite massive international meddling, interference and even direct attempts to subvert the electoral process.

Although the issues and events often overlap and coincide, I believe that the clearest way to present this chapter will be to address separately relations with Russia, the USA then the rest of the world. Of particular note in Belarusian international relations are those with Poland, China and with other socialist states such as Cuba and Venezuela.

Russia

Russia, as we have seen, has played a significant part in the history and development of Belarus. Russian is still the predominant language, and Russians make up the second largest ethnic grouping after Belarusians at 11.4% in 2005.[2] The 1994 presidential election in Belarus saw both Lukashenko and Kebich advocate closer ties with Russia, and ultimately Lukashenko's plan for a union was a significant factor in his overwhelming victory. The Union itself is best explained by Lukashenko in the following paragraph: *"The basic aims of the union are: the consolidation of the friendship and comprehensive co-operation, the improvement of the quality of life of our people, insuring of a steady social and economic development of the union member states, and not just separate states."*[3]

The Union makes provision for preferable trade conditions, and the lifting of visa restrictions between the two countries. It ought to be noted that Lukashenko apparently hoped to spread his notion of the socially oriented market economy to fulfil the above statement, which has not proved favourable to Russian business owners. In 2005 when trying to agree modifications to the draft constitution of the Union State, Lukashenko refused to approve amendments to the detriment of Belarusian sovereignty. He commented to Russian media that *"we will never agree to the Union State if the underlying principles are thrown under the hoof"* referring to each countries autonomy in internal affairs. Lukashenko continued by saying, *"the common things are foreign and defence policies. Everything else is the national priority- Russia's hoof won't smash the social policy of Belarus"*.[4]

As reported in the Russian daily, Kommersant, the basic disagreement was Putin's insistence of using the European Union as an model, whereas the Belarusians preferred to pattern the Soviet Union.[5] The actual Union has been signed in principle, but very little has actually been achieved in its construction. This is due to the reasons outlined above, particularly the Russian side's reluctance to be equal parties, and also that for the first years of his presidency Lukashenko not only had to struggle with his parliament, but also Boris Yeltsin.

Progress towards the Union has been generally no more constructive since Vladimir Putin's election to the office of President in 2000. Lukashenko's enthusiasm for the Union has not abated, but he has certainly lost a lot of faith in the Russian government's sincerity on the issue*. The union process has generally ground to a halt, with both sides reintroducing customs controls along their border in 2001. Added to this is the difficulty in reaching an agreement on a constitution for the Union State.

Politically the whole union project has been favourable to Lukashenko, as he has been able to reap some economic benefits, and also has gained support from a large part of the Belarusian, and Russian populations. In the mid 1990's, surveys in Belarus showed that 55% of Belarusians favoured the restoration of the Soviet Union. On another question 63% supported a simple union with Russia.[6] The Russian government initially attempted to establish a dominant position, due to their larger economic power, but Lukashenko has managed to maintain Belarusian dignity and independence whilst also gaining vital concessions from the Russians. Primarily the customs union signed in 1995 granted Belarus oil and gas at below market prices, guaranteeing a saving of 400 million US dollars per year in fuel costs.[7] The Russians for their part were allowed to operate several army bases, including an anti-missile defence base in Baranovichi in western Belarus. Lukashenko agreed to this small Russian military presence in Belarus, as he hoped the union would ultimately include a joint defence policy. The Russians were also grateful for the union in regard to closer access to the Kaliningrad† region, which following the end of the Soviet

---

* A point of note is that in 1999 Yugoslavian President Slobodan Milosevic expressed interest in joining the union as an observer state.

† Formerly Konigsberg.

Union had become a geographically isolated part of Russia on the Baltic Sea.

Lukashenko was well aware of the dire economic state of Belarus in 1994, but also knew the success it had enjoyed during the Soviet era. Thus by re-establishing preferential trade with Russia, Belarus was able to overcome some of its initial problems in relation to the collapse of the Soviet economy. Lukashenko highlighted this to Russian critics of the union reminding them that *"before the break up of the USSR, Belarus was known as one of the more economically developed republics, which subsidised the Soviet Union's budget"*.[8] By 1998 Russia was buying some 70% of Belarusian exports.[9] This has to be understood in context: i.e. Russia's market economy has little flexibility to 'do a favour' for its neighbour. Belarusian goods have been successfully competitive in terms of their cost, and quality. Despite the strategic advantages Russia was not benefiting economically to the same extent as the Belarusians. Belarusian goods are certainly sold on a grand scale in Russia, but the customs treaty minimised the Russian profits. The constant wrangling over small issues and the deliberate proposal of unacceptable elements into the discussions by the Russian side are aimed at drawing out the process of forming the Union. Russia knows that pressure on Lukashenko from the West may force him to accept less favourable terms from Russia, and also there is the added element of Putin's imminent end of term as President. Putin has declared no intention of proposing an amendment to the constitution (as Lukashenko had done) to remove the two term presidential restriction. However he potentially could step into the post of President of a Russia-Belarus Union, and thus preserve his power and personal influence.

Russia's presidential elections are due in 2008, and thus in 2005 serious discussion of a draft constitution for the Union began in Moscow. The problem of course for the Russians is how to keep power with Moscow, and not as is often mentioned, to allow Lukashenko to take power in the Kremlin. Such a situation is not as fantastic as it first appears. Independent Lithuanian sociologist Oleg Manayev surveyed the Belarusian people in 2006, and reported 44% of the population would like to see Lukashenko president of the Belarus-Russia Union. With Putin receiving 22%. The remainder was divided between various Belarusian and Russian political figures; particularly communists. Of note from the same survey, was that 52% of Belarusians still consider themselves 'Soviet Citizens' as opposed to Europeans.[10] Added to this an Associated Press report in 1997 admitted that Lukashenko's popularity did not end at the Russian border, describing him as *"a darling of* [Russian] *hard-liners"*.[11] This article is largely critical of Lukashenko, and starts with the misinformed statement that he had praised Hitler, but it does offer a valuable insight into the reasons for Lukashenko's popularity with workers in Belarus and Russia. Vladimir Martinenko a young collective farm worker near Minsk commented: *"He's young, he's energetic, and he's trying to do something for ordinary people, so of course he'll have opponents"*.[12] Such sentiments are echoed in Russia where away from Moscow and St Petersburg quality of life is generally poor and work opportunities few.

Lukashenko's political appeal in Russia is also quite genuine. At May Day parades his portrait has been seen with increasing regularity over the last few years. In 2006 it was seen in St Petersburg being carried by most socialist, and communist parties. In a Russian opinion poll of 1999 he was voted to be Russia's third most popular politician despite not being Russian! A Russian engineer, Viacheslav Shtruzhkov commented *"we all belong to the same big Soviet family"*.[13] An initiative group has even been formed in Russia that has proposed running Lukashenko as a candidate for the 2008 Russian presidential elections. Despite the fact that Lukashenko is technically ineligible to stand, the message of support is still clear.

Lukashenko is not unaware of his popularity in Russia, and has addressed groups of Russian workers and even military academies. Notably when speaking at the Vladivostok Marine Academy in the Russian Far East he delighted his audience with the promise that Belarus would continue to *"protect the glory of the Soviet Army"*.[14] Such talk is well received in Russia, a country shamed by its under funded crumbling military, which was once hailed as the mighty victor of the Great Patriotic War.

In its background study of Belarus, the British Helsinki Human Rights Group (BHHRG), asserts the Union to be essential to Belarusian economic interests, but also notes that *"the problem for Belarus will come if it becomes impossible to avoid the down side of economic involvement with Russia"*.[15] The BHHRG are essentially referring to corruption and Mafia activity. Thus the Union has the potential to be exploited both politically and economically. Another difficulty for Belarus is that it has to contend with the very powerful Russian energy companies, on whom the Belarusians are almost entirely dependent on in terms of fuel.

In April 2006 the Russian gas company 'Gazprom', declared that it was to raise gas prices in Belarus. The price hike would certainly hit the Belarusian economy hard, and the move was declared by the Belarusian economic commissioner Stepan Pisarevich to be both "*blackmail and outrageous behaviour*".[16] The promised price hike was to occur in December 2006, at the height of winter. However Gazprom appeared to be using this economic threat as leverage in their attempt to buy out the Belarusian gas transit company 'Beltransgaz'. The Russian company can certainly hold Belarus to ransom over gas supply, but the Belarusians are also able to use their supply pipelines to western Europe as a bargaining point. Ultimately the fuel 'crisis' tested both sides' commitment to the Union State, and also tested these commitments in the face of market forces.

This fuel crisis came to a head, with the Belarusians refusing to pay the increased price demanded by Russia. At the last minute (literally) Belarus and Russia agreed a new price for fuel. The price rise whilst not being the same as that paid in Ukraine, or western European countries was still significant to the average Belarusian household. In 2006 Belarus had been paying around $47 per thousand cubic metres of gas, Gazprom wanted to increase this for 2007 to $200. The deal brokered on the night of New Year's eve was $100, more than doubling the price of fuel. Western media crowed at Lukashenko's change of fortunes and predicted his downfall now he could no longer rely on cheap Russian energy to subsidise his economy. What was not reported was that Belarus had secured a 70% rise in transit fees from Russia to the west. Belarus and Russia also then failed to resolve oil transit issues diplomatically. Russian flexing of its economic muscles backfired, when by cutting off oil supplies to Belarus it also effectively halted supplies to Poland and Germany. This caused significant concern over the reliability of Russia as an energy supplier. Putin's response was to predictably blame the Belarusians, and rather suspiciously claim that the Russian government had been hoping to "*prompt Belarus to conduct free-market reforms*".[17] This certainly seems to be an afterthought intended to seek reconciliation with the Western countries affected. After all, the term 'free market' does not apply to the state monopolies that are the Russian Gazprom and Transneft companies.

The Russian position increasingly became seen as justifiable in that it had been 'subsidising' the Belarusian economy, and was now being blackmailed by its tiny neighbour. This again is a gross distortion of the reality. Even at the price of $47 per 100 cubic metres of gas Gazprom was still making profit margin of 20%.[18] Such a level of profit hardly qualifies as a subsidy. What this does illustrate though is how far Russia has moved from the Soviet principles of its recent past. Essential resources such as fuel are now charged, not at cost, or at a fair profit to maintain the industry and its workforce, but rather at whatever price the market can stand. Unfortunately for those in Belarus and Ukraine, the market in western European countries can stand much higher prices. Gazprom's greed meaning that even a 20% mark up that results in over $15 billion profit per year for Gazprom from Belarus is seen as insufficient.* Gazprom sells gas to western European countries for around $250 per 1000 cubic metres. Thus the Belarus price is not a subsidy, but rather is simply not profitable enough. This flexible pricing policy has resulted in two things, firstly significant price hikes in those countries who have politically distanced themselves from Russia. For example the 'Rose revolution' in Georgia has resulted in a market price of $235 per 1000 cubic metres. Which will have a severe impact in a country that already has the third worst human development index rating in Europe.

The second result is that Gazprom has amassed significant political control. Its chairman Dimitry Medvedev is also the Russian Federations deputy Prime Minister, and favourite to succeed Putin as President in 2008.

In 2001 Gazprom took over the Russian news channel NTV. Which as covered earlier spread the story of Lukashenko praising Hitler, and continues to play a part in broadcasting anti-Lukashenko media into Belarus. Lukashenko will not risk his social policy and country on a chance of heading the Union that may not pay off. Such a gamble is of course not out of the question for Putin, as one of his strongest bases for popular support has been his role in the war against terrorists and separatists in Chechnya. The prevailing political climate accepts vast spending on security, and 'the war on terror'. So-

---

* This is calculated from the 2004 Belarusian gas imports and $47 dollar price

cial spending is being reined in to allow for this. As President of the Union Putin's legacy could continue, but Lukashenko's would probably end with him. It is clear then that the success, or not of the Russia-Belarus Union has the potential to become key to the region. Certainly in geo-strategic terms in regards to fuel and its transit.

In a 2007 interview with the Reuters news agency Lukashenko made it clear that his vision of the Union was still alive, but that the economic base of the union needed to be restored. *"We are ready to give up any claims, financial, economic claims to the Russian Federation, if Russia for its part, takes similar steps. Mutual relations between states cannot be fitted into a usual bookkeeper's ledger account. They imply more than that"*.[19]

The United States of America

Belarus has come under severe criticism for its policies and practices under the leadership of Lukashenko. The loudest voice has been that of the US government and not that of the indigenous Belarusian opposition. US interests in, and concern for Belarus has its roots in Cold War politics, and specifically to when the Belarusian nationalists who had collaborated with the Nazis were allowed to set up their 'government in exile' in New York in the late 1950's. As a point of note there is also another Belarusian 'government in exile', which claims authority from the short-lived Belarusian National Republic of 1918. Such movements were obviously anti-communist, and were thus useful propaganda tools for any US administration during the Cold War era.

Following the collapse of the Soviet Union, many of these 'governments in exile' attempted but were wholly unsuccessful in entering politics in their former homelands. Almost all simply acknowledged the new governments. With one notable exception; following the election of Alexander Lukashenko, Belarusian nationalist groups abroad were revived by their sponsors. The fall of the Soviet Union coincided with the presidency of George Bush Senior. His term in the White House ended in 1993, the year before Lukashenko's election, and the peak of the BPF's popularity, with a climate of free market orientated nationalism in the former Soviet republics. 1993-2001 saw the new US President, Bill Clinton react to the lack of 'reforms' in Belarus. Clinton pursued the typical interests of any US administration, largely those of economic benefit to US business. Clinton also had command over US military actions in the Balkan wars, which were hugely unpopular in Russia and the other Slavic states. Clinton was of course succeeded by George W. Bush who has escalated the war of words with Minsk, going so far as to sign into law the 'Belarus Democracy Act' in 2004 (more on which later), and to order sanctions against Belarus in 2006.

The first sign of problems between the Lukashenko government and the USA came in 1994. Whilst European countries were at first optimistic about the new president who was not from the old Communist Party nomenclatura, the USA was immediately concerned by his pro-Russian stance, and pledge to restrain privatisation of public owned industry. US State Department head Jack Segal has commented that *"from the moment President Lukashenka [sic] assumed power...Belarus' relations with the US...have become increasingly difficult"*.[20] If it were needed, a flash point of direct confrontation occurred on September 12th 1995. On this day a gas balloon taking part in the 'Coupe Gordon Bennett' international balloon race was shot down by a military helicopter after straying into Belarusian air space. The balloon's two pilots were US citizens, and both died in the crash. The US government was furious, and an apology from Lukashenko to *"President Clinton, and the American people"*[21] was forthcoming. Russian TV offered an opposite story, claiming that Lukashenko had blamed the Americans. Two other balloons that strayed over Belarus landed unharmed, one of which was intercepted by another helicopter. The shot down balloon had not responded to radio calls, and the helicopter crew considered it to be unmanned.[22] The US Department of State still* officially declares that the Belarusians *"have not apologised or offered compensation for these killings"*.[23] The day after the tragedy, the Belarusian government released a statement declaring: *"The government of the Republic of Belarus expresses its regret over the air accident, which entailed fatalities. All steps taken by Air Defence troops to establish contact with the flying object- including activation of additional radar, repeated attempts to establish radio contact, a flyover by military helicopter to spot the pilots and firing of warning shots-did not bring any results"*.[24]

Lukashenko himself ordered an investigation into the incident on September the 13th. It ought to be remembered that Lukashenko had

---

* As of May 2007.

only been President for just over a year, and was at the time still establishing the role of the presidency. The actions of the air defence force ought not to be seen as a personal act by him.

It is a typical example of double standards that the US has expressed horror at these 'killings' and ignored the apologies to serve their own agenda. A comparative example of a misidentified target being shot down comes from July 1988. This incident saw the US Navy missile cruiser 'USS Vincennes' shoot down an Iranian Airways Airbus. The Vincennes was actually in Iranian territorial waters, and the civilian airliner was in a commercial air corridor. The shooting down of Iran Air flight 655 resulted in 290 civilian deaths, to which the USA has offered no apology. Furthermore the Vincennes crew was awarded combat ribbons, and the ship's air warfare co-ordinator received the Navy commendation medal for 'heroic achievement'. The cruiser returned to Boston to a heroes welcome, with a navy band playing and other vessels saluting with gunfire. A public affairs officer noted that *"Navy officials did not want the ship to sneak into port"*.[25]

Lukashenko represents the antithesis of the US dominated unipolar world, and thus without honesty or even irony the State department bemoans the lack of an apology for the 1995 balloon tragedy. This attitude is best summarised by George Bush Senior who as Vice President in 1988 made the following statement on Iran flight 655: *"I will never apologise for the United States of America, ever. I don't care what it has done. I don't care what the facts are"*.[26]

In 1996 the US State Department released a report on the human rights situation in Belarus containing few facts, and served principally as a justification for the conclusion it was required to draw. Namely that it was in the best interests of the USA to establish 'democracy' in Belarus. This was to be done not through diplomatic pressure, or co-operation with Belarusian government or political parties, but by creating and funding non-government organisations (NGO's).

1996 was the year where it became clear that the interests of the USA, and the agenda of President Lukashenko, were not compatible. The referendum of 1995 in particular showed that Lukashenko was not only reversing the changes made by the nationalists in 1991, but more importantly was protecting his own position legally. The referendum of 1996 further consolidated Lukashenko's power, and of particular concern to the USA was the question on the unrestricted sale of land. It was clear that Lukashenko was not in favour of the unrestricted sale of Belarusian land and importantly the enterprises that could create opportunities for easy profits, as was happening in other former Soviet republics. Lukashenko's socially orientated economy could in no way serve US business interests.

To this end, the Organisation for Security and Co-operation in Europe (OSCE) boycotted the referendum in 1996, though three members of the European Parliament did observe. One of these, British MEP Brian Cassidy declared a *"distaste for Lukashenko"*[27] before even leaving for Minsk. Brian Cassidy is an interesting and certainly not accidental choice to observe the referendum in Belarus. He is a Conservative and a devotee of the free market. Incidentally Cassidy applied to the EU for compensation for the costs of a pheasant shoot he had been forced to cancel in order to go to Minsk.[28]

Further to handpicking groups and individuals with the 'correct' opinion of Lukashenko to monitor elections and form NGO's in Belarus, the USA is also very particular about it's sources of information. A good example being the continued reliance on 'Radio Free Europe/Radio Liberty' (RFE/RL).

RFE/RL was founded in New York in 1949, its aim being to broadcast anti-communist propaganda beyond the 'Iron Curtain'. Funding came from the US Congress, via the CIA. Since 1994 its European operations have been almost exclusively aimed at Belarus. The RFE/RL mission statement makes interesting reading in terms of objectivity. This propaganda tool is declared to be *"a model for local media"*. Whilst pre-amble defines 'stability' as being *"based on democracy and free market economies"*.[29] Despite this commitment to democracy, Lukashenko's referendum of 1995, when over 70% of the people voted to change the Belarusian flag is described by RFE/RL as *"a heavy blow to democratic forces"*.[30]

At first glance it may not be obvious what the USA has to gain from interfering in Belarusian politics and internal affairs. Belarus is not rich in oil or any fuel, and nor does the government have vast reserves of hard currency or gold. The official US line is its concern for democracy and human rights within Belarus. This was the reason Belarus was added to the list of 'Outposts of Tyranny' in 2004, along with the following nations: Cuba, the Democratic People's Republic of Korea, Myanmar (Burma), Iran, and Zimbabwe. For this reason to be valid it would then follow that US intervention is only necessary in the internal affairs of the above nations, and that the rest of the world is thus more democratic and/or has a greater respect for the human rights of their citizens. However, the US maintains excellent relations with Saudi Arabia despite the fact that the unelected ruling monarchy allows only very restricted local elections (and these only began in 2005). Women in Saudi Arabia are not allowed to vote,[31] whilst criticism of the government, the forming of trade unions and public demonstrations are also forbidden by law.[32] The USA happens to be Saudi Arabia's biggest customer in the sale of oil.

This is just one example; another could easily be a reminder of how Yeltsin violently dealt with his elected parliament in 1993, only to be rewarded with IMF credits. The case of Israel and Palestine further raises concern over the US commitment to protecting human rights. Both Arabs and Israelis suffer as a result of a policy based on the provision of weapons rather than a meaningful attempt to end violence and establish a peaceful resolution to the conflict. The US commitment to the protection of human rights and democracy unfortunately comes second to economic concerns. Another charge levelled against Belarus by the USA was that it sold weapons to Saddam Hussein's Iraq. Lukashenko adamantly denied this to be the case. Again hypocrisy is simply ignored, as the USA itself had happily sold weapons to Iraq prior to the first gulf war, including chemical and biological weapons material.[33]

Lukashenko can be dismissed so readily as he is typically referred to as 'the last dictator in Europe' an 'authoritarian president' and a 'hard-liner', but who makes these accusations? The answer is usually media sources such as CNN, the BBC, the Wall Street Journal etc, however these terms have become a part of US government terminology too.

Neil Clark in London's Guardian newspaper highlighted glaring inconsistency in the application of such terms. He noted that Lukashenko, as well as Hugo Chávez of Venezuela are both frequently referred to by the media as 'hard-liners'. Clark's article is interesting in its observation of the fact that 'reformer', 'moderate' and 'moderniser' are terms used purely on the basis of a leaders economic policy being pro-Western, regardless of how extreme the rest of their programme is. One example cited by Clark is that of Hungarian Prime Minister Ferenc Gyurscany.

Gyurscany himself is a millionaire, and has pushed an ultra free market neo-liberal policy since his election. In 2004 he announced plans to privatise Hungary's health care system due to the cost of running it; but did find *"7.7 million pounds to buy air to air missiles from the US, and 34.5 million pounds to 'adapt' its armed forces to the demands of NATO and EU membership."* Clark's conclusion being, " *To many a policy of putting guns before health would be considered hard-line. But not the Western media who laud Gyurscany as a 'centrist reformer' "*.[34] It follows therefore that the USA is at best applying the terms 'human rights and democracy' selectively, or at worst is not interested in either.

What then is the USA interested in? The Saudis obviously provide a lot of fuel, as well as substantial investment in US corporations. Hungary may be abandoning the majority of its ten million citizen's access to health, but it is spending over 77 million US dollars on weapons. Lukashenko on the other hand does not compromise social policy, and nor does he provide vast amounts of fuel to the USA. However Belarus does have a vast state owned, and thus unplundered economy. Belarus also has oil refineries and oil transit pipes from Russia to western Europe. The result of foreign 'investment' in these industries would be predictable. For example the Russian government discovered in 2003 that its agricultural sector was unable to afford fuel for food harvesting and planting due to private companies primarily supplying the western European market.

As such the Belarusian oil refineries and pipelines are a very lucrative business opportunity in the same way as the Beltransgaz gas pipelines are. To put a figure to the potential profit that is being kept from private investors and redistributed into the Belarusian social fund, Prime Minster Sergei Sidorsky announced in 2006 that Belarus makes the equivalent of one billion US dollars per year from its oil refineries.[35]

Rising prices of all types of fossil fuels are an indicator, and reminder of their impending exhaustion, and also the lack of any serious attempts at finding alternatives. If wars are fought in the Middle East over oil, then there is no reason why the USA should not seek further control over European supplies and distribution too. Of the oil barrels used in the world each year the USA consume 40%, as well as over 20% of the natural gas and coal.[36] Further to fuel interests there is the fact that Belarus has a well educated workforce engaged in the production of high technology equipment, some of which is used in weapons systems. Therefore Belarus is not in the market for buying

US weapons when it is capable of making and indeed exporting its own. The eastern expansion of NATO has garnered a significant profit from re-equipping the former Warsaw pact countries with US weapon systems*. A pro-Western government in Minsk would not only provide the possibility for purchasing hi-tech weapons factories as well as their designers, but would also eliminate a rival arms trader worth around one to two billion dollars per year.[37]

Another key factor in the US policy towards Lukashenko is ideology. Throughout this book the social policies of Belarus have been compared with those of the USA and other developed nations. The reason for this is not in order to 'score points' but to underline the reason for the overt hostility and misinformation from the USA. If Belarus is indeed an Outpost of Tyranny it somehow manages to be so without threatening any other nations, whilst also preserving and improving the quality of life of its own citizens.

The key threat that Lukashenko poses is the success of his system, and the very fact that he presents a viable alternative to the US model of free market capitalism. His policy is one of independent development, and mutual support, as opposed to the neo-imperialism proposed by the highly influential US 'Project for a New American Century' (PNAC) think tank. The core prepositions of PNAC include "*American Leadership is good, both for America and for the world*" and to this end "*we need to increase defence spending significantly*".[38] It is quite clear how the PNAC intends to resolve any disagreements.

The PNAC at first glance appears to be a conspiracy theorists dream, or some kind of right wing splinter group, but it actually plays a significant role in US politics and government. The PNAC Statement of principles is signed by 25 prominent political figures and theorists, including Jeb Bush, Dick Cheney, Francis Fukuyama and Donald Rumsfeld. At the time of writing, sixteen members of the PNAC are in the presidential administration of George W Bush, including Paul Wolfowitz, president of the World Bank whose interest in Belarus has already been covered. With this in mind a clash between the USA and Belarus seemed inevitable. When Lukashenko declared to the UN that the world was unipolar, the USA will not have been insulted, but instead glad that he understood the facts.

Throughout the second half of the 1990's it became clear that Lu-

---

* In 2004 the USA made $18.5 billion from the sale of weapons.

kashenko could not be 'bought out' and was sincere in his aims of aligning Belarus with Russia. Thus the USA began to increasingly raise the issues of human rights and democracy through its media, and also legislature. Direct armed intervention, as seen in Vietnam, Afghanistan, and most recently Iraq has been one method used by the US to impose its dominance. However this has proved to be exceptionally unpopular with the public, and can often destroy the stability and very infrastructure of the state that is to be brought to heel. Ruined and volatile countries do not provide a very good market or 'window of opportunity' for foreign investment. More frequently US intervention/interference takes the form of covert action, and the destabilising of the government or country in question. This is usually accompanied by 'independent' media demonising the regime, thus establishing public hostility. Usually a legal basis is established for any intervention. This takes the form of an act approved by congress, with the aims of introducing 'democracy' or 'independence' to a country. Examples include the Belarus and Cuba Democracy Acts, as well as the Syria Accountability and the Lebanese Sovereignty Restoration Acts. (The Iraq Liberation Act of 1998 is an example of how a destabilised and weakened regime can be delivered a coup de grâce by military force).

Once legal basis (in US, seldom in international law) is established then typically the USA channels funds into opposition groups and media. Typical examples include the support for the Contra rebels in Nicaragua, as well as the refusal to hand over Luis Possada Carriles to Cuba or Venezuela to be tried in connection with the 1976 bombing of a Cuban civilian airliner. Commenting on this, Venezuelan President Hugo Chávez said in 2005 that, *"it is difficult, very difficult, to maintain ties with a government that so shamelessly hides and protects international terrorism"*.[39]

Once an opposition has been created or sponsored, then sanctions are usually brought to bear until ultimately the aim is that the government will collapse, either through elections or a 'peoples' revolution as seen in Serbia, Ukraine and Georgia. This model is adaptable and over time has seen variations, but ultimately the methods are very similar, and the goals identical, to establish in power a pro-Western government with a free market economy. It is almost irrelevant if the new government is actually any more democratic than the previous one.

A pertinent example would be the case of the 'Rose Revolution' in Georgia that saw Mikhail Saakashvili come to power in 2003. George W. Bush subsequently praised Saakashvili, saying *"thank you for setting such a good example, you and your people. I appreciate the reforms you have put in place here. Georgia has come a long way very quickly"*.[40] Saakashvili has pledged to join NATO, and as such Georgia has been granted over one million US dollars per year since 2003 to help pay for US weapons and training for its armed forces*. As well as allowing US military aircraft to access its airspace Georgia has even committed troops to Iraq.[41] The 'reforms' President Bush referred to above, actually prompted the organisation, Human Rights Watch, to send him an open letter in June 2006 raising their concerns. At the core of which were *"new legislation and policies on the treatment of prisoners, the use of force by law enforcement officers and judicial independence that run counter to the government's international human rights commitments"*.[42] The BHHRG has also raised concerns over Saakashvili's abuse of power and alleged corruption.[43] Despite this it is clear that the US administration is more than happy with their ally in Tblisi.

The example of the Rose Revolution is particularly pertinent to Belarus, as it was the model for the Ukrainian Orange Revolution, and was also unsuccessfully copied by the Belarusian 'Denim Revolutionaries' in 2006. The US media position on Belarus has already been mentioned, and from a BBC open forum on the subject, the majority of Western public opinion appears to be against Lukashenko.[44] Thus the next step for the USA was to establish a legal basis for intervention in Belarusian affairs. The moral objection to Lukashenko had to be politicised. The resulting Belarus Democracy Act was ultimately passed in 2004, but was preceded by legally dubious intervention and propaganda, particularly around the 2001 Belarusian presidential elections.

In April 2000 President Clinton appointed a new ambassador to Belarus, Michael Kozak. The significance of this and its implications ought not to be downplayed. Kozak in the 1970's was directly involved in the US campaign against the socialist Sandinista government of Nicaragua. Kozak also served as a special presidential envoy during the US invasion of Panama that saw the removal from power of CIA

---

* As in Hungary increased military spending has 'coincided' with reductions in areas such as education and health.

sponsored drug trafficker: General Manuel Noriega. Despite his CIA connections Noriega refused to provide military support to the Contra rebels in Nicaragua, which ultimately led to his downfall. Prior to being posted to Belarus, Kozak held the position of Chief of the Diplomatic Mission to Cuba. Thus it is fair to assume that Kozak was appointed to Belarus by no coincidence. His experience in regime change, and his dealings with Cuba, made him an ideal choice to represent US interests in Belarus. Kozak described Belarus as *"worse than Cuba"*[45] before even arriving in the country to present his ambassadorial credentials. Kozak however was not concerned by insulting an elected head of state, and quickly established a close working relationship with Hans-Georg Wieck head of the OSCE permanent Mission in Belarus.

David Chandler a senior lecturer in International Relations commenting on the 2001 presidential elections noted that Kozak and Wieck had worked on a plan to field a unified opposition candidate to oppose Lukashenko; in order to avoid dividing the votes between various parties.[46] Such a plan shows the complicity of the OSCE in US foreign policy, and exposes the fragile nature of the OSCE commitment to 'democratisation'.

Such intervention can hardly be considered democratic, as it perverts the choice of the Belarusian people into a straight decision of whether to support Lukashenko or not. Political debate is stifled by such a clumsy coalition. Chandler noted that *"If there had been a number of opposition candidates to choose between and Lukashenka* [sic] *had won less than 50% of the votes, the election would have gone to a second round and the opposition could have chosen which candidate or platform to support"*.[47]

This highlights the possible intention to exaggerate Lukashenko's victory margin, and thus call the election result into question. This certainly seems feasible when it is considered that the man selected by Kozak and Wieck was not actually the most popular opposition candidate. Belarusian opinion polls showed that the most popular of the opposition candidates was Semyon Domash who had the backing of the centre right parties, as well as the BPF. However the man chosen to head the opposition was the ill and ageing Vladimir Goncharik, whose position was centre left, and not obviously pro-Western.[48] Such a decision by the US ambassador (as well as a violation of international law) seems contrary to US interests, unless of course the aim was *not* to beat Lukashenko at the ballot box. On the last day of voting, Goncharik did not campaign or speak to Belarusian voters; but instead went to the Hotel Planeta in Minsk to denounce the expected result to the OSCE, and other observers from the Council of Europe and EU.[49]

The result of the election was unsurprisingly a victory for Lukashenko. He had the stability of the country, and also his handling of the economy behind him. He won with 75.6% of the votes cast. The conduct and controversies will be covered in the next chapter, but as a postscript to the result the BHHRG concluded that: "*far from promoting diversity and the development of democracy, the West has frozen any kind of real political life in Belarus. The opposition to the government is 'chosen', its leaders 'appointed', their every move dictated and funded from abroad. The sidelining of Semyon Domash's candidature in the presidential election is only the most recent example of a series of ill thought out choices, masquerading as democracy*".[50]

The claim that the opposition to Lukashenko was funded from abroad has not brought any denials, or rebuttals. In fact Kozak* had written a letter to the Times newspaper in London on the 3rd of September a few days before the election announcing that "*the [US] embassy funded 300 non governmental organisations (NGO's), including non-state media*". Although directly funding a political party was denied it was conceded that "*some of the NGO's were linked to those who were seeking political change*".[51] In Kozak's letter it was declared that the USA's "*objective and to some degree methodology are the same*" in Belarus as in Nicaragua some twenty years previously. The Times described this as "*an unusual admission*", adding that the Sandinista/Contra war had "*claimed at least 30,000 lives*".[52] Kozak's unusual admission also "*coincided with moves by the Bush administration to gain increased political influence in eastern Europe and the Balkans*".[53]

The comparison between US policy and methods in Belarus and Nicaragua is alarming. The Contra rebels systematically targeted the civilian population of Nicaragua, in order to disable the Sandinista government's social and land reforms with as little personal risk as possible. One of the many such examples being the Contra attack on the passenger boat 'Mission of Peace'. After allowing an Army patrol boat to pass by, the Contras opened fire on the civilian vessel killing

---

* Despite being a Clinton appointee, Kozak remained as ambassador to Belarus after George W. Bush's election to the presidency in January 2001. Kozak had previously worked with George Bush Senior as Acting Assistant Secretary of State for Inter-American Affairs.

two people, and wounding almost thirty more.[54]

How then could such guerrilla warfare be adapted to Belarus? The answer is relatively straightforward. Despite the claims of a dictatorship, Belarus does hold parliamentary and presidential elections, allows political marches, and also its borders are not closed. All this allows for the opportunity to 'import' activists who can cause maximum disruption during elections, and ideally turn protest marches violent. Images of riot police dispersing protestors on TV will always add substance to any claims of a police state. Incidentally this is somehow not the case with the Poll tax riots in the UK, Civil Rights marches in the USA or when Georgian President (and reformer) Saakashvili's riot police used machine guns to disperse protestors in 2005.

The first sign of this tactic in Belarus occurred in April 1996 at a sanctioned rally on the tenth anniversary of the Chernobyl disaster. The rally was dominated by Paznyak's BPF, and following his recent trip to Kiev to rally support was also attended by members of the Ukrainian National Association/Intra Party Assembly (UNA-UNSO). The fact that Paznyak went to another country to gain support for Belarusian nationalism is questionable in itself, but not as questionable as UNA-UNSO. This Ukrainian nationalist organisation is predictably anti-Semitic and xenophobic, but is probably most famous for sending paramilitaries to Chechnya to fight against the Russian army.[55] Following the inevitable clash with the Belarusian militia (police) 204 people were arrested including 17 members of UNA-UNSO.[56]

During the 1999 parliamentary elections US writer Chad Nagle observed an anti-Lukashenko protest in Minsk. His account is enlightening in that as a direct observer he estimated the crowd at around 2000, as opposed to the 10,000 he later heard in a Western news report. What he saw in the protest were *"male skinhead type youths singing soccer hooligan chants"* who were *"clearly spoiling for a fight".*[57] The importing, or hiring of troublemakers is clearly part of the strategy for unseating Lukashenko. The US sponsored NGO's financial dealings are conveniently vague. In fact it has been reported that Belarusian opposition leaders following the 2001 elections demanded to know *"where all the money donated by the West for the election campaign went".*[58]

The presence of UNA-UNSO in Belarus will not have gone unnoticed by Lukashenko. Their hatred of Russia makes them willing foot soldiers in any anti-Russian campaign. As such the Russia-Belarus union makes Lukashenko a target for their hostility too. As well as Chechnya, UNA-UNSO sent volunteers to fight in border conflicts in Transnistria and Georgia. Also of note is their prominent role in Ukraine's Orange Revolution, where they provided security for 'Orange leaders' and key supporters of Viktor Yushchenko.

The Israeli Stephen Roth Institute identified an organisation called the 'White Legion' to be *"the Belarusian version of the Ukrainian paramilitary UNA-UNSO"*.[59] Lukashenko had this and similar groups made illegal in 2004. A spokesperson for the ministry of justice declared that the *"activities of these organisations escalate social and political tension and are of an extremist and illegal nature. We know for a fact that there have been contacts between radical groups and representatives of foreign circles, which has a destabilising influence on domestic processes"*.[60] As in the case of the far right newspapers mentioned earlier, the Western media took the stance that by banning the White Legion, Lukashenko was stifling democracy; and accused him of liquidating NGO's in order to maintain power.[61] As well as the media, the US Department of State complained of the *"harassment and de-registration of NGO's"*[62] in its report on alleged Belarusian human rights abuses of 2004.

George Krol replaced Kozak in August 2003 as US Ambassador to Belarus. Krol seemed a much more appropriate choice than Kozak as an ambassador, as he is an expert on Russian and Soviet affairs, and speaks Russian too. Kozak's replacement was not due to his 'failure' to achieve regime change, in fact he had been quite successful in asserting US influence over the Belarusian opposition, and had caused the vote of 2001 to appear suspiciously supportive of Lukashenko. Kozak left a network of some 300 NGO's funded by the USA, which has been noted to be particularly high, equating to one organisation for every 30,000 Belarusians.[63] Kozak had also established a clear alliance between the OSCE mission and US embassy in Belarus.

In the USA it was taken for granted that Lukashenko had somehow cheated in the elections, after all even the OSCE condemned the result. Plans were then put into place to pass the 'Belarus Democracy Act' through congress. Senator John McCain was vocal in calling for its approval, and delivered a key speech against the 'Lukashenko regime'.

Before entering politics McCain served as a Navy pilot, and fought in Vietnam. Shot down and captured in 1967, he was subjected to continued torture until his release in 1973. This experience led him to make the statement that cost him many votes in his campaign for the 2000 Republican presidential candidacy: "*I hate the gooks, I will hate them as long as I live*".[64] His initial refusal to apologise for the word 'gooks' lost him a great deal of support and respect, particularly from ethnic minorities and progressive Americans. McCain is notable for amending George W Bush's Defence appropriations bill of 2005 to exclude grounds for legitimising torture by US forces in the war on terror. McCain is one of the driving forces behind US policy on Belarus; with Russian newspaper Kommersant crediting him with initiating the draft project for the Belarus Democracy Act.[65]

In November 2002 McCain declared that *"Alexander Lukashenko's Belarus cannot long survive in a world where the United States and Russia enjoy a strategic partnership and the United States is serious about its commitment to end outlaw regimes whose conduct threatens us"*. The conduct in question was that Belarus by having trade agreements with Iraq was therefore supplying arms to terrorists. McCain expanded on this theme adding that, *"September 11th opened our eyes to the status of Belarus as a national security threat"*.[66] The Belarusian connection to the predominantly Saudi terrorists seems to be known only to McCain, but the fact that he delivered the above speech to the US media, and Belarusian opposition leaders in Washington DC is notable. The conference itself was entitled 'Axis of Evil: Belarus-the missing link'. The aim of this is quite clear. Lukashenko cannot be discussed or evaluated objectively when he has been declared to be not only a dictator, but also as being involved with the September 11th terror attacks on the USA.

The fact that Belarus maintained diplomatic relations with Iraq was enough for McCain to make the above connection between the war on terror, and Belarus. The fact that the US National Commission on Terrorist Attacks refuted the Iraqi connection to September 11th did not stop McCain maintaining this tenuous link (and nor did it stop the US going to war with Iraq).[67]

However the seeds were sown and McCain went on to deliver anti-Lukashenko diatribes with gross distortions and opinions presented as facts. For example in August 2004 he declared that Lukashenko *"has ordered the disappearances of opposition activists and journalists. He runs Belarus as if it were the Soviet Union"*.[68] The cases of 'disappearing' activists and journalists has been covered in the previous chapter, but as to how McCain would know precisely what Lukashenko has 'ordered' is baffling. Commenting on this, Raphael Johnson of the American Journal of Russian and Slavic Studies said that Lukashenko is a threat "*because his policies, which contradict the standard ideology of the IMF at every point, have been successful far beyond most developing countries*".[69] Johnson also notes that the 'kicking out' of the IMF or World Bank essentially means the removal of US interference and control over a nation's economy.

Senator McCain creates quite a paradox when he accuses Lukashenko of stifling democracy and repressing the opposition, and yet was campaigning for the release of more US funds for Kozak's 300 NGO's. McCain also failed to acknowledge that at the time Belarus had 18 registered political parties of which Lukashenko controls none. Added to this fact is the damage done by Kozak and Wieck to the democratic process in Belarus by selecting just one opposition presidential candidate. The diversity of political parties is quite a stumbling block for criticisms of democracy in Belarus, as Lukashenko relies on parliamentary support from coalitions, and his presidential power is very dependent on the backing of parliament. Indeed in Lukashenko's consolidation of power it was the parliament who initially resisted democratic change.

However the lack of serious debate over Belarus meant that in October 2004 the US Senate approved and passed the Belarus Democracy Act. Upon signing the act George W Bush declared; "*The Belarus Democracy Act of 2004, which I signed into law earlier today, will help the cause of freedom in Belarus. This bipartisan legislation demonstrates America's deep concern over events in Belarus and a commitment to sustain those Belarusians who must labour in the shadows to return freedom to their country*".[70]

The aim is clear, the US wishes for its own definition of freedom to be used in Belarus, and it will financially support Lukashenko's opposition to achieve this. The fact that Belarusian politics have been simplified by US policy and Western media into Lukashenko versus 'the opposition' hides the reality of the situation in Belarus (and indeed politics as a concept). Any election or disagreement can be portrayed as a struggle between the dictator, and the 'democratic forces'. The actual politics and political parties of Belarus are not discussed, as this would erode the basis of the anti-Lukashenko position. Indeed democracy is not the ideal result of the Belarus Democracy Act, because the Belarusians would re-elect Lukashenko anyway.

Discussing the USA as a 'model democracy' Professor Chomsky noted that "*most* [democracies] *have not yet achieved the US system of one political party, with two factions controlled by shifting segments of the business community*".[71] This is particularly pertinent to the case of Belarus, it highlights that it is not how a person achieves or maintains power that is important to the USA. What is important are favourable circumstances for foreign (i.e. US) investment and business. (This also explains why Clinton and Bush used the same ambassador in Belarus without any problems in term of foreign policy).

The Act itself declares that the USA has a *"vital interest in the independence and sovereignty of the Republic of Belarus, and its integration into the European community of democracies"*.[72] The 'vital interest' has already been covered, but what is significant, and certainly not going to gain support from Russia, is the use of the words 'European community'. The act details the reasons for its own necessity and validity, and amongst these are exaggerations and deliberate distortions of the truth concerning various issues covered already. Including the declaration that: *"The Belarusian authorities actively suppress freedom of speech and expression, including engaging in systematic reprisals against independent media"*.[73] The fact that the majority of the media available in Belarus is independent is ignored, and again it is hoped that nobody will look too closely at the nature of the publications that have been acted against. Further to this point about the media, the act also bemoans the 'crackdown' on NGO's.

The act also quite bizarrely claims that: *"The Lukashenko regime has reversed the revival of Belarusian language and culture, including the closure of the National Humanities Lyceum, the last remaining high school where classes were taught in the Belarusian language"*.[74] Lukashenko has commented clearly on the necessity of preserving the Belarusian language, and the fact that it holds status as joint national language with the majority spoken language of Russian is hardly a reversal. The above quote, which is termed 'finding number 9' of the Belarus Democracy Act also makes a broad presumption as to what ought to be considered Belarusian culture. Great Belarusian writers, poets, artists and events are actually honoured by the 'Lukashenko regime'. However Lukashenko has not allowed Belarusian culture to be exploited in a nationalist sense at the expense of the other ethnic groups. The 'reversal' spoken of, in all probability is Lukashenko's belief that the Soviet era was culturally relevant to Belarus. The claim that Belarusian is not taught in schools is also bogus. In the academic year 2001-2002 of the 1.4 million Belarusian schoolchildren, over 400,000 were being taught in Belarusian.[75] The Belarusian education ministry also passed a decree in 2001 on 'additional measures for widening the sphere of the Belarusian language use'. This decree called for the foundation of Belarusian grammar schools in every region of Belarus and in each city district, as well as the opening of Belarusian departments in institutions of higher learning.[76] Again it is necessary to understand that the US is not acting from a position of moral superiority. Indigenous North American language and culture has hardly been promoted or protected by successive US governments.

The most disturbing finding is number five, which observes that: *"Viktor Gonchar, Anatoly Krasovsky and Yuri Zakharenka* [sic], *who have been leaders and supporters of democratic forces in Belarus, and Dmitry Zavadsky, a journalist well known for his critical reporting in Belarus, have disappeared and are presumed dead".*[77] These high profile disappearances have been discussed n the previous chapter, but it is noteworthy that the above 'finding' has not been abridged or edited. The fact that four people have 'disappeared' is considered reason enough to meddle in another countries internal affairs. Finding number 6 however, does elaborate on the above statement. It claims that: *"Former Belarus government officials have come forward with credible allegations and evidence that top officials of the Lukashenko regime were involved in the disappearances".*[78] These 'former officials' were not named or cited, and this 'credible evidence' was not revealed. Usually, in passing such an act Congress ought to have asked for the inclusion of such evidence. As it transpired the act was passed unanimously with very little debate. Ultimately the evidence is not important so long as the goal is achieved. The myth of Lukashenko 'death squads' serves as the Belarusian equivalent of Iraqi 'weapons of mass destruction'. The Act also cites state repression of religious institutions, despite the fact that the religious leaders within Belarus are unaware of the harsh treatment that US Congress presumes they suffer. The Jewish community is highlighted in finding number 10 as being harassed by the 'Lukashenko regime'. This despite the fact that the chief Rabbi of Belarus said in 2004 that he had *"no qualms with any aspect of Lukashenko's rule".*[79] The US based National Conference of Soviet Jewry also noted that in Belarus *"long suppressed Jewish life has rebounded and is flourishing".*[80]

In this spirit of ignoring what is actually happening in Belarus, the final two findings of the Belarus Democracy Act declare that the presidential election of 2001 had been *"fundamentally unfair and nondemocratic* [sic]" and that Belarus had not followed the criteria established by the OSCE.[81] The irony that in the said election it was the OSCE and US embassy that subverted the democratic process unsurprisingly failed to be mentioned. With this less than watertight case the US declared its solidarity with opponents of the 'Lukashenko regime'.

Section 3 of the Act follows the above 'findings' and details precisely what the US government is willing to spend its taxpayer's money on. It is declared that the Act aims *"to encourage free and fair presidential, parliamentary and local elections in Belarus, conducted in a manner consistent with internationally accepted standards and under the supervision of internationally recognised observers"*.[82]

Clearly only the OSCE observers opinions count. For example the BHHRG observed the 2001 presidential elections and found no evidence of government cheating, but were seriously concerned by the machinations of the US embassy and OSCE mission to Belarus. The BHHRG used the membership of the USA in the OSCE as an opportunity to monitor US midterm elections in 2002*. The conclusion drawn made a thinly veiled comparison to the Belarusian election the year before. *"The election seemed at best sloppy, so much so that even elections BHHRG has monitored in 'pariah' states of the ex-Communist bloc compared favourably in terms of cleanliness and order"*.[83]

Section 3 of the Belarus Democracy Act also gives authorisation for assistance *"to be provided primarily for indigenous Belarusian groups that are committed to the support of democratic processes"*.[84] This is the main point, and purpose of the act. It establishes a (US) legal basis for financing opposition to Lukashenko, but also with use of the word 'primarily', the opposition need not exclusively be within Belarus. This 'blank cheque' can be extended to groups such as UNA-UNSO, so long as their activities serve the goals of the Belarus Democracy Act. This is not supposition, or an exaggeration. The Act actually lists the activities it supports as:

1. *The observation of elections and the promotion of free and fair electoral processes.*

---

* Several OSCE observers were actually refused entry into US polling stations, in one case officials at a Republican Party headquarter threatened to call the Police if the observers did not leave.

2. *Development of democratic political parties.*
3. *Radio and television broadcasting to and within Belarus.*
4. *The development of non-governmental organisations promoting democracy and supporting human rights.*
5. *The development of independent media working within Belarus and from locations outside the country and supported by non state-controlled printing facilities.*
6. *International exchanges and advanced professional training programs for leaders and members of the democratic forces in skill areas central to the development of civil society; and*
7. *Other activities consistent with the purposes of this Act.*[85]

The key point here clearly being number 7, which has no conditions or restraints attached. Surprisingly the funding is just as vague. The President is authorised by the Act to take "*such sums as may be necessary*"[86] to carry out these goals.

As outlined in the third point above, another method of influencing 'regime change' in Belarus is by the funding of radio broadcasts into Belarus. RFE/RL already carry out this role, but other stations were also established, particularly in the run up to the 2006 presidential election (see next chapter). Added to the above methods of subversion and external propaganda the US also added sanctions against Belarus to its Democracy Act. Specifically no funds from the US Government including the Export/Import Bank, and overseas Private Investment Corporation should be made available to the government of Belarus. This is of course quite a wide hitting sanction in a country with a significant number of public owned industries. Added to this, the sanctions include the complete proscription of the US Trade and Development Agency from carrying out activities in Belarus. Furthermore the Act stipulates that the US will use its "*voice and vote*" against any international financial institution that attempts to extend financial assistance, technical assistance, or grants to Belarus.

Having learnt from its experiences in maintaining the internationally unpopular trade embargo on Cuba, the US does allow humanitarian assistance to continue.

Section 6 of the Act also calls on multilateral co-operation, meaning that the US hopes to take the aims and methods outlined above and persuade other countries, particularly European ones to adopt them too. This can be seen to be in effect by the negative approach to Belarus adopted by the European Union, as well as the anti-Lukashenko radio broadcasts and publishing emanating from Poland and the Baltic states.

As evidence was not on hand to justify a great deal of the 'findings' outlined in section 2 of the Act, section 7 stipulates that a report should be presented by the President of the USA to appropriate congressional committees within one year of passing the act. This report has to show all weapons related sales of the Republic of Belarus that could be connected to international terrorism. The President also has to report on *"The personal assets and wealth of Aleksandr Lukashenka* [sic] *and other senior leadership of the government of Belarus"*.[87] In response to this last point Slavic affairs specialist Prof. M.R. Johnson commented: *"Could one imagine the fallout if George W. Bush was to be forced to reveal his own personal finances such as his interests in the Carlyle Group? The Carlyle cult had as one of its major investors the family of Osama Bin Laden"*.[88] Lukashenko's own response to this was not dissimilar, addressing a government conference two days after the passing of the Act he commented: *"What do the parliamentary elections and referendum have to do with the President's income? Well I immediately ordered everything the government has paid me summed up and sent to America. And then our new parliament would gather and demand before the next elections that Bush publish his income. And then we'd compare. Would he send us that information do you think?"*[89]

The Act called upon Lukashenko to end all persecution of political opponents and the media and to hold free and fair elections. Congress also commended the *"democratic opposition in Belarus for their commitment to participate in the 2004 parliamentary elections as a unified coalition"*.[90] Again this seems contrary to the goals of achieving genuine democracy, There is an assumption that the diversity of political opinion should be polarised into a simple pro or anti-Lukashenko position. Whilst also acknowledging the Belarusian electoral process in the same sentence. Presumably an election is determined to be free or fair not by its conduct but simply by its result.

The immediate impact of the Belarus Democracy Act of 2004 was that US anti-Lukashenko rhetoric was given the 'legal base' that legitimised turning words into action. On the Belarusian side, the opposition groups welcomed the Act and the unlimited amount of revenue it promised. According to official Congress figures, US spending in Belarus for the fiscal year of 2004 was 8.1 million dollars, whilst its estimated total for 2006 is 11.9 million dollars.[91]

Lukashenko also commented on the Act being a *"present the Belarusian government could not wish for"*. Despite being insulted and angered by the contents of the Act, he observed that the Act damaged US interests in Belarus too. Explaining why the Act was a 'present' he added: *"This opus adds at least ten percent to the government's score"* addressing Bush directly he said, *"If you're nagging me for looking for an internal and external enemy, why would you give me reason to find that enemy abroad? Why are you giving me these chances?"*[92]

The Act certainly reinforces the image of the USA as an imperialist nation still fighting the Cold War. In a country such as Belarus that exhibits high levels of nostalgia for the Soviet Union and benefits from a strong economy with comprehensive social policy; the Act certainly does damage the reputation of the USA whilst vindicating Lukashenko.

The source of the Act also made for some cutting observations. Lukashenko described the US presidential elections as having the most archaic system in the world. *"There is no direct presidential election there. They elect the electors, and then the electors elect the president. As a result the incumbent president* [George W. Bush] *got fewer votes than the runner-up. Is that normal? And these same are concerned about the situation in Belarus!"*[93] Lukashenko was referring to the US electoral college system that in 2000 saw Al Gore receive half a million more popular votes, but George W. Bush win the presidency with five more electoral college votes. Other voting irregularities in this election prompted Lukashenko to respond by saying, *"they forgot they have enough of their own problems"*.[94]

Lukashenko also addressed the opposition who are to be the main beneficiaries of the Act, reminding them that they need more than US support to win power in Belarus. *"If the opposition has any realistic and promising ideas, they should first of all, recognise positive achievements in the Belarusian modern history and, secondly, condemn the challenges of Western countries against Belarus"*.[95]

On October 14th 2004 a joint statement was adopted and released by members of the Republican co-ordinating committee of Belarusian political parties and public associations. This was addressed to the citizens of Belarus, and the international community. The opening of the address declared that the *"stable and businesslike atmosphere in the Belarusian society on the eve of the parliamentary elections and all nation referendum is clearly against the grain of the governments of certain countries"*. As if there was any doubt as to the identity of these certain countries, the next sentence reads: *"The emergence of the so called Belarus Democracy Act can only be accounted for by a nervous breakdown of the US leadership. Regrettably the US Congress approved it"*.

The address reiterates the Belarusians frustration at outside meddling, and US double standards. Ironically the more pressure the US puts on Lukashenko the greater his support becomes. The address ends with the declaration that the co-ordinating committee declares *"that nobody shall prevent the Belarusian people from exercising its legitimate right and making a free and conscious choice on 17th October 2004, supporting the policy pursued by Alexander Lukashenko for a stronger and more prosperous Belarus"*.[96] The date in question refers to a referendum asking the people if they approved the removal of the existing two term presidential limit.

What ought to be noted is that a broad coalition of support had developed behind Lukashenko in Belarus. As an independent candidate he had been elected without the backing of a political party or organisation, nor was he a mouthpiece for businessmen or industrialists. To create stability and support, he had to do this by uniting factions, and pursuing both successful and popular policies. The show of support he receives in the face of adversity is authentic. No politician wishes their country to become isolated or a 'pariah', but in Belarus there is genuine conviction that their development is independent and beneficial.

Diplomacy is a vastly complicated and delicate issue, and the clumsy handling of foreign affairs by successive US administrations has only bred resentment. Lukashenko is a leader who has frequently settled issues by the medium of referenda; he takes democracy directly to the people, and is rewarded for doing so by genuine support. The USA has no provision in law for the holding of nation-wide referenda, only those at state level, thus no policy can actually be approved by the people. This is of tremendous democratic importance when politicians make decisions or take actions that were not part of an election manifesto. Essentially in most democratic societies the electorate votes in retrospect giving their approval, or not, to the acts carried out in their name by the party in power. This becomes acutely the case when the ideological position of political parties becomes increasingly unclear or 'grey'. (A good example would be the case of the 'New' labour Party in the UK).

The Belarus Democracy Act is only a small part of the pressure being applied by the US. Following the Belarusian Presidential elections in 2001, the US also put forward a motion to the UN condemning the conduct of the election, as well as alleged human rights abuses. Lukashenko declared in 1998 that nobody, but the Belarusians themselves would determine their own way of life. He compared Western interference with the 1941 German invasion and added that: *"Talking to us with force, provocations, blackmail and threats will not be allowed by anyone"*.[97]

This position was reinforced in 2004 when Belarus turned the political tables on the USA and proposed a draft resolution to the UN General Assembly attacking the US for its electoral conduct and human rights record.

Belarusian permanent representative to the UN Andrei Dapkiunas declared to the delegates to the 59th session of the UN General Assembly in New York. *"The delegation of the republic of Belarus has the honour to introduce a draft resolution 'Situation of Democracy and Human Rights in the United States of America'"*.[98] After a brief outline of the document Dapkiunas addressed the chairman with the following statement:

"By introducing this draft resolution Belarus does not intend to play a role of mentor of human rights. On the contrary, the proposed draft should be considered an action of last resort and a measure taken primarily in response to the draft resolution on Belarus initiated by the delegation of the United States. Introducing a country resolution we remain committed opponents of country resolutions in general. Our document is first and foremost an appeal to the common sense of distinguished members of this high assembly. We do not expect the United States delegation to take this initiative lightly or indifferently. Similar is our attitude to the US draft on Belarus. The most responsible way out of this mutual exchange of accusations would be the withdrawal of both drafts as well as any other country resolution from consideration by the Third Committee and concentration on real priority matters before the Committee".[99]

This statement is enlightening and logical. It shows that Belarus will not suffer pressure in silence, but also that it is willing to work with any other nation on an equal basis. It also shows that Belarus is capable of showing restraint, and rationalises its complaint as opposed to throwing down a direct challenge to the USA (This is in marked contrast to the Belarus Democracy Act). The timing of the Belarusian draft proposal was certainly intended to coincide with the Act, as much as it was a response to US criticism at the UN.

The draft resolution itself is a well presented document, and was certainly serious and accurate in its format and findings. I will not quote the entire document here, but the main concerns are: Electoral irregularities (particularly concerning the presidential election of 2000), the use of the death penalty for those under the age of 18 at the time of a capital offence, and also its use on the mentally ill. Civil rights infringements, and illegal detention and torture of suspected terrorists at the US military base in Guantanamo, and ill treatment, torture and deaths in custody of suspects under arrest or in US jails. This draft resolution served the purpose outlined by Dapkiunas in that it showed the USA that the methods it uses can also be applied to itself. Ultimately Belarus withdrew the draft resolution, satisfied that it had made its point without provoking an all out conflict with the USA. This is in line with Lukashenko's claim that Belarus is willing to work with any nation providing there is a basis of *"equality and mutual respect"*.[100] Belarusian deputy UN ambassador Aleg Ivanov informed the Reuters news agency that: *"Our main goal was to show that any country in the world can be accused like this"*.[101] He also commented that the Belarusian delegation had received a lot of support from other countries on this resolution, with six countries actually requesting to be co-sponsors of the draft. Ivanov did not rule out reintroducing this resolution adding that: *"We will not keep silent. We will not agree with such political pressure"*.[102]

As an interesting postscript to this draft resolution, not only was it supported by several 'small nations' but also from within the USA itself. The citizens of Washington DC cannot elect a representative to Congress, and nor do they have a representative in the Senate. This is a unique situation with no other capital city having no voting representation within government. 'Taxation without representation' is the motto that appears on Washington DC's new car licence plates.

Commenting on the Belarusian draft proposal the executive director of the Worldrights organisation, Timothy Cooper said: *"Now every nation on earth will learn America's dirty little secret - that there is no genuine and effective democracy for the residents of its capital city. It is now only a matter of time before the full weight of the world's diplomatic community is brought to bear on remedying these human rights wrongs. To bring that day closer, we call upon*

UN General-Secretary Kofi Annan to intervene and deploy the prestige of his high office to end the violations and win us nothing less than equal congressional representation".[103] It is certainly ironic that the pro-democracy legislation against Belarus was approved in Washington DC.

In November 2006, Belarus again became the subject of a US and EU sponsored country specific human rights resolution. True to their word, the Belarusians reintroduced their draft resolution in response to this further provocation. It is interesting to note that the USA only regards the UN as a body of authority when it serves US interests to do so. The dismissal of the UN over the invasion of Iraq sharply contrasts with US use of country specific resolutions. Senator John McCain went so far as to say that if the USA did not invade Iraq then it may be *"subordinating its power to the United Nations"*.[104] Of course it is expected that countries such as Belarus must subordinate their power to the UN or face the consequences.

Another war of words between Belarus and the USA erupted in January 2005 when nominee US Secretary of State Condoleezza Rice declared Belarus to be an 'Outpost of Tyranny' in a speech to the Senate Foreign Affairs Committee. The inability of the US to make its accusations that Lukashenko was somehow connected to world terrorism stick, shifted the US position to a highly contentious moral one. The Belarusian political model had to be shown to be ineffective and brutalising. US ambassador to Lithuania Stephen Mull used all of his diplomatic skills when he commented on Belarusian development as *"clearly abnormal"*. He also added that the US has *"no desire to force unwanted change on the Belarusian people"* and that they must *"make their own choices freely and based on exposure to a wide range of information, not state propaganda"*.[105] Again it must be noted that he is blindly repeating his own state's propaganda to consider that there is not a wide range of information available in Belarus. Surely the Ambassador to Lithuania ought to be aware that Belarusians actually receive Lithuanian TV broadcasts, as well as the fact that the BPF's newspaper 'Svaboda' is printed in Lithuania (Although the editorial team and writers are based in Minsk). However 'local experts' such as Kozak and Mull were able to put flesh on the bones of the theory of Belarus as an 'Outpost of Tyranny'.

The term 'Outpost of Tyranny' seemed to certainly be in the vein of the previous US grouping 'the Axis of Evil'. Tony Blair added 'Arc of Extremism' to these groups in a speech in 2006. Despite Senator

Mcain's seminar on Belarus being the 'missing link' in the Axis of Evil, Belarus has only managed to officially be labelled an Outpost of Tyranny. This may all sound ridiculous, and that quite simply, is because it is.

Lukashenko summarised this to a Wall Street Journal reporter, declaring that the term 'Axis of Evil' was *"unacceptable in international relations. One should not divide nations into good and bad. One must look into the matter first. Such statements will not contribute to international stability and relations between the states"*. Lukashenko also advised US politicians to take a more responsible approach to world affairs, noting that *"the policy of good will only contribute to America"*.[106] What is meant by this comment, is that very seldom is an issue 'black or white', and this is acutely the case when talking about a whole country. A genuine understanding of the reasons for the direction of a nation's development takes time and an understanding of its history and culture. This does not fit into a simple slogan, and ought not to be condensed for the 'news in 60 seconds'. However this reality does not fit with modern Western governments who rely so heavily on corporate media, and 'spin'. Hence labelling nations as evil or tyrannical is far simpler than trying to persuade people to support policies that need an involved and informed debate.

The National Assembly of Belarus issued a statement in early May 2005, which avoided mentioning the label 'Outpost of Tyranny', but instead referred to an *"intensification of the anti-Belarusian campaign"*. The statement condemned the flawed 'evidence' cited, and went on to mention that objective data showed the progressive development of Belarus in the social and economic fields. In reference to Condoleezza Rice's speech the statement declared: *"Recent intensification of the anti-Belarusian actions indicates a deliberate strategy of defamation of Belarus by the forces that don't like an independent policy of our country. The 'conductor' of these actions, striving for individual world domination is well known"*. These are strong words indeed, and although the USA is not named it is rather obvious who is being referred to as seeking world domination. The National Assembly statement also declared *"that using human rights rhetoric for advancing political and economic interests of one group of states at the expense of other states has no prospects and contradicts the very concept of human rights"*.[107] This is a clear and strong moral argument, and unsurprisingly was left without official answer by the US. However the new US ambassador to Belarus George Krol, could not resist the opportunity to tell the Belarusian press that they were conducting an anti-American campaign. As reported (again, apparently without irony) by RFE/RL, "*Krol noted that government-controlled media outlets portray US diplomats as spies whose only aim is to destabilise Belarus*".[108] Either Krol is commending the Belarusian media's accuracy, or is wholly unfamiliar with the actions of his predecessor. Much more likely is that his comments were intended for the foreign audience.

However it is significant that the US ambassador was able to freely express his opinions in state controlled publications within an 'Outpost of Tyranny'. In US - Belarusian relations a pattern has emerged of the US side making a broad criticism of Belarusian methods or practice, whilst the Belarusians compose a detailed response. The Western media however only tends to report the accusation, and not any rebuttal or explanation. In a meeting with the former Belarusian ambassador to the UK Alyaksei Mazhukhou, I was told that he frequently wrote to newspapers to respond to statements about his country. He noted that he had never had a letter printed, despite the fact that the British ambassador in Minsk was given frequent access to the press.

A Belarusian foreign ministry spokesman who directly responded to Condoleezza Rice's remarks lamented that "*her vision of the situation in Belarus is unfortunately too far from reality now*".[109] Lukashenko responding to President Bush's inauguration speech promise to carry freedom to every nation, said that some did "*not need their freedom, drenched in blood and smelling of oil*". Once again Lukashenko reiterated that he was not taking a hard line anti-US position, because "*the Belarusian people have not set these goals for me*". He further emphasised that Belarus was ready to co-operate with the US, and other NATO countries, but only if "*Belarusian national interests are observed, and only on an equal and mutually beneficial basis*".[110] Lukashenko's comments reveal his awareness of the democratic process, which does not fit with his label of 'dictator'. He was not elected on an anti-US platform, and thus has no pretensions to dogmatically oppose all things American. However nor was George Bush elected on the promise of pumping "*such sums as may be necessary*" into the Belarusian opposition. The uncomfortable reality is that the comprehensive social system of Belarus is being undermined by tax dollars from ordinary US citizens. The social policies outlined in Chapter 12 would not be possible if Lukashenko was allocating a significant percentage of the Belarusian GDP to opposition groups within the USA.

The Belarus Democracy Act, and 'Outpost of Tyranny' label kept up the pressure on Lukashenko, and ultimately were intended to have a significant influence on his next big challenge, a presidential election in 2006. This election was to be the culmination of all the efforts of the US in effecting regime change. NGO's and politicians financed and supported by the USA were to play their part, and the anti-Lukashenko groups were already talking of what colour to adopt for their revolution. Ultimately the 'revolutionaries' adopted the colour of blue, in reference to denim jeans, these supposedly being a symbol of US style freedom.

Leading up to the election Lukashenko made a startling claim in an interview with Russian journalists. He said he had received information that *"very big forces even in America and in Europe, even in Great Britain to my surprise, I've received this information quite recently, -many declare that if Lukashenko wins at these elections we'll recognise him de facto"*.[111] What became clear after the 2006 election, and in fact during it, was that Western countries were clearly no more willing to accept a Lukashenko victory in Belarus than they had been five years earlier.

The conduct of the election itself will be covered in the next chapter, but it is unsurprising that the 'unified opposition' candidate again received strong US and EU support. The popularity with the Belarusian electorate of the pro-Western candidate, Alexander Milinkevich, or of his platform was quite irrelevant to his US patrons. Instead it was presumed that the vast sums of money channelled into Belarusian NGO's would be used not to fight an election campaign, but instead to push out Lukashenko through mass protest in imitation of other 'colour revolutions' in eastern Europe. Despite the calm and orderly manner with which Belarusians went about their daily lives leading up to the election the US Deputy assistant Secretary of State (for European and Eurasian affairs) David J Kramer called upon all sides to *"avoid violence"*.[112] The Belarusian foreign ministry reacted with some concern to this, and a spokesman requested the US to share any information it had about possible planned violence. The Belarusians were right to be worried, in the run up to the election most Western media could not mention the election without speculating on a repeat of the Ukrainian Orange Revolution. It was also important that the above statement came from within the staff of Condoleezza Rice's Department of State. In April 2005 Ms Rice met with the leading figures in the Belarusian opposition movement. The meeting took place in Lithuania concurrently with a Nato meeting. She declared that the election was an *"excellent opportunity"*[113] for Belarusians to voice their will. This needs to be understood in light of the opposition leaders decision to organise street protests following the result. The opportunity then, is not to go out and vote, but instead to protest the results. Unsurprisingly several Belarusian Members of Parliament were concerned by Ms Rice's interference. Nikolai Cherginets compared the situation with that of the cold war, and accused the US Secretary of State of calling for the *"overthrow of a legally elected head of state"*.[114]

Milinkevich appears to have emerged from the aforementioned meeting as being the US approved candidate despite scoring single digit percentages in independent pre-election polls (In the actual election these polls proved accurate when he won 6% of the vote). Most surprising of all is that one of Milinkevich's election advisors was Terry Nelson, the man who directed George Bush's 2004 presidential campaign.[115]

Challenging Lukashenko's popularity was an almost insurmountable obstacle and thus in the words of a New York Times report in January 2006: "*Mr. Lukashenko's opponents seem not to be running an election campaign, as much as they are trying to organise an uprising*". Another article in February echoed this, reporting that Milinkevich "*is campaigning not for the presidency, but for an uprising*".[116] Again the US position of supporting democracy in Belarus is highly suspect when not only are they ignoring the fact that Lukashenko has genuine popular support from the people; but they are supporting a candidate who is seeking to take power via a revolution supported by a tiny percentage of the population. Lukashenko unsurprisingly won a huge share of the vote on 19th of March 2006, and the opposition was quick to stage its protests. The planned for 'Denim Revolution' failed to materialise, leaving the US wondering what to do next. The answer was to decry the results that even their own media had foreseen. Intermedia and Gallup/Balticmedia polls predicted huge Lukashenko wins. These agencies are notably independent and their results were reported by the Los Angeles Times, and the Times in London prior to the final result that was then decried by the same publications. The US responded quickly with an official press release from the White House saying *"we will not accept this result"*.[117] A spokesman from the Belarusian embassy in the USA replied that: *"The United States did not, does not and will not have a mandate to reject or recognise elections results in other independent states"*. He continued that *"in our country the President is elected by the people, and not in the street, but at the polling stations"*.[118]

The failure of their candidate to win the election, or to mastermind an alternative route to power led the White House to refer back to the Belarus democracy Act, and increase the sanctions already in place. On July the 27th the US congress introduced the Belarus Democracy Reauthorization Act of 2006. Essentially this Act serves to continue the initial aims of the original Act. The key point of its reauthorization is that the bill grants 20 million US dollars for the fiscal years, 2007 and 2008. To be used for democracy building organisations, whilst a further 7.5 million US dollars was additionally allocated for radio and television broadcasting into Belarus.[119] The specifying of funds appears to be an improvement on the previous 'such sums as necessary'. However the amount is around double the previous yearly contributions as detailed earlier.

Added to this is a ban on President Lukashenko as well as many other government officials from travelling to the USA. The EU having already banned Lukashenko from travelling to its member states. The immediate effect being that Lukashenko is unable to travel to the UN in New York. As will be seen later the other effect is that it pushes Belarus closer to other regimes that displease the US. Following Lukashenko's victory the USA again replaced their ambassador. George Krol being succeeded by Karen Stewart.

This overview of diplomatic relations between Belarus and the USA represents only a scratch on the surface of the complicated nature of US actions and policy in Belarus. As has been seen in previous chapters, and indeed will be seen again later, the USA has taken an extraordinary interest in Belarusian internal affairs. Many issues in regard to elections, economics and foreign policy all frequently involve a notable degree of US interference.

In a speech to Belarusian diplomats in 2004 Lukashenko acknowledged the position of the US as the centre of military, financial, economic, technical and political power in the world. *"Nonetheless the US has clearly misused its world leadership especially during the last years. Kosovo in Yugoslavia and Iraq are particularly odious examples"*.[120]

Lukashenko acknowledged that in the short term the relations with the USA were going to be difficult which transpired to be case. Lukashenko believes the solution must be found within the USA concluding that, *"in the long term, and in a broader sense we believe that changing their style of leadership is in the very interests of the US. Otherwise it would not be a leadership, but an aggressive dictatorship"*.[121]

Cuba and Venezuela.

The relationship between Belarus and Russia has not been as smooth as Lukashenko would like. Added to this is the dominance of the US position in Belarusian relations with Western Europe. Thus Lukashenko has had to look further afield for strategic allies.

One country that has faced the machinations of the US government for over forty years is Cuba. The close relationship between the Soviet Union and Cuba made an alliance between Lukashenko and Fidel Castro almost inevitable.

In September 2000, Lukashenko went on an official visit to Cuba in order to sign a friendship treaty, and establish the nature of the co-operation between the two countries. Whilst in Cuba it was agreed to increase diplomatic ties by opening embassies. Fidel Castro praised Lukashenko for his opposition to the dismantling of the Soviet Union, and also for not *"bowing to the IMF "*.[122] Lukashenko was also decorated by Castro with the Order of Jose Marti, which is the highest Cuban state award for foreign nationals. Castro observed that Belarus was a state that had maintained good relations with Cuba since the end of the Soviet Union. Lukashenko added that *"the former Socialist Republics didn't have the moral right to abandon Cuba"* and that they *"should now correct that mistake"*.[123]

In a statement sure to do little to improve Lukashenko's image in the eyes of the US administration he claimed that Fidel Castro, *"is a legendary leader whose thoughts and convictions are not only valid for Cuba, but for all of humanity"*. He added that Castro's life *"constitutes a manual for any world political leader"*.[124] It is not just Lukashenko's background as a political instructor that would have formed this opinion of Cuba's Marxist leader. Castro's pragmatism, adaptability, and commitment to socialism under the most adverse circumstances will have been both inspirational and influential on his Belarusian counterpart.

Following the collapse of the Soviet Union the Cuban economy became seriously isolated, and few believed that socialism could survive there. As Lukashenko consolidated his power and set about re-establishing a Soviet style social insurance system in Belarus, Cuba was always available as an example of a nation that maintained such policies under a US blockade and political isolation. In fact Belarus has been a particularly vocal opponent of the US economic blockade of Cuba. The US blockade began in 1962 (and was eventually codified into US law in 1992), and its maintenance is voted on annually by the UN, with the US using its power of veto to continue the embargo despite massive opposition. The only other country to consistently vote for the maintenance of the embargo is Israel (however Israel frequently breaks the embargo).

Relations between Belarus and Cuba are based on mutual respect and understanding, as well as shared values and beliefs. Cuban foreign minister Perez Roque announced on a visit to Belarus in 2003 that the country can *"count on the Cuban leadership"*. He also recognised that Belarus was pursuing its own independent policies and development and praised it for its *"steadfastness and persistence"*.[125] Lukashenko added that Cuba and Belarus *"have similar views on world affairs"*.[126] The Cuban embassy in Minsk was opened at the end of 2002 and bilateral trade and co-operation has increased. In 2005 a Belarusian delegation travelled to Havana in order to improve co-operation in the fields of health and science. This was followed in April 2006 by an official visit to Cuba by Belarusian Prime Minister Sergei Sidorsky. Belarusian exports to Cuba, despite the blockade are making their presence felt, particularly in terms of transportation and automotive spare parts, which have been in short supply in Cuba since 1962.

Some 90% of Belarusian exports to Cuba in 2005 were machine-engineering products. Mining equipment, trucks and tractors make up a significant part of other exports.[127] The dilapidated and obsolete equipment supplied to Cuba during the cold war and the pre revolutionary Cuban infrastructure is now being upgraded with these supplies.

Another supporter of Fidel Castro is Venezuelan president Hugo Chávez. The 'Bolivarian Revolution' in Venezuela is supportive of, and supported by socialist Cuba. Venezuela's oil wealth, once cynically exploited for the benefit of foreign companies, and a tiny elite is now being used to fund social programmes, aiming to improve life for

Venezuela's impoverished majority. Speaking of this new direction Castro said to Chávez: "*The struggle for dignity is called Bolivarianism in Venezuela; In Cuba this struggle is called Socialism*".[128]

With Chávez being an ardent supporter of Castro, as well as having previously been the victim of a US backed coup, it was inevitable that the Venezuelan and Belarusian leaders would develop closer ties between their countries. In June 2006 Adan Chávez, Presidential Secretary and former Venezuelan ambassador to Cuba, went to Belarus to pave the way for a presidential visit. Adan Chávez spoke of the possibility of forming an anti-imperialist block, and even of establishing an international court that could bring G.W. Bush to trial for war crimes. Adan Chávez is considered by some to be more hard-line than his younger brother with a background of involvement with left wing Venezuelan guerrilla forces.

At the end of July President Chávez himself made his official visit to Belarus. Lukashenko and Chávez found they shared a lot of common ground. With Lukashenko summarising: "*Both Belarus and Venezuela have many common interests and one main goal – securing higher living standards for their citizens and peaceful conditions for materialising constructive plans*".[129] Despite both countries having felt the weight of external pressure and criticism their solidarity was based not on necessity, but on their shared desire to pursue an independent line.

Chávez praised Belarus and its President, on arrival in Minsk he declared himself to be "*among friends and brothers*".[130] Chávez is often unpredictable and appeared to surprise Lukashenko when he announced that "*Belarus has transformed into reality Vladimir Lenin's slogan that we must end man's exploitation of man. We see a model of social development here that we have only begun to establish at home. We must defend the interests of man and not the domestic interests of capitalists, wherever they may be, in North America or Europe*".[131] This is high praise indeed, and the reference to Lenin was certainly not accidental. Hugo Chávez is a man who 'the left' in many countries respect and admire. Lukashenko for the most part is relatively unknown.

This raises an interesting question, and problem. Why is it that Castro and Chávez both hold Lukashenko's Belarus in high regard, with Chávez even commenting on using it as a model for Venezuela whilst some socialists in the West believe Belarus to be a police state run by a dictator? The answer is essentially down to the power, influence and focus of the media. Chávez receives far more press because of Venezuela's oil. When Chávez speaks, the world listens. Venezuela in 2004-2005 provided around 15% of the oil consumed by the USA.[132] As such any political change in Venezuela effects the USA, and thus the world.

The higher volume of interest in Venezuela almost inevitably produces more balanced reporting, and thus it is harder to manipulate facts, and publish outright lies. This still happens, but counter arguments are more readily available. In Belarusian affairs this is seldom the case. The fact that Spanish is more widely understood in Europe and the USA also is an advantage over Belarusian and Russian. Belarusian press releases usually only find a home on their embassies web pages, with newspapers having little interest in providing balance in their articles about 'Europe's last dictator'. The more coverage Chávez receives the higher are the chances that people will pick up on positive elements, and ask why he has taken the position he has. In Belarus only an election brings broad media coverage, and then not of the policies or programmes of the candidates, but a simpler black and white picture of 'democracy versus dictator'. To find positive and accurate information on Belarus/Lukashenko requires effort that few people have the time or inclination to carry out. One of the prime motivators for writing this book was to compile 'the other side of the argument' in one place, and provide people with the information needed for a genuine discussion and assessment of Belarus.

The agreements reached by Lukashenko and Chávez are the beginning of what promises to become a strategic partnership. Chávez explained *"here I've got a new friend and together we'll form a team, I thank you Alexander* [Lukashenko], *for your solidarity and we've come here to demonstrate our solidarity"*.[133] This solidarity is more than just words. Chávez noted that the Venezuelan oil industry was currently importing around ten billion US dollars worth of equipment and services *"and a good part of this money goes to the United States. We're sure Belarus can supply a good part of this equipment"*.[134] The economic advantage to Belarus would be significant, and Lukashenko also was pleased with the political ramifications too. He described the trade and strategic agreements reached as being "a *natural urge to depart from the unipolar model of the global order to a community of equal partners*".[135] To this end Belarus is a supporter of Venezuela's bid for a (non-permanent) seat on the UN Security Council. In a televised speech Chávez sent greetings to Lukashenko and thanked the Belarusian government for its *"firm support"* adding that: *"Belarus is a free country, Venezuela is a free country, and that puts us in sight of the US empire's ill fated objectives"*.[136]

Despite the rhetoric, both Chávez and Lukashenko have always made pains to distinguish between the US government, and its people. Chávez went so far as to sanction fuel supplies to poor families in the USA at 40% below the market price. Chávez like many others is not afraid to say that he believes the Iraq war was fought for access to oil, and not for the purpose of establishing democracy. However for Chávez, Iraq provides a clear example of what happens to oil producing countries that are not sympathetic to the needs and goals of the world largest oil consumer. With this in mind he has set about providing an effective armed force to defend the Bolivarian Revolution. Certainly a large proportion of this equipment and technology will come from Belarus. The head of Lukashenko's security council claimed that a deal had been struck that would bring Belarus almost a billion US dollars.[137] The possibility of such deals was in all likelihood the motivating factor for President Bush's Executive Order of June 2006 that declared Belarus to constitute *"an unusual and extraordinary threat to the national security and foreign policy of the United States"*.[138] Presumably the ability to defend yourself being the threat to US foreign policy.

The close relationship between Belarus and Venezuela has come at a key time in terms of energy disputes. The difficult negotiations between Belarus and Russia over gas prices throughout 2005/2006 has led Lukashenko to seriously consider looking to Venezuela for cheaper and more reliable fuel supplies. The Russian energy companies are reluctant to have their profits reduced by selling at a reduced rate to their eastern European neighbours. Also they are aware that a lower price can also lead to the client countries selling on a portion of the fuel at this same low price, thus undercutting the Russian companies and suppliers. The result of this is that Belarus can no longer rely on Russia for a preferential deal on its energy requirements. Price hikes in western Europe were quickly passed onto consumers by the gas suppliers, which is something Lukashenko cannot afford to do. Hence the ongoing negotiations between Russian energy firms, and the Belarusian government over selling control over, or a stake in, the Belarusian pipelines in exchange for lower fuel prices. Certainly Venezuela can supply part of the solution to the Belarusian problem, and

Hugo Chávez has proven that he is willing to make preferential deals for political goals, and not solely for economic ones. To this end Venezuela agreed in 2007 to lease oil producing land plots* to Belarus that will generate around 2 million tonnes of oil per year. In return the Belarusians are establishing a construction industry for Venezuela as well as providing industrial and agricultural specialists.[139]

The European Union

What has become clear through the ongoing energy disagreements is that Belarus is no satellite of Russia. Lukashenko has not sold the independence of the Belarusian people, and that any attempts from the Russian government to exert control over its Belarusian neighbour have been rebuffed. Lukashenko has kept true to his promise of pursuing international relations on a basis of equality and mutual respect. As such Lukashenko in November 2006 told Ukrainian journalists that Russia's price hikes on fuel were intended to put Belarusian financial entities in a *"disadvantageous position compared to Russian businesses"*.[140] Lukashenko's criticism of Russian businesses was not surprising although his proposed solution certainly was. Lukashenko suggested the possible forming of a Belarusian-Ukrainian union state. The degree to which this proposal was meant as a serious full union, or as a tool against Russian regional dominance and financial pressure remains to be seen. What is clear is that all of Russia's fuel supply pipelines to western Europe currently pass through these two countries. Lukashenko's suggestion of a joint policy on oil and gas issues including the possibility of applying a standard transit tariff certainly makes sense. Lukashenko summarised the practical nature of such a plan by saying, *"what if we pursued a single policy in talks with Russia on this matter? Would it be worse? It would be better. So let's do it"*.[141]

As covered earlier, Lukashenko has maintained close ties with Russia, but has been very aware that the Belarusian economy cannot rely on any one country for too great a share of its support. Thus from the beginning of his presidency, Lukashenko has carefully developed and maintained good relations with the two giant economies of India and

---

* In May 2007 Iran and Belarus agreed a similar deal on gas and oil producing land on Iranian territory.

China. Belarus is not isolated, and nor can it be. Its location between the EU and Russia is geographically and strategically important. The Lukashenko government has brought stability and economic growth, with foresight and planning. Belarus does not rely on one 'sponsor' and nor can it, or indeed any nation that wishes to pursue a truly independent model of development.

In a 2004 speech to Belarusian diplomats Lukashenko commented that of the Belarusian economy approximately 60% of the GDP is exported, and thus the talk of isolation did not take the facts of the modern world into consideration. Lukashenko is well aware of the significance of a countries economy as a geo-political factor, and one that is actually the prime reason for most military interventions and actions worldwide. This can be seen by the alarm shown in Washington when South American countries begin nationalising their own assets, or at the concern over the re-emergence of OPEC. As Lukashenko summarised: *"It is economy that defines a countries authority, status and role – not the possession of nuclear weapons, or weapons of mass destruction"*.[142]

Belarus maintains open economic relations with the world, and I have focussed primarily on the main strategic partners and opponents here. As opposed to listing every nations dealings with Lukashenko I have concentrated on the Union State with Russia, the colossal level of interest/interference from the USA, and the relations of solidarity between Cuba, Venezuela and Belarus. One more area of note is Belarusian relations with the European Union.

The EU for the most part has echoed and actively pursued the same agenda in Belarus as has the USA. The Eastern expansion of the EU has taken it right to the borders of Belarus, and this proximity has seen an increase in the dissemination of anti-Lukashenko information from the territory of Poland and the Baltic states. The historical reasons for this lie in the general hostility toward the Soviet system in the Baltics, and Poland. Belarusian respect and reverence for this period of their history is at odds with the experience of its western neighbours. Indeed in the Baltic States where anti-Russian, and anti-communist sentiment are often viewed as the same thing, aggressive nationalism and neo-Nazism are serious problems. In April 2005 a UN human rights Commission approved a resolution expressing concern over the building of memorials to the Waffen SS, a Nazi organisation declared to be criminal at the Nuremberg trials. The resolution was primarily aimed at Latvia, but in Estonia SS memorials are now in place (surprisingly the US voted against the resolution).

Poland, who after Belarus suffered the greatest proportionate loss of life during the war (one in four citizens) has no sympathy for the SS, it certainly has seen a dramatic increase in right wing groups and tolerance of xenophobia. Yet what is more important in Polish hostility toward Belarus is the fact that the Polish government is pursuing an incredibly Western looking agenda. IMF conditions are met without fail, subsidies are not granted to beleaguered farmers, the economy is being privatised on a vast scale, with the predictable result of huge nation-wide unemployment, and a subsistence level of survival in the Polish countryside. Added to this is a 'brain drain' of mass migration of young qualified workers to other EU countries. Poland is also noted to be the staunchest supporter of US policy in mainland Europe.

The diplomatic conflict between Poland and Belarus in 2005 was the most direct international confrontation of Lukashenko's time in government to date. Even the US interference has not come so close to a severance of diplomatic relations, which looked very possible in the case of Poland. The dispute grew out of an internal issue, and the issues span both social and foreign policy. In October 1990, when Belarus was still a part of the Soviet Union, the Polish minority established the Union of Poles in Belarus (UPB). This organisation sprung up in reaction to the BPF as well as the increasing nationalist sentiments which perestroika and glasnost had awoken. The UPB however, was a largely non-political organisation, and was far more culturally orientated. The Polish minority in Belarus principally live in the western regions, and make up approximately 3.9% of the population (396,000 people). Belarusian Poles, except for those in Minsk are predominantly a rural population, engaged in agriculture and small-scale industry. The UPB has 20 branches and some 22,000 registered members. As well as the UPB there are also 14 other registered Polish associations. These organisations publish 12 periodicals of which the UPB's daily has a circulation of 5,600 copies.[143] This is important to note in light of the common criticism over independent media availability in Belarus.

In March 2005 the UPB held its sixth congress where the issue of leadership and direction was raised. The existing leader Tadeusz

Kruczkowski was defeated in an election to be replaced by Andzelika Borys. Kruczkowski refused to accept the result of the vote claiming that it had not been carried out under the rules of the UPB, and that there had not even been any debate of the key issues at the congress. An appeal was lodged with the Belarusian Ministry of Justice.

The Ministry confirmed that irregularities had taken place under the UPB's own rules, and the ministry's diplomatic solution was simply that the UPB should hold a repeat congress, and have another vote. This however was not enough for Borys who turned to the Polish government for support. The possibility that this was the intention from the very beginning is not unlikely.

Borys claimed that the Poles in Belarus were now somehow being persecuted for their ethnic background, and a demonstration was staged. This was followed by a raid by Belarusian police on the headquarters of the UPB. Borys and several other new 'leaders' were arrested and charged with participating in an unsanctioned demonstration and also illegally meeting with a Polish Member of Parliament.[144]

The previous leadership was temporarily reinstated until the repeat congress could be organised. In an attempt to diffuse the situation. Kruczkowski announced that he would not seek re-election. He had been accused by his opponents of being pro-Lukashenko and anti-UPB. The Belarusian position was remarkably clear, that the vote needed to happen again following the rules of the UPB. With the 'favoured candidate' stepping down it is unclear how Lukashenko could be using this case to persecute the Polish minority. However Western media reports of the issue actually did use terms such as *"persecution"*[145] and one headline declared *"Lukashenko's War on Poles"*.[146]

The diplomatic row quickly escalated when Belarus expelled the Polish embassy's press secretary for involvement in 'anti Belarusian activity' with the UPB. The Poles responded in kind. Ultimately each country expelled three of each other's diplomats, before the Poles recalled their ambassador for 'consultations'. At the same time the Polish government appealed to British Foreign Secretary Jack Straw to intervene in his capacity as chair of the EU.

Any doubt about Poland's attitude to Belarus was removed with this gesture. Although this was the peak of the crisis, Lukashenko was clear as to where it may have been leading. *"We are heading into a serious confrontation. Of course the Americans, the West, will aim to destabilise the situation here in any possible way"*.[147] He was certainly correct in this assessment as the US State Department issued a press release in August 2005, and have since used the case as an example of human rights abuse in Belarus worthy of sanctions. It must be noted that the Belarusian Poles themselves were massively unaffected by the whole affair. Passions were not roused over the issue, as it was not representative of any greater persecution or ethnic policy. The Belarusian Poles could not be made to resemble the Kosovo-Albanians. Even the anti-Lukashenko political scientist and analyst Vitali Silitski admits that the dispute was between Belarus and Poland, and not of an ethnic nature. He commented that most ethnic Poles in Belarus "*are deeply apolitical; many barely noticed this conflict*".[148] This certainly tallies with the official Belarusian policy towards ethnic and national groups, with the Ministry of Education even editing and translating Polish and Lithuanian books for use in Belarusian schools.

In Poland however the public reaction was fierce. The 'Super Express' newspaper commented that Poland should "*support the opposition* [to Lukashenko] *openly*".[149] The direction that Poland is developing in is markedly different to that of Belarus. Of key importance is the strategic role that Poland could potentially occupy in eastern Europe. Dr. Federico Bordonaro* has suggested that Poland is aiming to become the regional leader, with its economy and trade firmly integrated with its neighbours to reduce Russian influence in Europe.[150] It is also interesting that in a poll carried out by sociologists in Poland, Tony Blair and George W. Bush were voted the most respected foreign politicians whilst Fidel Castro and Alexander Lukashenko were declared to be the least popular.[151] This highlights the gulf between Polish and Belarusian culture and their political development.

The close support that Poland has shown for US foreign policy is also important. With Silitski making the observation that Poland is far more involved in promoting change in Belarus than any other country "*including, perhaps, the United States*".[152] Although the USA is certainly providing the majority of the money for such endeavours, the Polish government also funds Polish groups within Belarus.[153] Additionally US funded Belarusian opposition newspapers and radio stations also operate from Polish territory.

---

* Dr. Bordonaro is a senior analyst with the Power and Interest News Report. An organisation that uses open source intelligence to provide conflict analysis services in international relations.

In fact it has been speculated that the failure of the EU to sufficiently support Poland in the diplomatic row with Belarus has a basis in the close relationship between the USA and Poland. Both France and Germany maintain good relations with Russia, and these countries were united in their opposition to the US led invasion of Iraq in 2003. Silitski pondered *"whether some at the EU will be happy with the situation because the pro-American Poles were finally whipped by someone"*.[154]

In Belarus the result of the whole affair was one of great indifference. The UPB still operates, and Belarusian Poles live their lives as before, in harmony with other Belarusians. In contrast the issue of Belarus, and Alexander Lukashenko in particular is of great political significance to Poland. Polish Prime Minister Marek Bielka's press service announced in the build up to the 2005 Polish elections that he had held talks to discuss the overthrow of Lukashenko with other regional leaders.[155]

With Poland being a member of both the EU and NATO, and a staunch supporter of the USA it is likely that further diplomatic rows will emerge between it and Belarus. What remains unclear and open to speculation, is the degree to which the UPB incident was engineered as a pretext for intervention along the lines followed by NATO in Yugoslavia. The Belarusian Ministry of Justice insisting on the congress of the UPB simply being re-held was certainly no draconian action that could justifiably cause an international incident. Indeed the fact that Belarus is singled out as being undemocratic by the USA and EU shows again the hypocrisy of these large world powers. The US refusal to express concern via the UN Human Rights Commission over the building of monuments to the SS in the Baltic States is a prime example. It was the USA that declared the SS to be a criminal organisation in the first place, and US prisoners of war murdered by the SS in Malmedy in 1944 formed one of the key pieces of evidence for this. However history and reality are not always important when superpowers choose their friends.

Although the USA is by far the largest financial supporter of the Belarusian opposition, the EU also awarded a German company some 2.4 million US dollars to broadcast anti-Lukashenko radio and TV to Belarus.[156] Again this represents another element of non state run media in Belarus, although it cannot be considered to be objective or independent. Also of note is the fact that EU members Latvia and Estonia are thought by many analysts to be less democratic than Belarus; yet these two countries are not only permitted entry to the EU, but also NATO. Sergei Markov the head of the Institute for Political Studies in Moscow commented in 2006, *"as far as sanctions are concerned, they should be imposed on Latvia and Estonia which have completely excluded 25% of their residents from political life"*.[157]

US President George W. Bush visited Latvia in 2005 on his way to Moscow for the 60th anniversary celebrations of the end of the Second World War. He again referred to Belarus as the 'last dictatorship in Europe' and a country that 'needed to be free'. Following a question from an Estonian journalist President Bush revealed the essence of his definition of freedom. *"I praise Estonia for being an open market economy that is a free society. And therefore, if you're a free society that embraces market economies, you'll rank very high with me and the United States"*.[158] This underlines that it is the economic freedom that is of the highest importance. Political freedom and human rights concerns in Estonia have never been seriously highlighted or addressed by the USA.

Despite the above Belarus has excellent trade relations with most of the world, particularly with India, China, Russia, and even the EU. Additionally the independent line of Belarusian development has brought close and influential allies in South America and the Caribbean. Lukashenko's visit to Havana in 2000, will certainly have increased his standing with, or possibly brought him to the attention of Venezuela's Hugo Chávez. The success of left wing parties* across South and Central America is largely inspired by the longevity of Castro's Cuba, and the progressive strides made by Chávez. This leftward shift in South America should be of significant benefit to Belarus, gaining further strategic and economic partners. Speaking in 2006 to the assembled members of the Non aligned Movement (NAM) in Cuba, Lukashenko said that they needed to work towards a more just world system. *"This is our main goal, to achieve it, we should have a clear program of actions to create gradually but irreversibly a multi-polar world"*.[159]

---

* The 2006 presidential election in Nicaragua was won by Daniel Ortega, the former head of the Sandinista government.

Chapter 15. Elections and the Belarusian Opposition.

"The opposition can take key or any other posts, only if this decision is made by the people".[1] A.G. Lukashenko.

To some degree the issue of opposition and elections has already been discussed however Belarus is notable in that its internal political affairs, and international relations are linked to an unusual degree. Few countries have such blatant outside influences in their domestic concerns. The aim of this chapter is to assess the nature of the Belarusian opposition, and the conduct of the democratic process in Belarus. Inevitably this will mean that in this chapter some issues covered previously will be revisited, but this is essential in understanding the nature of the Belarusian opposition, and the conduct of elections.

The term 'opposition' is exceptionally broad, but it is one used by all the key parties. Lukashenko uses it, as does the US Department of State, and even the alternative presidential candidates in Belarus. This however is a simplification of the political make up of Belarusian government and politics. Belarus has many registered political parties and NGO's, who have members in positions of authority and power within the Belarusian parliament and regional councils. In the USA or UK, the opposition is considered to be whichever of the two main political parties is not in power at that specific time. With Lukashenko not representing a party, the opposition therefore is termed to be those who actively oppose his programme and methods. The notion that Belarus is a totalitarian state, and that Lukashenko is a dictator becomes patently false when the internal opposition is studied, additionally the external interference in Belarusian politics has served, rather ironically, to weaken the opposition movement's development and popularity.

Opposition to Lukashenko was initially from the nationalists of the Belarusian Popular Front (BPF) as Lukashenko fought to consolidate his power, and establish a parliament that would work for Belarus and not only against its president, the influence of the nationalists further waned.

The people of Belarus were craving the stability that Lukashenko had promised them, and resented the BPF and the old nomenclatura in the parliament who appeared to be blocking this. The BPF was further discredited by its association with the Ukrainian ultra-nationalists of the UNA-UNSO mentioned earlier.

By the time that Lukashenko faced his second presidential election campaign in 2001 the Belarusian political landscape had changed immensely. As detailed in chapter 10, Lukashenko had consolidated his power through a referendum in 1996, and in 2000 parliamentary elections were held. These served as an indication of how future elections were to be conducted, the Organisation for Co-operation and Security in Europe (OSCE) for example showed it had already made up its mind on Lukashenko. The OSCE actually refused to observe the conduct of the parliamentary election of 2000, but along with the European Parliament and Council of Europe sent a team that did attend an opposition demonstration calling for a boycott of the vote.[2]

Despite not actually observing the elections the OSCE declared on the day after polling that: *"The 15th October parliamentary election process in Belarus failed to meet international standards for democratic elections"*.[3]

This decision was reached without any discussion with the independent observers who actually did monitor the election. In fact at the OSCE press conference one French MEP, (who had monitored the poll) Paul Marie Coûteaux, attempted to voice his opposition to the OSCE's official conclusion. He was ignored and then shouted down. The man who rather comically demanded *"Silence !"* was none other than OSCE chief Hans Georg Wieck, who ought to be familiar from the previous chapter.[4]

The conclusion of the British Helsinki Human Rights Group (BHHRG) who have monitored every election in Belarus to date is an interesting one. Referring to the OSCE conclusion the BHHRG commented that *"it will do great damage to Belarus' diplomatic position in Europe, and yet the authors of the report are themselves unelected and unaccountable"*.[5] In a further ironic twist US ambassador Kozak said on the 8th of November 2000 that he hoped the forthcoming presidential elections in Belarus would be *"just as free and fair as the American elections"*.[6]

The run up to the Belarusian Presidential elections of 2001 was a turbulent one. NATO intervention in Yugoslavia was a very fresh memory, and the noises of disapproval from abroad seemed to be causing alarm bells to ring in Minsk. In fact in Yugoslavia, the first Western funded and organised 'people power' revolt had succeeded in ousting Slobodan Milosevic. This pattern was to be repeated in what became known as 'colour' or 'velvet' revolutions in several eastern

European countries.

However Lukashenko is not Milosevic, and his situation in 2001 was very different to that of the former Yugoslav leader. Even the conservative US journal the 'National Review' conceded that the situation in Belarus was not as it was often presented, commenting that: "*To Western reporters, the opposition mouths the language of human rights; off camera, they admit that a power struggle is going on*". The article further notes that "*their appeals have been directed to foreign governments and busybody groups rather than to their countrymen. Since the referendum,* [1996. See chapter 10] *all the opposition did at home was to insist the president's supporters had 'massaged' the yes vote upward – though they admitted their own level of 8% was about right*".[7]

An important factor in ousting Milosevic had been the youth movement 'Otpor'. This movement had received substantial financial support from US organisations. Otpor served as the example to be followed in Belarus, with the formation in January of 2001 of the 'Zubr' (Bison) youth movement. Zubr at first was strongly linked to the BPF, possibly 'sharing' members, and certainly sharing political positions. Zubr is a nationalist organisation, and has participated in, and has organised anti-Russian demonstrations. However Zubr's main activity appears to be anti-Lukashenko graffiti. Lukashenko was more than familiar with the importance of Otpor's role in overthrowing Milosevic the previous year. In an address to the Belarusian administrative authorities just before the 2001 election, Lukashenko termed the current opposition as "*nationalist minded*" and that they would attempt to seize power by "*any ways and means*".[8]

Zubr was completely manufactured from the start, and as such is not a very useful guide to the sentiment of young people in Belarus, but rather an example of what some people can be paid to do and say. The Zubr leader Alexei Shidlovsky met with Otpor 'veterans' in February 2001 and continued to receive advice from them at US sponsored meetings in Poland, Lithuania and Slovakia. Shidlovsky commented that "*Otpor was the model for us. We have relations with the Western embassies we tell them what we're doing and planning*".[9]

The use of Otpor as an inspiration for Zubr turned out to be ineffective. The success of Otpor had been the lack of overwhelming support for Milosevic that enabled them to have more influence, in Belarus this was not the case. Commenting on Zubr as a factor in the 2001 presidential election Dr. Vitali Silitski conceded that "*in Belarus the opposition was very weak, and hardly electable. Zubr tried to mobilise the people to support a victory that was never achieved*".[10]

Added to the factor of weak opposition, must be the simple truth that Belarusian nationalism is not a viable political platform. Belarusian political movements and parties are well aware of this, with nationalist organisations being either reactionary (such as the BPF, formed during the Soviet era) or fringe extremists.

When it was announced that presidential elections would take place in September 2001 the opposition was divided and weakened by its adherence to nationalism as an alternative to Lukashenko. How far this was a genuinely Belarusian error, or the result of misinformed advice from abroad is open to speculation. A spokesman for the Belarusian Communist Party observed that: "*The US leadership and its European satellites will do everything to ensure that these elections are won by anyone – a liberal, a national extremist, a quasi-communist and so on – other than Lukashenko, who firmly supports the Belarusian people and does everything in his power to hinder the colonisers plans*".[11]

Three candidates actually stood for the Presidency in 2001. Against Lukashenko were Sergei Gaidukevich head of the Belarusian Liberal Democratic Party, and Vladimir Goncharik who stood as the candidate of the 'unified opposition'. As was mentioned in the previous chapter, of the opposition parties, and individual candidates Goncharik was not the most popular and seemed an unlikely and surprising choice to represent 'the opposition'. Goncharik himself was president of the Trade Union Federation in Belarus, and a former Central Committee member of the Communist Party of the Soviet Union, making him an unexpected choice for US support.

Goncharik was far from being the most obvious candidate for the opposition to rally around, particularly when the opposition included such diverse parties as the nationalist BPF, and the Belarusian Party of Communists (BPC). It is important to note that in Belarus there is the BPC and the Communist Party of Belarus (CPB), who since 1991 have held very different views on the president. The BPC is widely considered to be an opportunist party, who are communists in name only. This was shown when their leader, Sergei Kalyakin, informed election monitors that he favoured the cessation of state intervention in all economic matters, and even blamed the "*old, uneducated population*"[12] for the problems in Belarus. This position may explain the need for another communist party in Belarus.

The three likely candidates for the opposition to unite behind were Kalyakin, Goncharik and the former governor of the Grodno region Semyon Domash. (BPF leader Paznyak was self-exiled in the USA as of 1996). Kalyakin of the BPC was largely a confusing figure to the electorate, whilst any US support for the head of a communist party would be difficult to justify at home. This left Goncharik and Domash.

At first it seemed that Domash was the most obvious choice, and was certainly the more popular choice of Belarusian voters. Domash had considerable prestige in the western regions of Belarus, and was also quite well known in Minsk as a calm and constructive leader of the opposition. In fact Goncharik actually believed Domash to have taken the role of unified candidate in January 2001. Commenting on this he said, *"This morning I was already told that Mr. Semyon Domash has already announced himself the candidate from the joint political opposition. Well, let him do that! The matter is that I never viewed myself as the possible candidate for Presidency"*.[13]

Domash had support from the centre right, and thus was far more in tune with the Western model than the former Communist Party apparatchik and trade union boss Goncharik. Domash also appeared to have political and personal support from the BPF, Zubr and the United Civic Party of Belarus. Despite the personal popularity of Domash there was the problem that the opposition had little overall support, and that he represented too great a shift in political positions from Lukashenko for the tastes of the majority of Belarusian voters. This was noted by Wieck and Kozak, who also were aware that if Lukashenko was to win, then the margin of his victory had to look as suspicious as possible. Thus, the opposition leaders were, *"called to the US embassy"*.[14] Where it was decided that Domash was to be replaced by Goncharik. This version of events was also reported by the London Guardian newspaper, which personally credited Kozak with shifting support away from Domash to Goncharik.[15] The Belarusian media had also caught hold of this story and widely broadcast the interference in their democratic process by the OSCE and US embassy.

Once on board, Goncharik did not help his own cause by announcing in June 2001 that he had no objections to Belarus joining NATO and the EU.[16] Such a statement only served to show fealty to his sponsors, and was certainly not in tune with the wishes of a population who had previously given more than 80% of the vote to a man promising the exact opposite. Lukashenko made reference to the meeting at the US embassy, and specifically noted Wieck's role, "*he invited everybody for a conversation, including Gaidukevich, and determined: either all shall be in favour of Goncharik or let us take off all the alternative candidatures. Let Lukashenko remain alone*".[17] The key point here being the suggestion that all of the other candidates boycott the election. Thus making the wholes process, as well as any result apparently redundant. The headlines of a 'one party state' would have practically written themselves. This would have served as an extension of the 'Yugoslav model' being used by those who sought the removal of Lukashenko. A contestable result is required in order for a 'velvet revolution' to be successful.

In Serbia, Milosevic had not been able to win the required majority vote of over 50% to defeat the unified opposition candidate, Vojislav Kostunica. The huge demonstrations that followed came from Milosevic's refusal to accept the result and ended in his ousting. In Belarus this model needed slight adaptation, and one way was to ensure that Lukashenko won by as large a margin as possible in an attempt to discredit the results.

Another consideration is the attitude of the Belarusian people themselves, who for the most part are ignored by both the opposition and their Western sponsors. One Belarusian I interviewed shortly after the 2006 election made this comment: "*I don't want to live in the EU, I want to live in Belarus. If in March, Lukashenko told us Belarus would enter NATO, then we would have another president*". This is significant in that it shows how greatly Belarusians value their short history of statehood and independence. The same way that the nationalists have concern over losing sovereignty to Russia, ordinary Belarusians do not want to trade their independence for a place in the EU or NATO. This is why the history of Belarus is so important in understanding how Lukashenko wins elections and remains popular. It is simply naïve to presume that Belarusians do not know what is best for them, or that 'they ought to want to be like us'. Such arrogance combined with millions of dollars has still failed to convert a nation of only ten million inhabitants. As Lukashenko put it "*there will be no 'Kostunica' in Belarus*".[18]

For the Belarusian people there has been more than enough evidence of international tampering in their affairs. The opposition suddenly began producing large amounts of high quality printing, and as Lukashenko himself pointed out, the 'unified opposition' website was registered to an address in Texas USA.[19] Furthermore, Belarusian police in early 2001 confiscated computers being used by an unregistered newspaper. These computers appeared to have been provided by the US government. As reported by Jared Israel, *"rather than being embarrassed that his boss had been caught outrageously violating Belarusian sovereignty, State Department spokesman Richard Boucher demanded that Washington's computers be returned!"*[20]

Sergei Gaidukevich was the third candidate in the 2001 election, and he had also been invited to the US embassy meeting proposing a single opposition candidate, but had refused to agree to the plan. Gaidukevich as head of the Liberal Democratic Party of Belarus, thought that the decision was not his to make, and certainly not in the interests of his party. Gaidukevich is sometimes mislabelled as being something of a stooge for the President, because of his refusal to unite behind a single candidate. Although his politics are clearly different to Lukashenko's, Gaidukevich refuses to belittle Belarusian achievements, or to demonise the President. In 2001 Gaidukevich even criticised the Western backed candidate for having *"eighteen communists on his team"*.[21] This sheds a strange but illuminating light on the way that US foreign policy works. After all, had the USA not just spent over 40 years attempting to remove communists from power?

The vote itself was conducted in a calm and orderly manner. Perhaps only in Minsk was this not entirely the case. With opposition funds and support being particularly concentrated in the capital. This is necessary if an Otpor/Kostunica solution is to be achieved, this also keeps the opposition close to the eyes of foreign media. The BHHRG noted that domestic observers from various anti-Lukashenko groups created an antagonistic and suspicious atmosphere in the polling stations, and kept up a constant commentary on mobile telephones during the count. A practice incidentally, that is forbidden in most countries.

The official results of the election saw Lukashenko emerge with 75% of the vote, behind him came Goncharik with 15% and Gaidukevich with 2.5%. Unsurprisingly the opposition cried foul, but failed to even convince themselves. One example of this being a polling station in Minsk where the election committee was made up of Goncharik supporters from the Trade Union Federation. At this station where manipulation or fraud could hardly be expected to go Lukashenko's way, he still polled 61% against Goncharik's 35%.[22] In a rare admission the head of the Office for Democratic Institutions and Human Rights (ODIHR) of the OSCE, Gerard Stoudmann, acknowledged that there was *"no evidence of manipulation or fraud of the results"*. Similarly the Association of Central and Eastern European Election Officials confirmed that the election had been *"free and open in compliance with universal democratic institutions"*.[23] The OSCE officially denounced the election as being neither free nor fair, despite what had been said by Stoudmann. And it is ought to be remembered that the OSCE had refused to actually observe the vote. However of far more pressing concern was the spectacular failure of the opposition to gain genuine mass support, and importantly, where had all of the foreign money actually gone? Whilst Lukashenko was declaring his campaign and victory to have been *"elegant and beautiful"* Russian news channel NTV suggested that the opposition had simply pocketed the foreign cash.

As a sign of what was to come for Belarus, foreign 'independent' media picked up the OSCE report as gospel, with no attempt to validate its version of events. The BBC carried an article titled *'Belarus vote neither free nor fair'* parroting the OSCE conclusion. Tucked away in the article is an unexplored comment from the BBC correspondent in Minsk, saying that in reality Lukashenko had been *"widely expected to win"*.[24] The 2001 presidential election was a real test for Lukashenko, and his first experience of dealing with a large scale foreign intervention in his country.

The decision by the US government and the OSCE to support Goncharik as the democratic opposition candidate was a curious one. His apparently left wing base in the trade unions, and an alliance with the Belarusian Party of Communists, does not make him an obvious ally of the West. However he was certainly more malleable than Lukashenko had turned out to be, and presumably more so than Semyon Domash. The key lesson to be drawn from this meddling in the election was in the phrase; *"either all shall be in favour of Goncharik or let us take off all the alternative candidatures. Let Lukashenko remain alone"*. The importance of this being that if Lukashenko was going to win (as was widely predicted), then the result had to be made as questionable as possible. This method seems to have been applied again in 2006.

On December 16th 2005 a resolution was passed by the Belarusian parliament to set the date for the next presidential elections as March the 19th 2006. Lukashenko announced that he would stand for a third term. He also said that if he were not re-elected he would probably retire from politics, and that he would *"find what to do, and not interfere in* [the] *new president's activity"*.[25] However Lukashenko was quite convinced that he would not need to retire just yet.

The previous opposition candidates and leaders had disappeared from the political scene into obscurity. Having been unsuccessful in 2001 Goncharik, and even Domash were left to carry on where they had once been, in the Trade Union Federation, and as parliamentary deputies; whilst the West looked for a new face to represent the 'united opposition'. Significantly the BPF's founder Zyanon Paznyak announced himself as a contender, however he was unable to gain enough support to be registered as a candidate. Sergei Gaidukevich also announced his intention to stand for the presidency for the second time, which in effect showed that he had survived politically by not being a part of the contrived Western backed opposition. A lesson could have been learned here, but as before Gaidukevich, although a liberal democrat, was considered to be too independent of Washington and Brussels. (In fact Gaidukevich's party is a member of the 'Liberal International' and as such would certainly have been favourable to Europe). As in 2001 Gaidukevich was able to shed some light on the reason why he was not considered suitable for the 'unified opposition' candidacy. As reported by the BHHRG, *"he could have been the 'unified' opposition candidate himself if he had been prepared to rubbish Belarus but although he claimed there were problems to be addressed he admitted that much had been achieved"*.[26]

Lukashenko was riding high on a surge of popularity at the start of 2006. The economy was continuing to grow, and the benefits of this were being distributed widely and visibly to the people. Evidence of this can be seen in the comments of foreign election observers who returned to Belarus in 2006. One example being the comments made by Israeli parliamentary deputy Mikhail Gorlovskiy who noted that since his first visit in the 1990's *"these are two different countries. Progress is obvious"*.[27] Additionally, the All Belarus People's Assembly had held it's third session on March the second and third of 2006. This assembly is a form of direct democracy, described by the Belarusians as *"an open conversation with the nation"*.[28] As well as allowing representatives from all over the country to participate in general decisions and make proposals, it also serves as a platform for the president to report on the progress that has or has not been made in the country.

Lukashenko was able to announce that the goals set forth by the people at the second People's Assembly had been achieved and made reality. The reason for this success Lukashenko declared was simple: *"We have not embezzled the people's wealth, we have not got into burdensome debts. Relying on life itself, we have worked out our own model of development based on well balanced and thought out reforms. Without any sweeping privatisation and shock therapy. Preserving everything that was best in our economy and traditions"*.[29]

The opposition's constant call for 'democracy in Belarus' is greeted by most Belarusians with great scepticism. Particularly following a People's Assembly, and in the year of a presidential election. The People's Assembly certainly helped to cement support behind Lukashenko. The leader of the Belarusian section of the revived Communist Party of the Soviet Union enthused to an international audience in Belgium that the People's Assembly was a form of direct democracy *"unheard of in the West"*.[30]

Of course democracy is dependent on definition and interpretation. Belarusian entrepreneur Aleg Litvinovich, whom I interviewed in 2006 had this to say: *"The West likes Ukraine, because in Ukraine there is 'democracy'. I was in Ukraine a week ago, it does not have democracy, it has disorganisation and chaos. The West also likes Georgia, but Belarusians don't go to live in Georgia. The Georgians come here to live"*. This sentiment is genuinely popular, because it is easy for Belarusians to see the results for ordinary people of Western approved democracy.

Since 2001 the opposition have proved themselves to be a hardcore of activists seeking change, whose ranks are artificially buoyed by the large sums of Western money available. Lukashenko noted that these activists are frequently unemployed. *"Where have they taken their money from? Fighters for people's happiness so to say... They do fight by the way. One against the other, so as to demonstrate to the West who is the greatest enemy of Lukashenko and who is 'more democratic' in order to become a single* [candidate], *because in that case all the money will be flowing through them. This is the kind of fight they are waging"*.[31]

Alexander Feduta, a Belarusian independent journalist, who certainly does not support Lukashenko, argued that the US financing of the opposition was a mistake sure to backfire. He argued in 2001 that the USA had *"really helped the opposition financially so much, that the opposition has gone crazy. Name me another country where you get paid for being in the opposition"*. He also confirmed that funds had been stolen and misused lamenting that *"revolution is not done that way"*.[32] If it was obvious to those campaigning against Lukashenko that the 'unified opposition' was a foreign created and funded phenomena it was certainly obvious to the rest of the Belarusian people too. Thus when the Belarusian opposition rallied behind the very little known Alexander Milinkevich in 2006, the people watched very closely for any signs of foreign support. They didn't have to look too hard. As well as the fact that his campaign advisor was Terry Nelson (George W. Bush's campaign manager in 2004), Milinkevich was also invited to speak to the Polish Parliament in January 2006. Added to this he held a meeting with the EU foreign policy chief Javier Solana, European Parliament President Josep Borrell, and 25 other high level EU ministers in Brussels the same month. The importance of these two meetings is vast. Firstly, Milinkevich was the first Belarusian ever to address the Polish parliament, and he did so as an unelected individual with absolutely no authority behind him.

Secondly his visit to Brussels was highly controversial, particularly in light of the supposed neutrality of the EU in any internal affairs of a non-member state. Even the hostile Radio Free Europe/Radio Liberty acknowledged this embarrassing conundrum; how to support regime change without appearing to endorse any particular candidate. *"The answer, as it transpired over the course of the day, was to grant Milinkevich almost unprecedented levels of political access - while keeping it all very quiet"*.[33] Unfortunately 'very quiet' was not quiet enough. With the story being picked up across Europe, including of course, in Belarus. The excuse used was that Milinkevich was speaking to the EU ministers with first hand information on the political conditions in Belarus; whilst also requesting greater funding for foreign based radio and TV information broadcasts into the country. It requires quite a leap of faith to believe that an opposition candidate would present an unbiased version of events, particularly during an election campaign.

Milinkevich had emerged as the unified opposition candidate following a meeting with US Secretary of State Condoleezza Rice in Lithuania in April 2005. As reported in the Washington Post, on the agenda of the meeting was (again), *"unifying the opposition around a candi-*

date to challenge President Alexander Lukashenko".[34]

The fact that this had failed five years previous was apparently ignored. What Milinkevich did represent however, was a candidate who was wholly sympathetic to the aims of his sponsors. Surprisingly in one of the coldest winters on record Milinkevich made a campaign promise to end the preferential gas and fuel prices from Russia. All in the interests of the free market, and the cooling of the strategic partnership with Moscow.[35] It ought to be remembered that such a promise meant a raise in the average persons heating bill of some 70%. Since the Orange Revolution ended Ukraine's preferential deal in gas prices, ordinary Ukrainians have been severely effected. Fuel prices have gone up by 100%, and the cost of food is also rising. One Ukrainian pensioner commented that she spent her pension almost solely on her gas bill, and that *"already we can't afford to eat or drink properly. We can't afford to get sick and pay for medicine"*.[36]

At least in Belarus if Milinkevich ended the preferential fuel bills with Russia, people wouldn't have to worry about medical bills; or would they? Bluntly, the answer is yes. Despite the fact that the third All Belarus People's Assembly had decided to significantly increase spending on public health, and to continue with the progress made by the socially orientated economy. Milinkevich made the naïve policy declaration of his intention to introduce private health insurance. He concluded that private health care was preferable because, *"the person chooses what hospital and health care providers to use and this leads to competition among doctors"*.[37] Another way of looking at this is that those who can pay more will receive a higher standard of care. Leaving the poorest people with the 'least competitive' doctors. This would also inevitably lead to a concentration of the best services in the cities, particularly Minsk. Belarusian doctors becoming 'medical mercenaries' would also, as seen in the cases of Poland, the Czech Republic and Slovakia result in the economic migration of many of these to the West.

Milinkevich also declared his desire to take Belarus down the long road to EU membership. His election platform is an odd and rambling fantasy, of how Belarus would be under his leadership. Full of idyllic imagery, and unexplained promises. Here is an example, *"Many Belarusian families* [will] *vacation abroad. Others prefer domestic resorts and campgrounds. We save about 20 percent of our income, creating a foundation for family financial security. We are not afraid of losing our savings to inflation or unreliable banks. Inflation does not exceed 2 percent a year*".[38] Quite how this will happen is never explained, particularly in the light of the economic upheaval he has planned, including of course adding health insurance to people's outgoings. Milinkevich also predicts that many households will own more cars, but Belarus will be somehow 'greener'. Ultimately his platform is certainly worthy of reading as an example of how not to campaign to an educated electorate.

Belarusian media also observed that Milinkevich was frequently seen to be associating with 'anti-Russian' elements from the Baltic states and Poland. In summary the BHHRG remarked that: "*Without a clearly preferable economic model and consorting with foreigners who were notoriously anti-Russian – a xenophobia not shared by Belarusians – Milinkevich was courting a tiny share of the popular vote*".[39] Despite the obvious shortcomings in his programme, and a campaigning style of primarily addressing foreign politicians and journalists instead of Belarusian voters, Milinkevich was confident of a victory; but not in the polling booths.

Showing that little had changed in the use of the 'Yugoslav model' Milinkevich said in December 2005, "*if our campaign is successful, then we will get people out into the street*".[40] Indeed the hopes of removing Lukashenko from power were still pinned on a 'popular protest'.

Milinkevich himself, proved not to be particularly dynamic, and was described by some observers as "*weak and uninspiring*".[41] When opposition activists were asked what they actually knew about the man they were campaigning for, the standard reply given was "*he is the candidate of the unified opposition*".[42] Milinkevich's dour style contrasts sharply with that of the remaining candidate of 2006: Alexander Kozulin.

Kozulin put himself forward as a candidate on behalf of the Social Democratic Hramada movement. His political involvement with the Hramada however was noticeably short. He had been the rector of the Belarusian State University in Minsk until 2003, when he was sacked after an investigation into a corruption scandal. This meant that Kozulin was certainly well known in Belarus, and definitely more so than Milinkevich, but viewed negatively, and with an obvious axe to grind. The opposition and foreign media, at first were unsure of what to make of Kozulin, presuming he was a Lukashenko stooge to either discredit or divide the opposition vote. However as the election race began, it was clear that Kozulin was actively and very visibly campaigning.

Kozulin's campaign manager was none other than Myachyslau

Hryb, the former parliamentary speaker and acting head of state in 1993. Since this time, Hryb has been a particularly outspoken critic of Lukashenko. Hryb confirmed to the BHHRG that Kozulin did have a higher profile than Milinkevich, and that he was also campaigning more vigorously. Although it ought to be noted that Kozulin's methods were certainly unusual. He made frequent complaints to the Belarusian electoral commission and also disrupted meetings of Lukashenko supporters. At one point he made a display of stamping on a photograph of the President.[43] These highly visible and confrontational tactics however did make him a regular feature in the Belarusian media in the run up to the vote. Also converting the sceptics from believing him to be a Lukashenko stooge, to considering him a serious alternative to Milinkevich.

The opposition website 'Charter97' even discussed the possibility that Milinkevich and Kozulin were playing a 'good cop – bad cop' routine. And foreign election observers noted that activists at Kozulin's campaign headquarters were actually wearing Milinkevich lapel badges.[44] This theory is certainly a possibility, particularly in view of what Kozulin said in his election broadcast on Belarusian television.

Each candidate had been allotted television and radio time plus the publication of their material by state owned media. Again refuting the claim made by Milinkevich to the MEP's in Brussels that the opposition had *"no access to radio and TV channels, or the printed press"*.[45] In fact Lukashenko chose not to directly campaign, but instead to allow himself to be judged on his record, and the programme of the All Belarus People's Assembly. Added to this he did not take the TV and Radio slots allocated to him and offered them instead to his opponents.

Kozulin, in one of his television appearances chose the tactic of personal insults and allegations against Lukashenko. In an unedited thirty-minute rant Kozulin ripped up a photograph of Lukashenko, as well as making allegations that the president was a corrupt dictator. He then declared that Lukashenko had a lover and an illegitimate child.[46] This speech when viewed alongside Milinkevich's 'promised land of milk and honey' platform certainly does fit with the 'good cop - bad cop' theory. After the election Lukashenko was asked if he intended to sue Kozulin for libel, his response being; *"isn't getting 2% of the vote punishment enough?"*[47]

As well as Kozulin's provocative broadcast the opposition also did not shy away from breaking the electoral code of the country. One example being Milinkevich's attendance at a rock concert in Minsk where the MC urged the attendees to vote for the unified opposition candidate. Despite the fact that campaigning 24 hours ahead of the vote is prohibited. One observer also noted that the event was as much a political rally as it was a concert, and commented that the music was predominantly *"thrash metal with strong nationalistic themes"*.[48] An opposition newspaper also decided to publish the inflammatory anti-Islamic cartoon originally printed in Denmark that had caused outrage and violence across the world. Publishing the cartoon had been expressly forbidden under Belarusian laws against inciting religious and racial hatred*. However the opposition in Belarus is actively sympathetic to the aims of its sponsors, and in fact the Charter97 website shows fourteen activists with English language banners declaring *"America we are with you!" "Liberation of Iraq!"* and *"down with tyrants!"*.[49] All this whilst waving the old red and white Belarusian flag alongside a US one. Interestingly the only journalists present in the photos are from the Russian channel NTV.

As can be seen, the opposition took a position that was at odds with that of the history and experience of the Belarusian people. Milinkevich's popularity was undoubtedly effected negatively by his association with foreign powers, whilst Kozulin's antics represented the worst elements of any electoral process, and made him appear incredibly unsuited to the role of head of state.

This left Gaidukevich, although he represents the very real maturing of the political process in Belarus, his party and position does not enjoy massive popular support. Gaidukevich's Liberal Democratic Party is fully involved in the democratic process, and does not boycott elections, nor fall behind unified opposition candidates. Quite simply because it stands for what it believes in, as opposed to basing its whole position on being in opposition to Lukashenko. It is also of note that Gaidukevich did not have an English language website for his campaign, unlike Kozulin, and Milinkevich (who had several). The reason for the use of English by the opposition is closely linked to the distortion of events in Belarus by Western media. The moulding of popular opinion is not uniquely applied to Belarusians, but also to

---

* Muslim Tartars from the Crimea settled in Belarus in the 14th century. In 2006 there were around 100,000 practising Muslims in Belarus.

Western Europeans and North Americans. Resulting in their support of "*the propaganda onslaught conceived by their own countries intelligence services. In short, Western 'democracy aid' was being used to shape public opinion in the donor countries – especially the United States*".[50] This quote is from the executive summary of the election observers of the BHHRG. It certainly is a fair conclusion when it is considered that even the right wing British newspaper the 'Daily Telegraph' acknowledged that Lukashenko may win with as much as 80% of the popular vote due to his genuine popularity.[51] Whilst also running stories with headlines such as *'Little Stalin' Tightens Grip On Belarus*, and *Belarus Dictator Keeps Misery of Soviet Era Alive*.[52] This paradox is hardly surprising, when journalists frequently have limited independent sources, and conflicts of interest. Journalists who wish to report the news also have to conform to the editorial bias of their publication. Journalist and media critic Ben Bagdikian has written extensively on the effects of the concentration of Western media in the hands of a few private corporations. He noted that in 1984 fifty companies owned the majority of the media available in the USA, and by 2006 that number was down to five. The result of this is increasing "*manipulation of news to pursue the owners other financial goals*" which ultimately, particularly in light of fealty to advertisers, leads to "*the promotion of conservatism and corporate values*".[53] Thus the most powerful tools of influence are being used to promote a purely selfish outlook based on consumerism and the ignoring of any negative effects that this may have on others. This 'free and independent' media is therefore not necessarily in the best position to be purely objective about the system in Belarus, which represents a serious challenge to the existing Western social order, i.e. an order that allows the concentration of capital and influence in the hands of a tiny minority of the population.

In a 2007 interview with German newspaper 'Die Welt' Lukashenko discussed the nature of the independent media in regard to Belarus. He noted that the media bears a huge responsibility, declaring that the "*media can act like firearms*" and "*journalists can kill both democracy and a totalitarian system and cause damage to a society*".[54]

What was being driven at here is the link between media power and responsibility. Lukashenko added that in Belarus hostile Western and Russian media "*sweep with fire our country from the west to the east and from the east to the west*".[55] Thus the media campaign against Lukashenko serves a dual purpose. It attempts to destabilise the situation within Belarus, whilst seeking public acquiescence for doing so in the countries responsible.

This brings us to the conduct of the poll. The 2006 presidential election was condemned by the OSCE as (once again) neither free nor fair, and the US government refused to recognise the result. The official result was as follows: Lukashenko 82.6%, Milinkevich 6%, Gaidukevich 3.5%, and lastly Kozulin with 2.3%. The result certainly does show what appears to be an unlikely show of support for the incumbent. As discussed previously this may have actually been the intention, and is also not entirely surprising given the weak manifesto and methods of the opposition. It is important to note that whilst doubt was cast on the scale of Lukashenko's win, the OSCE recognised without complaint a 97% result for Saakashvili in Georgia, 93% for Heydar Aliev in Azerbaijan and 89% for Kurmenbek Bakiev in Kyrgyzstan. The key difference between these leaders and Lukashenko is not human rights or democratic processes, but rather political orientation. The case of Georgia has already been mentioned, but Bakiev is notable for residing over a country rife with corruption, with several Members of Parliament also having been murdered. Aliev has reportedly gained a vast personal and family fortune from oil revenue in a country which ranks 99th in the UN human development index. However Aliev did sign a huge contract with an international oil consortium of ten companies including Exxon Mobil and BP. Again this harks back to the earlier mentioned article concerning 'hard liners and reformers'.

The OSCE must come under the same scrutiny as do the nations it observes. How can an independent organisation declare elections free or fair based not on the conduct of the poll, but rather on the policies of the candidate who wins? The answer is relatively simple and ought not to be too surprising given the work of Hans Georg Wieck mentioned in the previous chapter. OSCE observers are actually nominated by the governments of the member states (which also includes the USA). With many of these in the employ of diplomatic and security services.[56] As such not only are *"they professionally bound to follow government policy"*[57] but also receive substantial per-diem payments for their work. US Congressman Alcee Hastings headed the OSCE observer mission in Belarus and he summarised after the poll that: *"As politicians who have fought elections themselves, parliamentarians have particular expertise in political campaigns and electoral processes, bringing added credibility to the conclusions of OSCE observation missions*".[58] This is particularly enlightening from a Democrat Congressman from Florida, the focus of the US presidential election scandal of 2000. Also Hastings himself has a less than inspiring background in terms of 'credibility'. He was a judge before he became a Congressman, however he was impeached in 1989 by the US House of Representatives for corruption and perjury. Among his 17 high crimes and misdemeanours was his alleged solicitation of a $150,000 bribe.[59] In its report the House of Representatives accused Hastings of acts of corruption that "*strike at the heart of our democracy*".[60] Thus Hastings makes an interesting, if unusual choice to head a commission investigating the fairness of the democratic process in other countries.

The OSCE's conclusion that the election was neither free nor fair was based on some hurriedly reached conclusions, primarily based on the campaign stage, as opposed to the vote. The interim report No2 is an interesting model of the level of objectivity shown by the OSCE. One example being the complaint that Milinkevich's campaign platform was not printed in the state owned publications because he failed to meet the deadline provided by the campaign regulations. However the other three candidates *did* have their platforms printed, simply by meeting the deadline. The OSCE also expressed concern that media coverage of the All Belarus People's Assembly could be used to promote Lukashenko, and indeed some speakers at the assembly had (unsurprisingly) "*endorsed the president's political programme*".[61]

The OSCE report was also critical of the Belarusian election code that limits campaign spending to the almost 67,000,000 Belarusian Roubles (around $31,000) allocated to each candidate by the state. It is clear that the opposition have far greater funds available should that be required, but what the report fails to address is the benefit of having a set limit on electoral spending; particularly when these funds are from the state. An election campaign in any country is an expensive undertaking, and for independent candidates without a lot of spare cash the costs are quite prohibitive. George W. Bush's campaign in 2004 spent over 345 million dollars, whilst his rival John Kerry spent over 309 million.[62] As can be seen, the man who spent the most won; as was the case four years previously. In fact in the US mid term elections of 1998 around "*95% of winning candidates outspent their competi-*

tors".[63] This of course has a huge impact on the democratic process. Who is supplying the money and what is their agenda? In the case of the 1998 election mentioned above corporate contributions outweighed those of labour unions by twelve to one.[64] As such, the interests of ordinary workers are unlikely to be prevalent over those of their wealthy bosses. This essentially limits political ambition in the USA to the very wealthy, and representatives of the business community. In Belarus to campaign for the presidency all that is needed is a platform capable of attracting 100,000 signatures of support; and the state will allocate an equal share of funds for a campaign.

The OSCE report did concede that the Belarusian Regional Electoral Commission offices were *"well equipped and have a variety of general information. Including candidate biographies and voter education materials"*.[65] This report seems to have more of an issue with the electoral rules (which all candidates have to abide by) than with any vote rigging or intimidation. The comments regarding increased coverage of Lukashenko in the state media are certainly valid, even though the report admits; *"mostly he was covered in his role as president"*.[66] Yet the report fails to acknowledge the opposition's complete monopoly of opinion in non-state media, and particularly the hostile radio and TV broadcasts aimed specifically at overthrowing Lukashenko.

The conduct of the campaign and the vote was not solely monitored by the OSCE. As well as independent observers, the CIS also sent a delegation. Despite the dramatically conflicting reports, it is interesting that the OSCE conclusion is the only one that has been covered and accepted as the truth by Western governments and media. The Belarusian government was not insensitive to the OSCE report either. The Ministry of Foreign Affairs issued a statement covering the election itself, and the observer's findings. They highlighted that the elections were monitored by over 30,000 domestic, and more than 1200 international observers. It was also made clear that these international observers were invited by, and not forced upon Belarus. This includes the OSCE-ODIHR delegation. The Ministry noted that by *"inviting the OSCE mission the Belarusian side sought once more to make sure whether the OSCE-ODIHR was capable of approaching its work responsibly and professionally, and make an objective assessment of the elections"*.[67] Needless to say the Belarusians were disappointed; and went as far as to conclude that the election monitors of the OSCE team served as *"an instrument for pronouncing verdicts formulated in advance from outside"*. As such the Belarusian government believes that reform is needed within the OSCE to make it a truly objective and respected organisation. It is important to note that among the criticisms of the OSCE's methods was the *"neglect of the opinion of their own observers – members of the mission, while formulating the findings and conclusions"*.[68]

As at the previous election the OSCE report appeared to be describing a different vote than the one observed, or simply, as described above exaggerated problems within the election code that effected all candidates equally. Tahir Kose a Turkish MP and election observer made the comment that: *"The mood of the Belarusians at the election is much more important than impressions of people who have come here"*. He added that the election was *"organised at a good level I found nothing to criticise. People are eager to go to the polls"*. Most significantly he also noted that he had been in discussion with OSCE observers who had also *"failed to reveal any serious violations?"*[69] during the campaign. An observer from Moldova echoed this position. Sergei Nazarija* saw the huge amount of external influence and pressure being brought to bear in Belarus. Of this he declared, *"I do not think pressure on any country, be it Moldova or Belarus, can radically shift the opinion of the electorate. Whatever it will be, I think the entire world should respect the choice of the Belarusians. We should respect it"*.[70] He also saw no pressure form the authorities on the electorate, and this included in the state owned media.

This opinion was echoed from an unlikely source. Michael Morgulis president of the US Christian Bridge International NGO declared the elections to be *"truly democratic"*.[71]

In fact such opinions and quotes were repeated by various election observers from the West, who had gone to Belarus believing dictatorship myth. Frank Creyelman of the Belgian senate was so impressed he hoped to share his positive impressions and experience of Belarus with his colleagues on his return to Belgium. This is an important point of note. The Belarusian system offers a genuine alternative to the 'development' plans of the World Bank and IMF, and also stands as an inspirational social model. Creyelman said: *"When I was going here I expected to see a different picture which I formed relying on the information in Western mass media: that every voter would have somebody behind his back who*

---

* Sergei Nazarija: Director of the Strategic Analysis and Forecasting centre, and a respected historian and writer.

would control his vote. *The things I have seen U-turned my impression about Belarus*".[72] This position was reinforced by Lithuanian observer Victoras Shugurovas who commented that the foreign media had "*lost the information war*",[73] by what he actually saw in the country.

Of course these opinions were not included in or addressed by the OSCE report, and nor was the findings of the BHHRG who compiled a comprehensive study. The CIS delegation report was also ultimately positive, but was dismissed amongst claims of bias toward Belarus. The OSCE however, with its history of direct meddling in the internal affairs of Belarus, was not considered to have any possible bias by Western media or governments. The CIS report so eagerly dismissed or ignored did however contain some criticisms and many enlightening findings. The CIS observer mission was in Belarus not only to monitor the final poll, but also the early stages of the election, including the collection of signatures for the proposed candidates. The CIS report recognised the extraordinary levels of access granted to all accredited observers including the OSCE and independents. The CIS mission actually worked closely with that of the OSCE, establishing co-operation in regard to issues of law, organisation of the election, and media monitoring.

The CIS observers found some evidence of misconduct at the stage of collecting signatures. Amongst these were some falsifications as well as technical flaws. One important example given is that in five electoral regions over 15% of signatures in Support of Milinkevich were found to have been falsified. Added to this Kozulin's campaign was found to have submitted inauthentic lists to 19 territorial commissions as well as in Minsk.[74] Also in violation of the electoral law, Milinkevich and Paznyak (probably in competition at the time) were actively campaigning for the next (voting) round, even though this was whilst the signature collection was still underway and as such, was a violation of the electoral code.

Once the campaign proper began, the CIS observers commented on the even and equal campaigning opportunities granted to all candidates. Local administrations provided premises for the candidates and their teams to conduct meetings with voters and also allocated places from where campaign literature could be disseminated. Despite this it was noted that Milinkevich's campaign team made numerous attempts throughout the campaign to arrange unauthorised meetings. The purpose of which can be reasonably assumed to have been to cause a confrontation with the authorities. On 17th of March, Milinkevich and Kozulin jointly held a meeting in Minsk where CIS observers witnessed *"appeals for illicit actions"*.[75]

On the day of the vote the CIS mission toured the polling stations and alongside the comments in the visitors books from OSCE observers, reported their satisfaction with the conduct of the election.

Although the CIS report does include individual criticisms, such as some people filling in their ballots before going into the voting booths, and at one polling station the booth was too small. When the observers pointed this out, the authorities acted upon the advice and rectified any problems. The CIS mission also observed the count, and was happy to report that there were no violations.

The independent observers of the BHHRG told a very similar story to the CIS delegation. They concluded that *"it is to be hoped that the Belarusian people can be left alone to sort out their own problems without yet more meddling from politicians and journalists discredited for their clumsy, failed interference in the affairs of others"*.[76] Ultimately this was to be the undoing of the opposition. Western backing provided enormous funds, but also brought with it the legacy of failed intervention in Iraq, as well as the dismal results of the other 'velvet revolutions' in eastern Europe. Nation building must come from within, civil society and culture cannot be exported with scant regard for the history and collective experience of a country. In Belarus the biggest mistake of those who wish to change its policies and direction is by associating these with one man: Lukashenko. The reality is that the obstacle to opening up Belarus to profit hungry companies and oligarchs is actually the Belarusian people themselves.

As summarised in the BHHRG report, *"instead of denouncing the Belarusian economic model, civil society activists ought to be encouraging neighbours to adopt it. But sadly there is no money in promoting a real civil society "*. Russian political scientist Gleb Pavlovsky took a similar position in an interview in February 2006, when he stressed that *"the society is the only controller of the elections, not the observers"*.[77]

When Lukashenko had declared that he had no need to rig the election in order to win he was telling the truth. In February he was scoring a rating of 60% even according to opposition figures! With over 30,000 election observers and such an approval rating, cheating would have been exceptionally counter productive. In fact in an inter-

The Last Soviet Republic

view with Ukrainian journalists in late 2006 Lukashenko claimed that his margin of victory had been played down to provide a more 'European' result.[78]

The actual voting was not the end of the issue. The people had voted for Lukashenko, but for the opposition the fight was only just beginning. The real show was to be the post election protests. The mass protest that had been planned failed to materialise. The first night of protest brought around 10,000 people to central Minsk. This is a significant number, but importantly is still less than 1% of the people who had voted for the opposition. The cold weather certainly played a part in the low turnout, but as ought to be remembered the 'Orange Revolution' protests in Kiev took place in sub zero temperatures with around half a million participants. The police were conspicuous by their low profile. They stood off a few streets away, ready to move in the event of any serious criminal activity, but far enough away as to not cause a conflict. The protest numbers massively dwindled after the first night, despite the appearance of the British, and several other EU ambassadors in a show of support that was highly questionable in terms of their diplomatic status.[79]

The protesters set up tents on the square and over the week camped out in protest. Milinkevich occasionally turned up to offer his support, but was notably lacking in leadership skills. Following the large protest on Monday night the numbers tailed off dramatically. Those whose loyalty had been bought quickly disappeared leaving the hardcore of the opposition activists to sit out the week in October Square. Police eventually removed around 150 people on the Friday. Those who were detained by the police were kept in custody for between 5 to 15 days, before being released.

Amongst those arrested were Lithuanians, Poles, Ukrainians, Russians, Georgians, and even Canadians, as well as Belarusians. This international contingent was noticed by Belarusian activists, who discovered that often they could not communicate with their fellow protesters. The clearing of the square was carried out in a remarkably restrained manner, and it became apparent that Milinkevich's boast to stay with the protesters until the end, had been a hollow one.

This was not the end of the protest however, as the following Saturday was the anniversary of the Imperial German declaration of independence for Belarus in 1918. Again opposition protests and demonstrations were planned. This time there was a clash with the police in a Minsk park. Riot police dispersed the crowd with smoke, as well as making a baton charge. The crowd was successfully dispersed with the only serious injuries reported being policemen after opposition activists started throwing glass bottles.[80] This clash was widely reported as being the Belarusian government's crackdown on the election protest, despite this being a separate event. The rally that Milinkevich had envisioned bringing out the 10,000 crowd of Monday night did not materialise, and only turned violent when Kozulin, in the words of Milinkevich made *"more than a mistake"*. This being to urge protestors to storm the city police station in order to release those detained the night before, and calling for *"the government's overthrow, and Lukashenko's death"*.[81]

The European Union quite rightly issued a statement that it was *"appalled"*, but unfortunately for the wrong reasons, as it went on to insist that Kozulin be *"released immediately"*.[82] Would any EU country show clemency to political leaders who actually attempted to storm a government building whilst calling for the overthrow of government and the death of the head of state? As if to indicate an answer to this question, during the same week France saw huge protests over a law to make it easier for employers to sack young workers being broken up by riot police using tear gas and rubber bullets. Thus, the methods used to disperse people demanding job security were harsher than those used on a crowd seeking the overthrow of the government. In contrast to Belarus, at no point in the reporting of the French clashes were the words 'dictator' or 'police state' used.

The presidential election had finally been decided, the opposition had lost the vote, and had also failed to carry out an insurrection. The 'Yugoslav model' had met its match. The reason for this, as Lukashenko explained is because *"Belarus has strong immunity, which is based on effective power, a strong social policy, and a dynamic economy that does not serve individual oligarchs, but the welfare of all the people"*.[83]

Conclusion: The Historical Choice of Belarus.

"Belarus is a sovereign European country, and it will never lose its independence. I often say: we do not claim the lands that belong to others, nor are we going to yield to anyone a piece of our own lands".[1] A.G. Lukashenko.

In 2003 Alexander Lukashenko delivered a lecture at the Belarusian State University in Minsk. The lecture was entitled the 'Historical Choice of Belarus' and was intended to explain the reasons for the development and direction of Belarus as a sovereign nation.

Sovereignty and history are the key points in understanding Lukashenko and Belarus. Belarusian independence was not seriously demanded, or expected at any point in its history. The Belarusian nationalist movement has always been marginal and except for the BPF in the early 1990's has been of little real influence. The Belarusian Soviet Socialist Republic was the first time that Belarus actually functioned as a nation, although its independence from Moscow was exceptionally limited. However Belarusians for the first time were governing themselves, and were able to rely on the financial support of their neighbours to establish industry and institutions of public health and education. Also the Belarusian farmers took to collectivisation with relative ease, seeing the benefits of collectivisation over the semi-feudal system which had preceded it. Mechanised agriculture, and the communities that the collective farm created were a huge step forward for the Belarusian people. Great advances were also made culturally, despite the constant wrangling over the status of the Belarusian language. Of importance in understanding the language issue is the fact that such a huge proportion of Belarusians were illiterate in 1917, that it was Russian teachers and texts that were sent by the Soviet government to remedy this in as short a time as possible. However the Soviet government was not insensitive to the reality of the historical make up of Belarus, and as such the first emblem, and Red Banner Order[*] of the republic had 'workers of the world unite!' and 'BSSR' written in Yiddish, Belarusian and Russian.

The Soviet Union's impact on Belarus was huge, in fact any attempt to ignore or dismiss this period of its history would be more than naïve. Belarusian nationalists argue as to which day is the most impor-

---

[*] The first and highest Soviet award of the time.

tant date in Belarusian history, the 1918 German declaration of an independent Belarus, or the day in 1991 when Belarus withdrew from the Soviet Union. There is no doubting that the end of the Soviet Union was a colossal day in Belarusian history, but ultimately it was not a positive day. As has been covered, the immediate effect on all republics following the collapse of the USSR was that of chaos, unemployment, and a huge cultural step backwards. For Belarusians the situation was acute, with few natural resources and an ineffective and increasingly corrupt government.

Belarus transformed very little between 1991 and 1994, as the Soviet system was not practically replaced by anything else. Belarus had no equivalent of Boris Yeltsin willing to bully and fight anything and anyone who stood in the way of his 'reforms'. Belarus was also one of the most militarised areas in Europe with thousands of Soviet Army troops stationed there, as well as nuclear weapons*. This military presence lent some stability to the republic, but also represented logistical problems in terms of allowing troops to return home, and feeding and housing them whilst they were in Belarus.

Stability in Belarus was temporary at best, and a steady slide into chaos was predicted. As such the new constitution called for the office of president to be established. The intention being clear, that the nation needed an identified leader. The power struggle between factions in the Supreme Soviet and Council of Ministers had to be resolved.

The idea that an outsider could win the election was not considered, and came as a shock to the established political elite in Belarus.

Lukashenko won the presidency in 1994 due in part for his record as a fighter of corruption, but far more for what he believed in and promised. Whilst other politicians were talking about what they could change, Lukashenko was stressing what elements needed to be preserved. The Communist Party of the Soviet Union may have disintegrated, but its core principles and ideals have not. That does not mean that Lukashenko declared the intention to restore communism in Belarus, because he was more than aware that the circumstances had changed. The end of the Soviet Union and 'communist block' in eastern Europe was so cataclysmic for the nations involved that some change was going to be necessary for survival. The programme of re-

---

* Lukashenko oversaw the final removal of all nuclear weapons from Belarus in November 1996.

form in Belarus undertaken by Lukashenko is one of change, only where change is necessary, and the preservation and improvement of the best traditions of the Belarusian past.

Although Lukashenko has conceded that he is authoritarian in style, he also affirms that the constitution and people of Belarus cannot allow him to be a dictator. As covered, the Constitutional Court remains as a very real check on his power, and is a body he does not control. As for the Belarusian people, far from being brutalised by his power they are the basis of it. Lukashenko drew complaints from his rivals for the frequency with which he would call referendums, but what this showed is that even at a time when he was in no position to be seriously accused of misconduct in the counting of votes, he could call on the people to confirm his direction and intentions.

Lukashenko himself acknowledged that it was the people themselves who had *"upheld the principle of social justice"* and *"did not vote for aggressive nationalism, but for historically shaped bilingualism"*.[2] The notion that Lukashenko is forcing the Russian language on a nation who already predominantly speak it; or that he maintains unjust control over the economy in order to pump money into the education and health sectors (in a country where very few could afford to pay for these services) is ridiculous. Yet just these pretexts have been used as a basis for intervention by the rich and powerful against the poor and the weak. The economic direction pursued by Lukashenko is a direct legacy of the Soviet Union. The profit from state run enterprises are not solely used to reward the directors, but is channelled back into the state coffers and divided up amongst the country through the social fund and government investment. Hence the popularity with the Belarusian people of the 'socially orientated market economy'. Social policy in the Soviet Union was a guarantee of coverage from 'the cradle to the grave' and as such was a positive experience for the people of Belarus. This historical element is preserved by Lukashenko, and though Belarusians are not rich in dollar terms they certainly get a fair deal for the work they do. As the economy grows, so does the quality of life for all in the country, and this is where the dictatorship issue comes in. Lukashenko is only a dictator in terms of the economy. He will not sell off lucrative enterprises and land to foreign investors because Belarusians not only need the revenue more, but also because in the 1996 referendum he promised not to. As already detailed the USA and EU maintain more than cordial relations with many leaders who are far from democratic, and who preside over their impoverished populations from the luxury of their palaces and offices. Leaders who abuse their own populations with US bought weapons are certainly more tolerated by 'the leaders of the free world' than Lukashenko has been. In recognition of Milinkevich's campaign and activities around the 2006 presidential election, the EU awarded him the Sakharov prize for human rights for his 'fight for democracy in Belarus'. (Milinkevich incidentally dedicated his prize for democracy to Alexander Kozulin the man whose less than democratic credentials were discussed in the previous chapter).

This leads us neatly to the Belarusian opposition. The so-called 'democratic forces' who use anything but democratic methods, and have become an industry all of their own. For many being in the opposition is simply too lucrative to actually want to see an end to Lukashenko. 'Independent' western media has for the most part proved itself no more objective or impartial than the worst examples of state owned propaganda from history; whilst US interference in Belarus has been excessive, unsubtle, and mismanaged. Apart from the provisions of the Belarus Democracy Act it is also particularly dubious from a legal point of view. Under international law more so, but then the US attitude to international law has been practically one of contempt*. Further to the attempted destabilisation of the internal situation in Belarus, the US military has recently installed missile bases on the territory of Poland and the Czech Republic, seen both as a defence against and a threat to Belarus and its Russian neighbour.

Belarus has never been an imperial power. It has never had pretensions to regional dominance, and as such has historically been swallowed up by aggressive neighbours. Battles have also been fought on its territory by Swedish, French and German troops. As such sovereignty is of enormous value to Belarus, as is independence. Not independence in terms of a rejection of all that has happened previously, but more as a recognition of a lesson learned from history. The Belarusian model of development is such that the positive achievements of the Soviet Union are acknowledged, whilst the negative experiences of history are learnt from. Belarusians have not taken vengeance on

---

* E.g. in 2005 the Oxford Council on Good Governance think tank accused the US government of deliberate and consistent breaches of international law, and violations of human rights.(3)

the perceived wrongdoers of history, ethnic Poles and Russians live in Belarus peacefully, as do Belarusian Jews, in spite of the decimation of their population between 1941 and 1944.

The collective experience of Belarusians as victims of foreign imperialist ambitions, and of course of the horror and genocide during the Great Patriotic war means that peace and progress are the goals of the Belarusian people. As such a dictatorship would not be tolerated for long; whilst the notion that Lukashenko is a fascist is absurd in the extreme.

The lesson of history has been learned in Belarus, and the model of development being pursued is one of the greatest benefit to the greatest number, this of course creates a cause for concern in nations who see the world as their sweatshop.

US and EU travel bans are now in place on Lukashenko and many of the government's top officials. Illustrating that rather than attempt any rational dialogue or transparent discussions on an equal basis, the West would rather isolate Lukashenko and hope his voice cannot be heard by those who may see through the hypocrisy and lies of their own leaders. The success of the Belarusian model of development is the genuine concern, not any fabricated human rights issues. Belarus is a country with phenomenally low unemployment and an equally comprehensive social welfare programme, and citizens of the USA and EU contribute their hard-earned tax money to discrediting, and it is planned to ultimately bring down this system.

This is not Belarusian state propaganda, but can be actually seen by anyone who chooses to freely enter or leave Belarus. There are no secrets for Lukashenko; independent charities, human rights organisations, and of course individuals can visit hospitals, orphanages, and even prisons. Opposition activists* and foreign visitors freely travel around the republic, and often through it to its neighbours. Opposition newspapers are freely and widely available, and even distributed on some flights into Belarus, and of course offer absolutely no balanced or objective view of the situation in the country.

The interviews I have conducted with Belarusian people themselves confirm that they are politically aware, and able to freely assess their government and its direction. One comment I received, (which is

---

* The opposition even hold a congress in Minsk. In 2007 Milinkevich opposed the idea of collective leadership for the opposition and refused to enter into any dialogue with Lukashenko. 600 delegates were in attendance.

typical) was "*I and all my family voted for him* [Lukashenko] *all three times. In some cases I don't like him, but in fact he is a great leader. I remember that time when our country was 'in a deep hole'. Now we live suitably. And I think this is a merit of the whole of our people and Lukashenko personally. Some people say that all the elections were faked-up. But it isn't true - this is truly the choice of our nation*".*

Belarusians are aware of the part they have played in their country's recovery since 1991, but also that Lukashenko has enabled them to do this. Lukashenko's refusal to sell out his country to the forces of 'globalisation' and instead to protect the interests of his people is what led political analyst Stephen Millies to comment that although labelled an Outpost of Tyranny *"for workers everywhere Belarus is an outpost of resistance"*.[4]

---

* From an open ended interview with Sergei Kurashov in 2006.

Appendix.

Full text of the Speech given by Alexander Lukashenko (to huge applause) at the High-Level Plenary Meeting of the 60th Session of the UN General Assembly in New York, 15 September 2005.

Mr. President,
Ladies and Gentlemen,
To have an honest look at today's world is the reason why state leaders have convened here at the United Nations. Together we must gain the understanding of the main thing: do we lead our countries and mankind along the right path? We should answer this question for ourselves and our nations. Without that we have no chance to get out of the deadlock that we are in.

Fifteen years have passed since the break-up of my country, the USSR. That event dramatically changed the world order. The Soviet Union, despite all mistakes and blunders of its leaders, was the source of hope and support for many states and peoples. The Soviet Union provided for the balance of the global system.

Today the world is unipolar with all the consequences stemming from this.

The once prosperous Yugoslavia was devastated and disappeared from the map of Europe.

The long-suffering Afghanistan became a hotbed of conflicts and drugs trafficking.

A bloody slaughter in Iraq is continuing to the present day. The country has turned into a source of instability for the vast region.

Iran and North Korea are looked at through gun sights.

Belarus is a nation just like the majority represented in this hall. Having emerged from the debris of the Cold War, Belarus became a state of advanced science and technology inhabited by ten million highly educated and tolerant people. The UN ranked us as a developed country with a high level of human development.

Like you, what we need from the world is peace and stability. Nothing more. The rest we shall create ourselves through our own efforts.

My country is free from conflicts. Different nations and nationalities peacefully coexist in Belarus each practising religions of their own and having their own way of life.

We do not cause any trouble for our neighbours, neither through territorial claims nor trying to influence their choice of the way of development.

We gave up our nuclear arms and voluntarily relinquished the rights of a nuclear successor to the USSR.

Today we shall sign the Convention for the Suppression of Acts of Nuclear Terrorism. We also declare that we have decided to sign the Additional Protocol to the Agreement between the Republic of Belarus and the International Atomic Energy Agency for the Application of Safeguards in Connection with the Treaty on the Non-Proliferation of Nuclear Weapons.

We have established a lasting and successful union with Russia as our very close neighbour.

We build our country using our own wits and on the basis of our own traditions.

But it is obvious that this very choice of my people is not to everyone's pleasure. It doesn't please those who strive to rule the unipolar world.

Wonder how?

If there are no conflicts – they are invented.

If there are no pretexts for intervention – imaginary ones are created.

To this end a very convenient banner was chosen – democracy and human rights. And not in their original sense of the rule of people and personal dignity, but solely and exclusively in the interpretation of the US leadership.

Has the world really become so black-and-white, deprived of its diversity of civilisations, multicoloured traditions and ways of life meeting the aspirations of people?

Of course not! The simple thing is that it is a convenient pretext and an instrument to control other countries.

Regrettably, the United Nations, though it belongs to us all, allows itself to be used as a tool of such policy. I am saying this with particular bitterness and pain as President of the country that co-founded the UN, after sacrificing the lives of one third of its people during the Second World War for the sake of our own freedom and the freedom of Europe and the entire world.

The Human Rights Commission keeps mechanically stamping resolutions on Belarus, Cuba and other countries. Attempts are being made to impose such resolutions also on the UN General Assembly.

But how can the United Nations be minding imaginary 'problems' while unable to see true disasters and catastrophes - of the calibre and nature which nobody other than the UN as a community of civilised nations can cope with and restore justice and order?

Let us give a glance at the world as it is.

Quite recently, in the room next to ours we were shown maps and graphs allegedly depicting weapons of mass destruction in Iraq. Were those weapons found?

They do not exist. In the meantime, Iraq was razed with bombs, devastated, people brought to utmost despair. Terrorists are threatening to use weapons of mass destruction against cities in Europe and America.

Has there been an open and independent trial under UN supervision of the Guantanamo prisoners? How many of them are there and who are they?

Who will defend the rights of the Abu Graib victims and punish all of their torturers without exception?

Afghanistan was ravaged with rockets and bombs under the pretext of finding Bin Laden. Was the world's 'number one terrorist' captured? Where is he now?

He is at large, but Afghanistan and Iraqi territories began to generate hundreds and thousands of international terrorists.

Foreign troops occupied the independent Afghanistan but the drugs production grew ten-fold. Did those troops enter the country for this purpose?

Today, Belarus, Tajikistan, Russia and other former Soviet states are literally flooded with a wave of 'traditional' drugs from Afghanistan meeting a wave of previously unknown synthetic drugs from Europe.

The leaders of the destroyed Yugoslavia and Iraq were put behind bars on groundless, absurd and far-fetched accusations. This was a very opportune way to conceal the truth about annihilation of their countries.

The trial of Milosevic was made into a caricature since long ago. Saddam Hussein was abandoned to the winner's mercy, like in barbarian times. There is nobody to defend their rights except the UN, their states no longer around, destroyed.

They should be released to be able to defend freely their rights, honour and human dignity.

AIDS and other diseases are ravaging Africa and Asia.

Poverty and deprivation have become a real and not a virtual weapon of mass destruction, moreover – a racially selective one.

Who will be able to stop this?

Who will insist that the United States of America put an end to its attempts against Cuba and Venezuela? These countries will independently determine their lives.

Trafficking in persons has become a flourishing business. Sexual slavery of women and children are seen as a common thing, almost a norm of life. Who will protect them and bring to justice consumers of 'live commodity'?

How can this disgrace to our civilisation be done away with?

This, in short, is the distressing account of the transition to the unipolar world.

Was it for that purpose that we established the United Nations?

Is it not high time for the UN to put an end to internal corruption scandals and get down in deed to address anguish and misery of the world? The answer to this question, in our view, is very clear.

Let us be honest to the end. We cannot bury our head in the sand like an ostrich.

In the end, the UN is us.

Therefore, it is up to us to take the destiny of the world in our own hands.

We must realise that the unipolar world is a world with a single track, a one-dimensional world.

We must become aware that the diversity of ways to progress is an enduring value of our civilisation, the only one that can ensure stability in this world.

The freedom of choice of the way of development is the main precondition for a democratic world order. This is exactly what this organisation was established for.

I do hope that the mighty of the world will understand this too. Otherwise, the unipolar world will ultimately strike them back. Great American Presidents Woodrow Wilson and Franklin Roosevelt, who stood at the roots of the League of Nations and the United Nations, were conscious of that.

Should we agree between us on this principal point, then we would succeed in implementing the principles of multipolarity, diversity and freedom of choice both in reality and the UN documents that we must abide by. We would protect the world from terrorism and the vulnerable, women and children, from slavery. We would protect all those unprotected.

It is then that the UN would become the organisation of the genuinely united nations. This, and not the numerical increase of the Security Council membership, is precisely the core of the UN reform.

I thank you.

Notes.

Chapter 1

1. Lukashenko. A.G. (2004). *Address by the President of the Republic of Belarus A.G. Lukashenko to the Belarusian People in View of Declaring the Referendum.* Press Service of the President of the Republic of Belarus.

2. Zaprudnik. J. (1993). *Belarus: At a Crossroads in History.* Westview Press. USA. (Condensed from chapter 1).

3. Ibid. Page 35.

4. Wikipedia. (2005). *The Pale of Settlement.* Wikipedia online Encyclopaedia. Available from: http://en.wikipedia.org/wiki/Pale_of_settlement (For a short history of the Pale of Settlement *'The Jews'* by Chaim Bermant is recommended).

5. Ibid.

6. Marples. David R. (1999). *Belarus: a Denationalised Nation.* Harwood Academic Publishers. Holland. Page 2.

7. Kahan. S. (1989). *The Wolf of the Kremlin.* Robert Hale. London.

8. Zaprudnik. J. (1993). *Belarus: At a Crossroads in History.* Westview Press. USA. Page 97.

Chapter 2

1. Lukashenko. A.G. (2002). *Press Release on the Event of October Revolution Day.* Press service of the President of the Republic of Belarus.

2. Marx. K, and Engels F. (1975). *Manifesto of the Communist Party.* Progress Publishers. Moscow. Page 51.

3. McAuley. M. (1977). *Politics and the Soviet Union.* Penguin, UK. Page 23.

4. Marples. David R. (1999). *Belarus: a Denationalised Nation.* Harwood Academic Publishers.

Holland. Page 2.

5. Zaprudnik. J. (1993). *Belarus: At a Crossroads in History.* Westview Press. USA. Page 65.

6. This was further explained by Lenin in his *Preliminary Draft Theses on the National and Colonial Questions.* (V.I. Lenin Collected Works, vol31, pages 146-147).

7. Zaprudnik. J. (1993). *Belarus: At a Crossroads in History.* Westview Press. USA. Page 67.

8. Marples. David R. (1999). *Belarus: a Denationalised Nation.* Harwood Academic Publishers. Holland. Page 3.

Chapter 3.

1. Lukashenko. A.G. (2005). *Speech to the 60th Session of the United Nations.* Press service of the President of the Republic of Belarus. Available online from: www.belembassy.org

2. Commission of the C.C. of the C.P.S.U. (B) (1939). *History of the Communist Party of the Soviet Union (Bolsheviks).* Foreign Languages Publishing House. Moscow. Pages 227-228.

3. Marx. K, and Engels F. (1975). *Manifesto of the Communist Party.* Progress Publishers, Moscow. Page 96.

4. Zaprudnik. J. (1993). *Belarus: At a Crossroads in History.* Westview Press. USA. Page 76.

5. Weinberg. R. (1998). *Stalin's Forgotten Zion.* University of California Press. Berkeley. Page 15.

6. Ibid. Page 16.

7. Marples. David R. (1999). *Belarus: a Denationalised Nation.* Harwood Academic Publishers. Holland. Page 6.

8. Zaprudnik. J. (1993). *Belarus: At a Crossroads in History.* Westview Press. USA. Page78.

9. Weinberg. R. (1998). *Stalin's Forgotten Zion.* University of California Press. Berkeley. Pages 16-17.

10. Ibid. Pages 20-21.

11. Davies. R. W. (1980). *The Industrialisation of Soviet Russia I. The Soviet Offensive; the Collectivisation of Agriculture, 1929-30*. Harvard University Press. Cambridge, Massachusetts. Pages 4-5.

12. Craine. B. Et-al. (1967). *A History of Civilisation*, Vol.2 3rd edition. Prentice Hall New Jersey. Page 285.

13. Marples. David R. (1999). *Belarus: a Denationalised Nation*. Harwood Academic Publishers. Holland. Page 7.

14. Kudrayashov. N. (1987). *The Brest Fortress*. Raduga Publishers. Moscow. Page11.

15. Vakar. N.P. (1956). *Belorussia: the Making of a Nation*. Harvard University Press. Cambridge, Massachusetts. Page142.

16. Marples. David R. (1999). *Belarus: a Denationalised Nation*. Harwood Academic Publishers. Holland. Page 7.

17. Zaprudnik. J. (1993). *Belarus: At a Crossroads in History*. Westview Press. USA. Page 86.

Chapter 4.

1. Lukashenko. A.G. (2004). *Alexander Lukashenko Visits Stolbtsy District*. Press service of the President of the Republic of Belarus.

2. Grey. I. (1979). *Stalin. Man of History*. Weidenfeld and Nicholson. U.K. Page 246.

3. Marples. David R. (1999). *Belarus: a Denationalised Nation*. Harwood Academic Publishers. Holland. Page 9.

4. Martens. L. (1994) *Another View of Stalin*. EPO. Antwerp, Belgium. Page 60.

5. Ibid. Page 61.

6. Marples. David R. (1999). *Belarus: a Denationalised Nation*. Harwood Academic Publishers. Holland. Page 9.

7. Ibid. Page 10.

8. Davies. R. W. (1980). *The Industrialisation of Soviet Russia I. The Soviet Offensive: the Collectivisation of Agriculture, 1929-30*. Harvard University Press. Cambridge, Massachusetts. Pages 13-14.

9. Zaprudnik. J. (1993). *Belarus: At a Crossroads in History*. Westview Press. USA. Page 87.

10. Ibid.

11. Marples. David R. (1999). *Belarus: a Denationalised Nation*. Harwood Academic Publishers. Holland. Page 11.

12. Ibid.

13. Ibid.

14. Zaprudnik. J. (1993). *Belarus: At a Crossroads in History*. Westview Press. USA. Page 88.

15. Marples. David R. (1999). *Belarus: a Denationalised Nation*. Harwood Academic Publishers. Holland. Page 13.

16. O'Donnell. J.S. (1999) *A Coming of Age: Albania Under Enver Hoxha*. Columbia University Press. New York.

17. Kudrayashov. N. (1987). *The Brest Fortress*. Raduga Publishers. Moscow. Page11.

18. Zaprudnik. J. (1993). *Belarus: At a Crossroads in History*. Westview Press. USA. Page 89.

Chapter 5.

1. Lukashenko. A.G. (2005). Address by President of the Republic of Belarus A.G. Lukashenko at the Minsk garrison parade in commemoration of the 60th Anniversary of the Victory in the Great Patriotic War. Press Service of the President of the Republic of Belarus.

2. Axell. A. (2001). Russia's Heroes. Constable Publishers. London.

3. Martens. L. (1994) Another View of Stalin. EPO. Antwerp, Belgium. Page 237.

4. Zaprudnik. J. (1993). *Belarus: At a Crossroads in History*. Westview Press. USA. Page 95.

5. Ibid. Page 97.

6. Ibid.

7. Aktion Reinhard Camps. (2005). *The Minsk Ghetto*. Online. Available from: http://www.deathcamps.org/occupation/minsk%20ghetto.html

8. Stalin. J.V. (1941). *Stalin Speaks*. The Communist Party of Great Britain. London.

9. Lukashenko. A.G. (2004). *Address by President of the Republic of Belarus A.G. Lukashenko During the Visit by Presidents of Belarus, Russia, and Ukraine to the State Memorial Complex "Khatyn"*. Press Service of the President of the Republic of Belarus.

10. Zaprudnik. J. (1993). *Belarus: At a Crossroads in History*. Westview Press. USA. Page 99.

11. Embassy of the Republic of Belarus. (2005). *July 3- The independence day of the Republic of Belarus*. Press release.

12. Silitski. V. (2005) *A Partisan Reality Show*. Transitions Online. Available from:
http://www.tol.cz/look/TOL/article.tpl?IdLanguage=1&IdPublication=4&NrIssue=115&NrSection=4&NrArticle=14025

13. Aktion Reinhard Camps. (2005). *The Minsk Ghetto*. Online. Available from: http://www.deathcamps.org/occupation/minsk%20ghetto.html

14. Silitski. V. (2005) *A Partisan Reality Show*. Transitions Online. Available from:
http://www.tol.cz/look/TOL/article.tpl?IdLanguage=1&IdPublication=4&NrIssue=115&NrSection=4&NrArticle=14025

Chapter 6.

1. Lukashenko. A.G. (2007). *Congratulation on the Victory Day*. Press release, 8th of May 2007. Embassy of the Republic of Belarus in the United States of America. Available online from: http://www.belarusembassy.org/

2. Zaprudnik. J. (1993). *Belarus: At a Crossroads in History*. Westview Press. USA. Page 103.

3. Ibid.

4. Belarus Guide. (2004) *Partisan Resistance in Belarus in Belarus During World War Two*. Virtual Guide Online. Available from: http://www.belarusguide.com/history1/WWII_partisan_resistance_in_Belarus.htm

5. Feldgrau.com (2006). *Research on the German Armed Forces 1918-1945*. Online Statistics and Numbers. Available from: http://www.feldgrau.com/stats.html

6. Marples. David R. (1999). *Belarus: a Denationalised Nation*. Harwood Academic Publishers. Holland. Page 18.

7. Ibid.

8. Zaprudnik. J. (1993). *Belarus: At a Crossroads in History*. Westview Press. USA. Page 104.

9. Marples. David R. (1999). *Belarus: a Denationalised Nation*. Harwood Academic Publishers. Holland. Page 19.

10. Zaprudnik. J. (1993). *Belarus: At a Crossroads in History*. Westview Press. USA. Page 105

11. Ibid. Page 106.

12. Ibid.

13. Marples. David R. (1999). *Belarus: a Denationalised Nation*. Harwood Academic Publishers. Holland. Page 20.

14. Ibid.

15. Central Board of Statistics of the Belarusian SSR. (1986). *The National Economy of the Belarusian SSR: Statistical Yearbook*. Minsk. Page 162.

16. Zaprudnik. J. (1993). *Belarus: At a Crossroads in History*. Westview Press. USA. Page 107.

17. Stuk. A. & Sapozhkov. Y. (1982). *Byelorussia*. Novosti Press agency Publishing House. Moscow. Page18.

18. Ibid. Page 44.

19. Zaprudnik. J. (1993). *Belarus: At a Crossroads in History*. Westview Press. USA. Page 114.

20. Stuk. A. & Sapozhkov. Y. (1982). *Byelorussia*. Novosti Press agency Publishing House. Moscow. Page72.

21. Ibid. Page 58.

Chapter 7.

1. Lukashenko. A.G. (1998). *Belarus Tomorrow*. East European Development Association. Geneva. Page 3.

2. Lenin. V.I. (1970). *What is to be Done?* Progress Publishers. Moscow. Pages 59-60.

3. Reader's Concerns. (1990). *Stalin: For and Against: Soviet People on Stalinism and its consequences*. Novosti Press Agency Publishing House. Moscow.

4. Morrison. D. (Ed). (1988). *Mikhail S. Gorbachev: An Intimate Biography*. Time Books. New York.

5. Marples. David R. (1999). *Belarus: a Denationalised Nation*. Harwood Academic Publishers. Holland. Page 27.

6. Ibid. Page 28.

7. *Ibid. Page 56.*

Chapter 8.

211

1. Lukashenko. A.G. (2003). *Address by President of the Republic of Belarus at a seminar on matters of ideology participated by top–level officials of the central and local government bodies March 27, 2003*. Press service of the President of the Republic of Belarus.

2. Marples. David R. (1999). *Belarus: a Denationalised Nation*. Harwood Academic Publishers. Holland. Page 71.

3. Belapan. (2006) Belapan Chronicle. *Presidential elections in Belarus*. Online. Available from: http://elections.belapan.com/president2006/eng/show.php?show=48760

4. Ibid.

Chapter 9.

1. Lukashenko. A.G. (1998). *Belarus Tomorrow*. East European Development Association. Geneva. Page 5.

2. Zaprudnik. J. (1993). *Belarus: At a Crossroads in History*. Westview Press. USA. Page 212.

3. Marples. David R. (1999). *Belarus: a Denationalised Nation*. Harwood Academic Publishers. Holland. Page 32.

4. Ibid. Page 33.

5. Zlotnikov. L. (2005) *Into the Noose of Populism*. 'Belarusi I Rinok'. Available online from: www.br.minsk.by/book/zlot.htm

6. Lvov. D.S. (1997). *Belaruskaya Dumka*. 'Belarusian Concept' Journal. 11.

7. Zlotnikov. L. (2005) *Into the Noose of Populism*. 'Belarusi I Rinok'. Available online from: www.br.minsk.by/book/zlot.htm

8. Catalinotto. J. (2000). *Belarus: NATO's Next Target?* Workers World. Available online from: http://workers.org/ww/2000/belarus1102.php

9. Bulachov. D. (1992) *Speech at the Ninth Session of the Twelfth Supreme Soviet of Belarus, Bulletin no.24*. Cited by Zaprudnik (1993). Page 166.

10. Zaprudnik. J. (1993). *Belarus: At a Crossroads in History.* Westview Press. USA. Page 168.

11. Marples. David R. (1999). *Belarus: a Denationalised Nation.* Harwood Academic Publishers. Holland. Page 70.

12. Lukashenko. A.G. (1998). *Belarus Tomorrow.* East European Development Association. Geneva. Page 17.

13. Ibid. Page 18.

Chapter 10.

1. Lukashenko. A.G. (1998). *Belarus Tomorrow.* East European Development Association. Geneva. Page 37.

2. Marples. David R. (1999). *Belarus: a Denationalised Nation.* Harwood Academic Publishers. Holland. Page 73.

3. Biely. A. (1997). *Belarus: Real or Fictitious Nation?* History Today, April 1997.

4. Stiglitz. J.E. (2002). *Globalisation and its Discontents.* W.W. Norton &co. New York.

5. Lukashenko. A.G. (2006). *Opening Remarks at the 3rd All Belarusian Peoples Assembly.* Available online from the National State Teleradio Company of the Republic of Belarus at: http://www.tvr.by/eng/news.asp?id=15458&date=02.03.2006%2015:09:00#6

6. Marples. David R. (1999). *Belarus: a Denationalised Nation.* Harwood Academic Publishers. Holland. Page 91.

7. Samuel. S.P. (2003). *Belarus: Facts.* Kavaler Publishers. Minsk. Page 41.

8. Mulvey. S. (2001) *Europe's Last Dictator?* BBC News profile of Alexander Lukashenko. Available online at: http://news.bbc.co.uk/1/hi/world/europe/116265.stm

Chapter 11.

1. Lukashenko. A.G. (1998). *Belarus Tomorrow*. East European Development Association. Geneva. Page 48.

2. Gowans S. (2001). *US Ambassador Admits Washington is Subverting the Belarus Presidential Election*. Media Monitors Network. Online. Available from: www.mediamonitors.net/gowans25.html

3. Zlotnikov. L. (2005). *Into the Noose of Populism*. 'Belarusi I Rinok'. Available online from: www.br.minsk.by/book/zlot.htm

4. Oreshko. A. (2003). *Economic Blues*. Belarus Reporting Service No 02, 31 Jan 03.

5. Lukashenko. A.G. (1998). *Belarus Tomorrow*. East European Development Association. Geneva. Page47.

6. Chomsky. N. (1989). *Necessary Illusions*. Pluto Press. London. Page 198.

7. Ibid.

8. Marples. David R. (1999). *Belarus: a Denationalised Nation*. Harwood Academic Publishers. Holland. Page 36.

9. Zlotnikov. L. (2005). *Into the Noose of Populism*. 'Belarusi I Rinok'. Available online from: www.br.minsk.by/book/zlot.htm

10. U.S Department of State. (2005). *Country Profile: Belarus*. Available online from: https://www.cia.gov/cia/publications/factbook/geos/bo.html

11. Belarusian Ministry of Foreign affairs. (2004). *Main Social and Economic Indicators of the Republic of Belarus*. Minsk.

12. Ibid.

13. Marples. David R. (1999). *Belarus: a Denationalised Nation*. Harwood Academic Publishers. Holland. Page 39.

14. Lukashenko. A.G. (1998). *Belarus Tomorrow*. East European Development Association. Geneva. Page47.

15. Belarusian Ministry of Foreign affairs. (2004). *Main Social and Economic Indicators of the Republic of Belarus.* Minsk.

16. Embassy of the Republic of Belarus. (2005-06). *Belarusian Economy in the First Half of 2005.* Also: *Socio-Economic Development of Belarus – January to September 2006.* Available online from: http://www.belarusembassy.org/

17. Ibid.

18. Belarusian Ministry of Statistics and Analysis (2006). *Living Standards: Main Indicators Relating to Living Standards.* Available online from: http://belstat.gov.by/homep/en/indicators/uroven.htm

19. Pravda.Ru. (2006). *Branded Dictator, Lukashenko is Deeply Loved by Many Belarusians.* Pravda: 17/03/06. Available online from: http:english.pravda.ru/world/77456-0

20. Embassy of the Republic of Belarus. (2004). *Belarusian Economy in the First Half of 2004.* Available online from: http://www.belarusembassy.org/economic/economy_6_2004.htm

21. Ibid.

22. Embassy of the Republic of Belarus. (2005). *Belarusian Economy in the First Half of 2005.* Available online from: http://www.belarusembassy.org/economic/economy_6_2005.htm

23. Ibid.

24. World Bank. (2005) *Belarus: Window of Opportunity.* Available online from: http://web.worldbank.org/WBSITE/EXTERNAL/COUNTRIES/ECAEXT/BELARUSEXTN/0,,contentMDK:20726033~pagePK:141137~piPK:141127~theSitePK:328431,00.html

25. Whittell. G. (1999). *Belarus Leader Calls for Missile Sell Off.* Free Republic News Forum. Available online from: http://www.freerepublic.com/forum/a3817d35c26f5.htm

26. Worldwide Tax. (2005). *Poland Unemployment Rates.* Available online from: http://www.worldwide-tax.com/poland/pol_unemployment.asp

27. IMF. (2006). *Republic of Belarus.* IMF Country Report No. 06/314 August 2006. Available online from: http://www.imf.org/external/pubs/ft/scr/2006/cr06314.pdf

28. Lukashenko. A.G. (2007). *Interview to Reuters News Agency*. 7th February 2007. Available online from: http://president.gov.by/en/press39040.html

29. Kommersant Daily. (2005). *Lukashenko Finds Comrades in China*. Kommersant December 7th 2005.

30. Lukashenko. A.G. (2005). *Interview by President of the Republic of Belarus A.G. Lukashenko to Representatives of the Mass Media of the Peoples Republic of China*. November 28, 2005. Available online from http://president.gov.by

31. Catalinotto. J. (2000). *Belarus: NATO's Next Target?* Workers World. Available online from: http://workers.org/ww/2000/belarus1102.php

Chapter 12.

1. Lukashenko. A.G. (1998). *Belarus Tomorrow*. East European Development Association. Geneva. Page 48.

2. Higgins. A. (1998). *Disaffected Russians Turn for Advice to Voice of Belarus*. The Wall Street Journal. 10/01/98.

3. Ibid.

4. Marx. K. Engels. F. Lenin. V.I. (1967). *On Scientific Communism*. Progress Publishers. Moscow. Page 462.

5. Lukashenko. A.G. (1998). *Belarus Tomorrow*. East European Development Association. Geneva. Page 49.

6. Ibid.

7. Rodriguez. A. (2005) *Alcohol Destroying Rural Russia*. Chicago Tribune. Available online from: http://www.mosnews.com/commentary/2005/12/15/alcoholism.shtml

8. Ibid.

9. Bennett. K. Et-al. (2005). *Coalfields Regeneration: Dealing with the Consequences of Industrial Decline*. The Policy Press. Bristol.

10. Lukashenko. A.G. (1998). *Belarus Tomorrow*. East European Development Association. Geneva. Page 49.

11. Lukashenko. A.G. (2005). *Procurement of Brewer's Barley Discussed at the Presidential Meeting*. October the Fifth 2005. Press Service of the President of the Republic of Belarus.

12. NationMaster.com. (2005). *Distribution of Family Income- Gini Index*. Available online from: http://www.nationmaster.com

13. Embassy of the Republic of Belarus in the United States. (2004). *Social and Labour Policy*. Available online from: http://www.belarusembassy.org/

14. BBC News. (2006). *Man Utd. Sign £56.5m AIG shirt deal*. Available online from: http://news.bbc.co.uk/1/hi/business/4882640.stm

15. Embassy of the Republic of Belarus. (2005). *Belarusian Economy in the First Half of 2005*. Available online from: http://www.belarusembassy.org/economic/economy_6_2005.htm

16. Ibid.

17. Lukashenko. A.G. (1998). *Belarus Tomorrow*. East European Development Association. Geneva. Page 45.

18. Ibid. Page 46.

19. Pravda. (2004). *Russian Education System Declines in Comparison with Soviet era*. Pravda 21/10/04.

20. United Nations Development Programme. (2004). *Human Development Report. Cultural Liberty in Today's Diverse World*. UNDP. New York.

21. Eason G. (2006). *Teachers to Fight Trust Schools*. BBC News. Available online from: http://news.bbc.co.uk/1/hi/education/4914014.stm

22. Ibid.

23. Samuel. S.P. (2003). *Belarus: Facts*. Kavaler Publishers. Minsk. Page 146.

24. Vetokhin. S. (2004). *Education in Belarus*. (National Report of the Republic of Belarus). Ministry of Education of the Republic of Belarus National Institute for Higher Education. Page 19.

25. Lukashenko. A.G. (1998). *Belarus Tomorrow*. East European Development Association. Geneva. Page 49.

26. Embassy of the Republic of Belarus. (2005). Social Policy and Labour Policy. Available online from: http://www.belarusembassy.org/

27. Palast. G. (2003). *The Best Democracy Money Can Buy*. Constable and Robinson Limited. London. Page 3.

28. Vetokhin. S. (2004). *Education in Belarus*. (National Report of the Republic of Belarus). Ministry of Education of the Republic of Belarus National Institute for Higher Education. Page 39.

29. Cherniavka. I. (2004). *Old-School Propaganda*. International War and Peace Reporting. March 2004. Available online from: http://baj.ru/2004/Mar/z310304e.asp

30. Lukashenko. A.G. (1998). *Belarus Tomorrow*. East European Development Association. Geneva. Page 77.

31. Lukashenko. A.G. (2003). *Message by the President of the Republic of Belarus to Belarusian People and Parliament of the Republic of Belarus*. April 16th 2003. Press service of the President of the Republic of Belarus.

32. Medvedev. M. (2001). *Last love of Belarusians*. Available online from: www.vitryssland.nu/loveluka.html

33. Office of National Statistics (2004). Cited by BBC Scotland. Available online from: http://news.bbc.co.uk/1/hi/scotland/3746162.stm

34. The Department of Trade and Industry. (2000). *Work and Parents: Competitiveness and Choice*. Green paper. Available online from: http://www.dti.gov.uk/er/g_paper/index.htm

35. Lukashenko. A.G. (1998). *Belarus Tomorrow*. East European Development Association. Geneva. Page 50.

36. Ibid.

37. *The Constitution of the Republic of Belarus. With alterations and addenda adopted at the Republican referendum of November 24,1996*. Available online from: http://ncpi.gov.by/eng/legal/V19402875.htm

38. United Nations Human Development Report 2004. *Cultural Liberty in Today's Diverse World*. Page 157. Available online from: http://hdr.undp.org/reports/global/2004/?CFID=863198&CFTOKEN=56943836

39. Lukashenko. A.G. (1998). *Belarus Tomorrow*. East European Development Association. Geneva. Page 93.

40. United Nations Human Development Report 2004. *Cultural Liberty in Today's Diverse World*. Page 157. Available online from: http://hdr.undp.org/reports/global/2004/?CFID=863198&CFTOKEN=56943836

41. World Health Organisation. (2005). *Make Every Mother and Child Count*. Available online from: http://www.who.int/whr/2005/en/

42. United Nations Human Development Report 2004. *Cultural Liberty in Today's Diverse World*. Page 157. Available online from: http://hdr.undp.org/reports/global/2004/?CFID=863198&CFTOKEN=56943836

43. UNAIDS. (2006). *Addressing AIDS Challenges in Belarus*. Joint United Nations Programme on HIV AIDS. 20th October 2006. Available online from: http://www.unaids.org/en/MediaCentre/PressMaterials/FeatureStory/20061025_Bellarus_en.asp (See also: *Report on Socio-economic development of Belarus January – September 2006*. At: http://www.belarusembassy.org/).

44. World Bank. (2004). *Belarus: Poverty Assessment. Can Poverty Reduction and access to Services be sustained?* Main Report. Europe and Central Asia Region Human Development Sector Unit. Report No.27431-BY Page ix.

45. Ibid. Page 76.

46. Ibid. Page 61.

47. Ibid. Page 57.

48. Nagle. C. (2000). *Belarus: Oasis in the Heart of Europe*. Available online from: http://www.antiwar.com/nagle/pf/p-n012601.html

Chapter 13.

1. Lukashenko. A.G. (2005). *Statement by President of the Republic of Belarus Alexander Lukashenko at the 60th Session of the United Nations General Assembly*. Press Service of the President of the Republic of Belarus.

2. Lukashenko. A.G. (1998). *Belarus Tomorrow*. East European Development Association. Geneva. Page 38.

3. Shannon. M (1999). *In the Heartland*. Australia/Israel and Jewish Affairs Council. The Review. November 1999. Available online at: http://www.aijac.org.au/review/1999/2411/heartland.html

4. Permanent Delegation of the Republic of Belarus to the OSCE. (2004). *Statement by Ambassador Viktor Gaisenak, Head of the Delegation of the Republic of Belarus, at the OSCE Conference on Anti-Semitism*. Berlin 28-29 April 2004. Document PC.DEL/326/04

5. Ibid.

6. Ibid.

7. Ibid.

8. The Stephen Roth Institute. (2001). *Anti-Semitism Worldwide 2000/1: Belarus*. Tel Aviv University. Available online from: http://www.tau.ac.il/anti-semitism/asw2000-1/belarus.htm

9. Lukashenko. A.G. (1998). *Belarus Tomorrow*. East European Development Association. Geneva. Page 38.

10. Nassor. A. (2005). *African Student Killed Near Metro Station*. The St. Petersburg Times. Issue 1134(100). Thursday December 29th 2005.

11. Bullough. O. (2006). *Russian Skinheads Intimidate Foreigners*. Reuters. Available online from

the Moscow News at:
http://www.mosnews.com/commentary/2006/02/14/foreignerslive.shtml

12. Jordan. M.J. (2004). *Jews get by in Belarus, but they feel the authorities watchful eye*. JTA. Available online from: http://ncsj.org/auxpages/030504jta_belarus.shtml

13. Embassy of the Republic of Belarus in the USA. (2005). *Belarus' Mass Media in Figures*. Available online from: http://www.belarusembassy.org/

14. Belarusian Ministry of Foreign Affairs (2002). *Main Social and Economic Indicators of the Republic of Belarus*. Minsk.

15. Franchetti. M. (2006). *Violence Feared as Europe's Last Dictator Clings to Power*. The Sunday Times. February 12th 2006. (This is just one of many such articles!)

16. Commentary to the law of the Republic of Belarus "*On introduction of changes and amendments to several legislative acts of the Republic of Belarus on the issue of strengthening responsibility for acts against a person an public security*". (2006). Available online from: http://www.belarusembassy.org/

17. Ibid.

18. Cited by the British Helsinki Human Rights Group (1997). *Belarus: Pariah or Victim?* Available online from http://www.bhhrg.org

19. Petina. L. (2000). *Women's Movement in Belarus. Formation, Development, Problems*. Available online from: http://www.cacedu.unibel.by/widm/eng/WMov.htm

20. Medvedev. M. (2001). *Last Love of Belarusians*. Available online from: www.vitryssland.nu/loveluka.html

21. The Constitution of the Republic of Belarus. With alterations and addenda adopted at the Republican referendum of November 24,1996. Available online from: http://ncpi.gov.by/eng/legal/V19402875.htm

22. Ibid.

23. United Nations Committee on Elimination of Discrimination against Women. (2004). *Campaign Needed to raise Awareness of Women's Human Rights in Belarus: But Delegation Says Increased*

Opportunities Have Provided Diverse Possibilities for Women's Participation in All Spheres of Life. Press Release WOM1430.

24. Malarek. V. (2003). *The Natashas. The New Global Sex Trade.* Viking. Canada.

25. Associated Press. (2005). *Update 2: Belarus Moves to Limit Online Dating.* AP. 12.14.2005, 1027AM.

26. Ibid.

27. Lagnado. A. (2001). *Why the Rural Millions Love a Dictator.* New Statesman 17th of September 2001. Available online from: http://www.newstatesman.com/200109170014

28. Embassy of the Republic of Belarus in the USA. (2006). *Weekly Digest of Belarusian News.* 31st of October 2006. Available online from: http://www.belarusembassy.org/news/index.htm

29. British Helsinki Human Rights Group. (1997). *Belarus: Pariah or Victim?* Available on line form http://bhhrg.org

30. UCSJ (2003). *Lukashenko Denies Praising Hitler.* Union of Councils of Jews in the Former Soviet Union. News December 9th 2003.

31. British Helsinki Human Rights Group. (1997). *Belarus: Pariah or Victim?* Available on line form http://bhhrg.org

32. Amnesty International. (2002). *Belarus.* Available online from: www.amnesty.org

33. Amnesty International. (2002). *United Kingdom.* Available online from: www.amnesty.org

34. Amnesty International. (2002). *USA.* Available online from: www.amnesty.org

35. Clark. N. (2006). *You Cannot be Serious: The Belarus Saga Exposes the Hollowness of the West's Support for Human Rights and Democracy.* The Guardian March 27th.

36. Prima News Agency. (2000). *Former Chairman of the Belarusian National Bank Lives in London.* 7th March 2000. Available online from: http://prima-news.ru/eng/news/news/2000/7/3/20745.html

37. Karbalevich. V. (1999). *Yuri Zakharenko: Disappearance or Political Terrorism?* Available online

from: http://www.ucpb.org/eng/library/weremember/zakharenko.shtml

38. Cited by BHHRG. (2001). *Belarus Presidential Election, September 2001*. Report by the British Helsinki Human Rights Group. Available online from: www.bhhrg.org

39. Gulak. O. (2000). *The Law of Power Replaces the Power of Law - Political Repression in Present Day Belarus*. Belarusian Helsinki Committee. Available online from: http://www.vitryssland.nu/picnicrapport.html

40. Ibid.

41. Cited by BHHRG. (2001). *Belarus Presidential Election, September 2001*. Report by the British Helsinki Human Rights Group. Available online from: www.bhhrg.org

42. Gulak. O. (2000). *The Law of Power Replaces the Power of Law - Political Repression in Present Day Belarus*. Belarusian Helsinki Committee. Available online from: http://www.vitryssland.nu/picnicrapport.html

43. Amnesty International. (2000). *Possible 'Disappearances' in Belarus*. Report, 1st of January 2000. Available online from: http://web.amnesty.org/library/Index/engEUR490032000?OpenDocument&of=COUNTRIES%5CBELARUS

44. Cole. V. (1999). *Belarus Update*. International League for Human Rights. Volume 2, No.39. September 1999. Available online from: http://www.ilhr.org/belarus/u39.htm

45. Ibid.

46. Ibid.

47. Amnesty International. (2000). *Possible 'Disappearances' in Belarus*. Report, 1st of January 2000. Available online from: http://web.amnesty.org/library/Index/engEUR490032000?OpenDocument&of=COUNTRIES%5CBELARUS

48. Inter-Parliamentary Union. (2006). *Belarus. Case No BLS/55 – Viktor Gonchar*. Resolution adopted by consensus by the IPU Governing Council at its 178th session. Nairobi, 12th of May 2006. Available online from: http://www.ipu.org/hr-e/178/Bls05.htm

49. Cole. V. (Ed). (1999). *Belarus Update*. International League for Human Rights. Volume 2, No.39. September 1999. Available online from: http://www.ilhr.org/belarus/u39.htm

50. Ibid.

51. Podoliak. M. (1999). *Political Contract?* Belarusskaya Gazette #85. 14th of May 1999. Available online from: http://www.ucpb.org/eng/library/weremember/zakharenko.shtml

52. Cole. V. (Ed). (2001). *Belarus Update*. International League for Human Rights. Volume 4. No19. May 2001. Available online from: http://www.ilhr.org/ilhr/regional/belarus/updates/2001/19.htm

53. Committee to Protect Journalists. (2004). *Belarus: Mother of Missing Journalist Requests New Investigation of the Case*. 5th of August 2004. Available online from: http://www.cpj.org/news/2004/Belarus05aug04na.html

54. Cole. V. (Ed). (2000). *Belarus Update*. International League for Human Rights. Volume 3. No31. July 2000. Available online from: http://www.ilhr.org/ilhr/regional/belarus/updates/2003/31.htm

55. Ibid.

56. Ibid.

57. Committee to Protect Journalists. (2006). *Journalists in Prison*. Available online from: http://www.cpj.org/attacks06/pages06/imprison_06.html

58. Lukashenko. A.G. (2002). *Interview by the President of Belarus to the Wall Street Journal Staff Reporter*. Available online from: http://www.president.gov.by/en/press13376.print.html

59. Ibid.

60. Lukashenko. A.G. (2001). *Address of the President of the Republic of Belarus at the Republican Conference on the Tasks of Executive and Administrative Authorities Under the Present Day Conditions*. Press Service of the President of the Republic of Belarus. Available online from: http://president.gov.by/en/press11521.html#doc

61. BHHRG. (2000). *Belarus 2000: Parliamentary Elections*. Report available online from:

www.bhhrg.org

Chapter14.

1. Lukashenko. A.G. (2005). *Statement by President of the Republic of Belarus Alexander Lukashenko at the 60th Session of the United Nations General Assembly.* Press Service of the President of the Republic of Belarus. Available online from:
http://www.belarusembassy.org/political/statement050916.htm

2. The CIA World Factbook. (2005). *Belarus.* Available online from: www.cia.gov

3. Lukashenko. A.G. (1998). *Belarus Tomorrow.* East European Development Association. Geneva. Page 21.

4. Kommersant. (2005). *Lukashenko Attempts to Avoid the Moscow Hoof.* Kommersant Daily November 24th 2005.

5. Ibid.

6. Marples. David R. (1999). *Belarus: a Denationalised Nation.* Harwood Academic Publishers. Holland. Page 109.

7. Ibid. Page 111.

8. Lukashenko. A.G. (1998). *Belarus Tomorrow.* East European Development Association. Geneva. Page 20.

9. Wagstyl. S. (1998). *Belarus: Leader Offers Soviet Style Solution.* Financial Times. October 23rd 1998.

10. Manayev. O. (2006). *Strengthening pro-"wide Europe" attitudes in Belarus.* Cited by Pravda 28th April 2006. (Article title: Belarusians want Lukashenko to rule Russia too).

11. Associated Press. (1997). *Belarus' President Inspires Fear, Loathing, Admiration.* 22nd June 1997. Available online at: http://chronicle.home.by/9706/970622.htm

12. Ibid.

225

13. Higgins. A. (1998). *Disaffected Russians Turn for Advice to Voice of Belarus*. The Wall Street Journal. 10/01/98.

14. Ibid.

15. British Helsinki Human Rights Group. (1997). *Belarus: Pariah or Victim?* Available online from: www.bhhrg.org

16. Tomberg. I. (2006). *Gazprom to raise gas prices for Belarus from 2007*. Novosti News Agency. Russia. Available online from: http://en.rian.ru/analysis/20060410/45529226.html

17. Associated Press. (2007). *Lukashenko Says Belarus Faces Difficult Years After Russia Raises Energy Prices*. International Herald and Tribune 19th January 2007. Available online from: http://www.iht.com/articles/ap/2007/01/19/business/EU-FIN-Belarus-Economy.php

18. Embassy of the Republic of Belarus in the USA. (2007). *Statements Regarding Russian Losses Running Into Billions Because of Gas Agreements With Belarus Are Contrary to Reality*. Press Release 9th January 2007. Available online from: http://www.belarusembassy.org/

19. Lukashenko. A.G. (2007). *Interview to Reuters News Agency*. 7th February 2007. Available online from: www.president.gov.by

20. Cited by the British Helsinki Human Rights Group (1997). *Belarus: Pariah or Victim?* Available online from http://www.bhhrg.org

21. Ibid.

22. Federation Aeronautic Internationale. (1996). *Statement on the Official Report into the Belarus Balloon Incident*. FAI.

23. US Department of State. (2006). *Background note: Belarus. Bureau of European and Eurasian Affairs*. April 2006. Available online from: http://www.state.gov/r/pa/ei/bgn/5371.htm

24. Hamilton. T. (1995). *Tragedy in Belarus*. Balloon Life. Available online from: http://www.balloonlife.com/publications/balloon_life/9510/tragedy.htm

25. Chomsky. N. (1989). *Necessary Illusions*. Pluto Press. London. Page 34.

26. Ghasemi. S. (2004). *Shooting Down Iran Air Flight 655 (IR655)*. (George Bush quote is from

Newsweek, August 15th 1988). Available online from: http://www.iranchamber.com/history/articles/flight_655.php

27. Cited by the British Helsinki Human Rights Group (1997). *Belarus: Pariah or Victim?* Available online from http://www.bhhrg.org

28. Ibid.

29. Radio Free Europe/ Radio Liberty. (2005). Mission Statement.

30. RFE/RL (2006). *Belarus Votes 2006. Candidates Spotlight*. Available online from: http://www.rferl.org/specials/belarus_votes/bios/Lukashenka.aspx

31. Ghattas. K. (2005). *Saudi's first Exercise in democracy*. BBC news Riadh. Available online from: http://news.bbc.co.uk/1/hi/world/middle_east/4252305.stm

32. Human Rights Watch. Saudi Arabia. World Report 2001. Available from: www.hrw.org

33. US Senate Committee on banking, housing and urban affairs. *Second Staff Report on US Chemical and Biological Warfare-Related Dual-Use Exports to Iraq and The Possible Impact on the Health Consequences of the War*. Available online from: http://www.gulfwarvets.com/arison/banking.htm

34. Clark. N. (2005). *Reformers and Hard-liners. What do Iran, Venezuela and Belarus have in common?* The Guardian Tuesday July 12th, 2005.

35. Council of Ministers of the Republic of Belarus. (2006). *Sergei Sidorsky: Belarus rakes in USD 1 billion every year in oil refining revenue*. Press release 1st August 2006. Available online from: http://www.government.by/en/eng_news01082006.html#n1

36. United States Geological Survey. (1998). *US Energy and World Energy Statistics*. Central Region Energy Resources Team. Available online from: http://energy.cr.usgs.gov/energy/stats_ctry/Stat1.html#ConsumptionUvsW

37. Rettman. A. (2006). *EU should target Belarus arms trade, expert says*. EU Observer. Available online from: http://www.data.minsk.by/belarusnews/032006/576.html

38. Project for the New American Century. (1997). Available online from: http://www.newamericancentury.org/

39. BBC. (2005). *Chávez Considers Breaking US Ties*. BBC News 23rd May 2005. Available online from: http://news.bbc.co.uk/1/hi/world/americas/4571957.stm

40. US Department of State. (2005*). Bush, Saakashvili Salute Georgia's Transition to Democracy*. 10th May 2005. Available online from: http://usinfo.state.gov/special/Archive/2005/May/10-770443.html

41. Berrigan. F. Et al. (2005). *US Weapons at War 2005: Promoting Freedom or Fuelling Conflict? US Military Aid and Arms Transfers Since September 11*. Arms trade Resource Centre. A World Policy Special Report. June 2005. New York. Available online from: http://www.worldpolicy.org/projects/arms/reports/wawjune2005.html#11

42. Human Rights Watch. (2006). *Open Letter to President Bush*. June 27th 2006. Available online from: http://hrw.org/english/docs/2006/06/27/georgi13683.htm

43. British Helsinki Human Rights Group. (2005). *Rose Revolutionary Justice*. Available online from: http://www.bhhrg.org/CountryReport.asp?ChapterID=773&CountryID=10&ReportID=252&keyword=

44. BBC. (2006). *Have your Say: Were Belarus Elections Free and Fair?* Available online from: http://newsforums.bbc.co.uk/nol/thread.jspa?threadID=1352&&edition=1&ttl=20060820141226

45. Nagle. C. (2000). *Belarus: Oasis in the Heart of Europe*. Available online from: http://www.antiwar.com/nagle/pf/p-n012601.html

46. Chandler. D. (2001). *Dictating Democracy in Belarus*. Spiked online. 12th October 2001. Available from: http://www.spiked-online.com/Articles/00000002D26F.htm

47. Ibid.

48. Ibid.

49. Ibid.

50. BHHRG. (2001). *Belarus Presidential Election 2001*. Report. Available online from: http://www.bhhrg.org/CountryReport.asp?ChapterID=176&CountryID=4&ReportID=55&ke

yword=

51. Cited by Israel. J. (2001). *Tough Measures Justified in Belarus*. Available online from: http://www.tenc.net/news/tough.htm

52. Lagnado.A. (2001). *US Adopts 'Contras policy' in Communist* [sic!] *Belarus*. The Times (UK). 3rd September 2001.

53. Ibid.

54. Chomsky. N. (1989). *Necessary Illusions*. Pluto Press. London. Page 57.

55. Marples. David R. (1999). *Belarus: a Denationalised Nation*. Harwood Academic Publishers. Holland. Page 83.

56. Ibid.

57. Nagle. C. (2000). *Belarus: Oasis in the Heart of Europe*. Available online from: http://www.antiwar.com/nagle/pf/p-n012601.html

58. BHHRG. (2001). *Belarus Presidential Election 2001*. Report. Available online from: http://www.bhhrg.org/CountryReport.asp?ChapterID=176&CountryID=4&ReportID=55&keyword=

59. The Stephen Roth Institute. (1997). *Belarus: Annual Country Report 1997*. Tel Aviv University. Available online from: http://www.tau.ac.il/Anti-Semitism/asw97-8/belarus.html

60. Tonkacheva. E. (2004). *Liquidation of NGO's in Belarus: a Means of Maintaining Power*. European Foundation Centre. Available online from: http://www.efc.be/cgi-bin/articlepublisher.pl?filename=ET-SE-01-04-1.html

61. Ibid.

62. US Department of State. (2004). *Country Report on Human Rights Practices 2004*. Available online from: www.state.gov.

63. Israel. J. (2001). *Tough Measures Justified in Belarus*. Available online from: http://www.tenc.net/news/tough.htm

64. Nevius. C.W. et-al. *McCain Criticised for Slur*. San Francisco Chronicle, 18th February 2000.

65. Cited by Johnson. R. (2005*). On Belarus and Lukashenko: An Answer to Senator John McCain (R-AZ)*. The American Journal of Russian and Slavic Studies.

66. Embassy of the United States of America in Minsk Belarus. (2002). *Senator McCain Speech to the New Atlantic Initiative Conference on Belarus*. November 14th 2002. Available Online from: http://minsk.usembassy.gov/html/mccain.html

67. BBC. (2004). *Bush Disputes 9/11-Iraq Findings*. 17th June 2004. Available online from: http://news.bbc.co.uk/1/hi/world/americas/3816699.stm (Includes link to the National Commission on Terrorist Attacks on the United States report).

68. Cited by Johnson. R. (2005*). On Belarus and Lukashenko: An Answer to Senator John McCain (R-AZ)*. The American Journal of Russian and Slavic Studies.

69. Ibid.

70. Bush. G.W. (2004). *Statement on the Belarus Democracy Act of 2004*. Available online from: http://www.whitehouse.gov/news/releases/2004/10/20041020-14.html

71. Chomsky. N. (1989). *Necessary Illusions*. Pluto Press. London. Page 22.

72. Belarus Democracy Act of 2004. (2004). The full text is available online from: http://www.charter97.org/eng/news/2004/10/27/act

73. Ibid.

74. Ibid.

75. Dzitsevich. L. (2002). *Language Education and Time*. Frantsishak Skaryna Belarusian Language Society. Available online from: http://tbm.org.by/eng/speeches/dzitsevich.html

76. Ibid.

77. Belarus Democracy Act of 2004. (2004). The full text is available online from: http://www.charter97.org/eng/news/2004/10/27/act

78. Ibid.

79. Jordan. MJ. (2004). *Living in Europe's Last Dictatorship, Belarus Jews Face Unique Challenges.* Jewish Telegraph Agency March 2004.

80. Ibid.

81. Belarus Democracy Act of 2004. (2004). The full text is available online from: http://www.charter97.org/eng/news/2004/10/27/act

82. Ibid.

83. British Helsinki Human Rights Group. (2002). *Florida revisited: An Account of the US Midterm Elections.* Available online from: http://www.bhhrg.org/CountryReport.asp?CountryID=56

84. Belarus Democracy Act of 2004. (2004). The full text is available online from: http://www.charter97.org/eng/news/2004/10/27/act

85. Ibid.

86. Ibid.

87. Ibid.

88. Johnson. R. (2005). *On Belarus and Lukashenko: An Answer to Senator John McCain (R-AZ).* The American Journal of Russian and Slavic Studies.

89. Cited by Charter 97. (2004). *Lukashenko Lambastes* [sic] *Belarus Democracy Act.* Available online from: http://www.charter97.org/eng/news/2004/10/07/lamb

90. Belarus Democracy Act of 2004. (2004). The full text is available online from: http://www.charter97.org/eng/news/2004/10/27/act

91. Congressional Research Service (2006). *CRS Report for Congress. US Assistance to the Former Soviet Union.* March 16th 2006. US Library of Congress.

92. Cited by Charter 97. (2004). *Lukashenko Lambastes* [sic] *Belarus Democracy Act.* Available online from: http://www.charter97.org/eng/news/2004/10/07/lamb

93. Ibid.

94. Ibid.

95. Weekly Digest of Belarusian News. (2004). *National News. Alexander Lukashenko: "Belarus Democracy Act" is Interference in the internal Affairs of Belarus*. November 18th 2004. Available online from: http://www.belarusembassy.org

96. Address by the Members of the Republican Co-ordinating Committee of Political Parties and Public Association's Leaders to Citizens of the Republic of Belarus and the International Community. (2004). [Co-signatories include the heads of various political parties as well as trade unions, the Belarusian Red Cross, and the League of Human Rights Protection]. Press release. Available online from: http://www.belarusembassy.org/

97. Sayenko. L. (1998). *Belarus Leader Criticises West on Independence Day*. Reuters. Minsk. July 3rd 1998.

98. Dapkiunas. A. (2004). *Introduction to Draft Resolution "Situation of Democracy and Human Rights in the United States of America"*. New York, 10th November 2004.

99. Ibid.

100. Pravda. (2003). *Lukashenko: Belarus to Develop Relations with USA on Mutual Respect Basis*. Pravda 22nd October 2003. Available online from: http://newsfromrussia.com/world/2003/10/22/50703.html

101. Fine L. (2004). *Belarus' Decision at UN*. Cited by: Weekly Digest of Belarusian News. November 18th 2004. Available online from: http://www.belarusembassy.org/news/digests/111804.htm

102. Ibid.

103. DC Vote. (2004). *Republic of Belarus Introduces UN General Assembly Resolution Condemning US Government for Violating Political Rights of Residents of the District of Columbia by Denying them Equal Representation in Congress*. DC Vote media centre press release November 8th 2004. Available online from:
http://www.dcvote.org/media/release.cfm?releaseID=146&keywords=draft%20resolution

104. Chomsky. N. (2000). *Rogue States. The Rule of Force in World Affairs.* Pluto Press. Page 14.

105. Mull. Stephen. D. (2005). *US and Lithuanian Interests in Promoting Democracy in Belarus.* Lithuanian Foreign Policy Review 2005/ 1-2 (15-16). Available online from: http://www.lfpr.lt/05.phtml

106. Press Service of the President of the Republic of Belarus. (2002). *Interview by the President of Belarus to the Wall Street Journal Staff Reporter.* Available online from: http://www.president.gov.by/en/press29302.html

107. Radio Free Europe/ Radio Liberty. (2005). *US Accuses Belarus Media of Anti US Campaign.* November 16th 2005. Available online from: http://www.rferl.org/featuresarticle/2005/11/14904384-3556-4ea5-94a8-515228b5e7e6.html

108. Weekly Digest of Belarusian News. (2005). *Belarusian President Criticises President Bush's inauguration Speech.* January 21st 2005. Available online from: http://www.belarusembassy.org/news/digests/012105.htm

109. Ibid.

110. Ibid.

111. Press Service of the President of the Republic of Belarus. (2005). *Verbatim of the Press Conference held by President of the Republic of Belarus A.G. Lukashenko for Mass Media Representatives from Russia's Regions.* Available online from: http://president.gov.by/en/press10939.html#doc

112. Majidi. M. (2006). *Belarus in the Crosshairs: US Government Orchestrates Anti-Lukashenko Opposition.* Socialism and Liberation magazine. May 2006. Available online from: http://socialismandliberation.org/mag/index.php?aid=612

113. BBC News. (2005). *Rice Backs Belarusian Opposition.* Thursday April 21st 2005. Available online from: http://news.bbc.co.uk/1/hi/world/europe/4470221.stm

114. Ibid.

115. Majidi. M. (2006). *Belarus in the Crosshairs: US Government Orchestrates Anti-Lukashenko Opposition.* Socialism and Liberation magazine. May 2006. Available online from: http://socialismandliberation.org/mag/index.php?aid=612

116. Cited by Gowans. S. (2006). *Lop Sided Lukashenko Win Anticipated as Legitimate Outcome*. Available online from:
http://www.williambowles.info/guests/2006/0306/lopsided_lukashenko.html

117. BBC News. (2006). *US Rejects Poll Results*. 20th March 2006. Available online from:
http://news.bbc.co.uk/1/hi/world/europe/4824642.stm

118. Embassy of the Republic of Belarus in the United States of America. (2006). *Commentary to the Press Secretary of the Ministry of Foreign Affairs of the Republic of Belarus to the Belarusian mass Media on the Statements Made by the Official representatives of the white House and the State Department with Regard to the Results of the Presidential Elections in Belarus*. Press release. Washington, D.C. March 23rd 2006.

119. Belarus Democracy Reauthorization Act of 2006. Full text available from:
http://www.govtrack.us/data/us/bills.text/109/h/h5948.pdf

120. Lukashenko. A.G. (2004). *Foreign Policy of the Republic of Belarus in the Modern World*. Available online from:
http://www.ebrdrenewables.com/sites/renew/Lists/EBRD%20Master%20Spreadsheet/DispForm.aspx?ID=197

121. Ibid.

122. Cole. V. Ed. (2000). *International League for Human Rights: Belarus Update*. ILHR. Volume 3 Number37 September 2000.

123. Radio Havana Cuba. (2000). *President of Belarus Underscores Similar Opinions Between his Country and Cuba*. RHC, 5/9/2000. Available online from:
http://www.radiohc.org/Distributions/Radio_Havana_English/.2000/2000_sep/Radio_Havana_Cuba-05_September_2000_21:30

124. Ibid.

125. Associated Press. (2003). *Belarus Calls For End to US Embargo on Cuba*. 31st of March 2003. Available online from: http://www.cubanet.org/CNews/y03/mar03/31e4.htm

126. Ibid.

127. Council of Ministers of the Republic of Belarus. (2006). *Sidorskiy: Belarus-Cuba economic*

relations will boost bilateral co-operation. News: 21st April 2006. Available online from: http://www.government.by/en/eng_news21042006.html

128. Cited by Gott. R. (2005). *Hugo Chávez and the Bolivarian Revolution*. Verso Books. London. Page 124.

129. BelaPAN news agency. (2006). *Lukashenko Expects Relations With Venezuela to Develop into Long-term, all-round Partnership*. Available online from: http://bhtimes.blogspot.com/2006/07/hugo-chaves-comes-to-minsk-interview_26.html

130. Nezhdanny O. (2006). *Hugo Calls on Lukashenko: Venezuelan President Visits Minsk*. Kommersant July 25th 2006. Available online from: http://www.kommersant.com/page.asp?idr=527&id=692409

131. Ibid.

132. Auken. B.V. (2005). *Venezuela Demands US Hand Over CIA Terrorist For Trial*. WSWS. Available online from: http://www.wsws.org/articles/2005/jun2005/posa-j17.shtml

133. Mather. S. (2006). *Venezuela and Belarus forge 'Strategic Alliance'*. Venezuelan Analysis July 25th 2006. Available online from: http://www.venezuelanalysis.com/news.php?newsno=2021

134. Ibid.

135. Ibid.

136. Associated Press. (2006). *Venezuela Gains support from Belarus in Bid for UN Seat*. 5th September 2006. Available online from: http://www.data.minsk.by/belarusnews/092006/17.html

137. Associated Press. (2006). *New US Ambassador says Washington wants to be 'reliable friend' to Belarus*. International Herald and Tribune September 18th 2006.

138. Executive Order of the President of the USA. (2006). *Blocking Property of Certain Persons Undermining Democratic Processes or Institutions in Belarus*. June 16th 2006. Available online from: http://www.whitehouse.gov/news/releases/2006/06/20060619-3.html

139. National Legal Internet Portal of the Republic of Belarus. (2007). *President will make official visit to Venezuela soon, Hugo Chávez will come to Belarus afterwards*. Press release 30th of March 2007.

Available online from:
http://law.by/work/EnglPortal.nsf/0/0A57F20DA8448CDCC22572AE0035EA98?OpenDocument

140. Maksymiuk. J. (2006). *Belarusian President Proposes Union With Ukraine*. RFE/RL. November 27th 2006 Volume 10 number 217. Available online from:
http://www.rferl.org/newsline/2006/11/5-not/not-271106.asp

141. Ibid.

142. Lukashenko. AG. (2004). *Foreign Policy of the Republic of Belarus in the Modern World*. Speech to the heads of Belarusian Diplomatic Missions. 15th September 2004. Available online from: http://www.ebrdrenewables.com/sites/renew/Lists/EBRD%20Master%20Spreadsheet/DispForm.aspx?ID=197

143. Embassy of the Republic of Belarus in the United States of America. (2005). *The Republic of Belarus' View of the Current and Latest Developments in Belarusian – Polish Relations*. Press release 13th of September 2005. Available online from: www.belembassy.org

144. Druker. J. (2005). *Belarus Targets Ethnic Polish Group*. ISN Security Watch, 11th August 2005. Available online from: http://www.isn.ethz.ch/news/sw/details.cfm?ID=12429

145. Ibid.

146. Maunk A. (2005). *Lukashenko's War on Poles*. Axis Information and Analysis. Available online from: www.axisglobe.com

147. Ibid.

148. Silitski. V. (2005). *Making Lukashenka Think Twice*. Belarus News and Analysis. Available online from: http://www.data.minsk.by/belarusnews/082005/115.html

149. Cited by BBC News. (2005). *Belarus-Poland Row Stirs up Press*. Available online from: http://news.bbc.co.uk/1/hi/world/europe/4728051.stm

150. Bordonaro. Dr.F. (2005). *The European Union's Tough Message to Belarus*. Power and Interest News Report 16th November 2005. Available online from:
http://www.pinr.com/report.php?ac=view_report&report_id=399&language_id=1

151. Cited by Charter 97. (2004), *Poles Dislike Castro and Lukashenka*. Available online from: http://www.charter97.org/eng/news/2004/08/16/love

152. Silitski. V. (2005). *Making Lukashenka Think Twice*. Belarus News and Analysis. Available online from: http://www.data.minsk.by/belarusnews/082005/115.html

153. Ibid.

154. Silitski. V. Cited by Druker. J. (2005). *Belarus Targets Ethnic Polish Group*. ISN Security Watch, 11th August 2005. Available online from: http://www.isn.ethz.ch/news/sw/details.cfm?ID=12429

155. Trukhachev. V. (2005). *Polish PM Starts the Pre-Election Attack on Belarus*. Pravda online. 26th August 2005. Available online from: http://english.pravda.ru/world/20/92/370/16051_Lukashenko.html

156. Millies. S (2006). *Belarus Beat Back Bush*. Workers World, March 26th 2006. Available online from: http://www.workers.org/2006/world/belarus-0330/

157. Markov. S. cited by RIA Novosti. (2006). *Belarus no less Democratic than Latvia, Estonia – Analyst*. Available online from: http://en.rian.ru/world/20060323/44723845.html

158. Goldstein. F. (2005). *Bush Agenda in Europe Hatchet Man for Wall Street Looters Downplays USSR Role in Defeating Hitler 60 Years Ago*. Workers World, May 12th 2005. Available online from: http://www.workers.org/2005/world/russia-0519/

159. Lukashenko. A.G. cited by Belaruski Novosti. (2006). *Lukashenko Calls on Non Aligned Movement to Become 'Independent Global Centre of Political Force'*. Available Online from: http://www.naviny.by/rubrics/inter/2006/09/16/ic_articles_259_147990/

Chapter 15.

1. A.G. Lukashenko. (2006). Cited by Belapan. *Lukashenko: Only the People Could Allow Opposition Members to Serve in Government Positions*. Available online from: http://www.naviny.by/rubrics/inter/2006/11/17/ic_articles_259_148713/

2. BHHRG. (2000). *Belarus 2000: Parliamentary Elections*. Report available online from: www.bhhrg.org

3. Ibid.

4. Ibid.

5. Ibid.

6. Ibid.

7. Almond. M. (1996). *Scorpion Battle – Politics in Belarus*. National Review December 23rd 1996. Available online from: http://www.findarticles.com/p/articles/mi_m1282/is_n24_v48/ai_18971886

8. Lukashenko. A.G. (2001). *Address of the President of the Republic of Belarus at the Republican Conference on the Tasks of Executive and Administrative Authorities Under the Present Day Conditions*. Press Service of the President of the Republic of Belarus. Available online from: http://president.gov.by/en/press11521.html#doc

9. Traynor. I. (2001). *Belarussian [sic] foils Dictator-Buster…For now*. The Guardian. Friday September 14th 2001. Available online from: http://www.guardian.co.uk/Archive/Article/0,4273,4256816,00.html

10. Silitski. V. (2005). *Outposts of Tyranny: Belarus*. Interview for the Washington Post. April 10th 2005.

11. Shkolnikov. L.G. (2000). *Address to the International Meeting of Communist and Worker's Parties in Athens*. Available online from: http://www.solidnet.org/cgi-bin/agent?parties/0100=belarus,_communist_party_of_belarus/belarusint3.doc

12. Cited by BHHRG. (2001). *Belarus Presidential Election, September 2001*. Report by the British Helsinki Human Rights Group. Available online from: www.bhhrg.org

13. Goncharik. V. (2001). *Interview with the International Information Services*. 24th January 2001. Available online from: http://www.belarusnews.de/nachrichten/2001/report/980342110.shtml

14. Chandler. D. (2001). *Dictating Democracy in Belarus*. Spiked Politics 12th October 2001. Available online from: http://www.spiked-online.com/Articles/00000002D26F.htm

15. Traynor. I. (2001). *Belarussian* [sic] *foils Dictator-Buster...For now.* The Guardian. Friday September 14th 2001. Available online from: http://www.guardian.co.uk/Archive/Article/0,4273,4256816,00.html

16. Labarique. P. (2001) *Belarus Under Pressure.* Non aligned Press Network. 15th February 2005. Available online from: http://www.voltairenet.org/article30033.html#nh10

17. Lukashenko. A.G. (2001). *Address of the President of the Republic of Belarus at the Republican Conference on the Tasks of Executive and Administrative Authorities Under the Present Day Conditions.* Press Service of the President of the Republic of Belarus. Available online from: http://president.gov.by/en/press11521.html#doc

18. Ibid.

19. Ibid.

20. Israel. J. (2001). *Tough Measures Justified in Belarus.* The Emperors New Clothes, 3rd September 2001. Available online from: http://emperors-clothes.com/news/tough.htm

21. BHHRG. (2001). *Belarus Presidential Election, September 2001.* Report by the British Helsinki Human Rights Group. Available online from: www.bhhrg.org

22. Chandler. D. (2001). *Dictating Democracy in Belarus.* Spiked Politics 12th October 2001. Available online from: http://www.spiked-online.com/Articles/00000002D26F.htm

23. Ibid.

24. BBC News. (2001). *Belarus Vote Neither Free nor Fair.* BBC 10th of September 2001. Available online from: http://news.bbc.co.uk/1/hi/world/europe/1534621.stm

25. News Service of the Republic of Moldova. (2005). *Lukashenko is Convinced he will Serve Another Term.* Available online from: http://politicom.moldova.org/stiri/eng/7488/

26. BHHRG. (2006). *Belarus: Brokeback Revolution. Why did Voters Reject the Denim Revolution?* Available online from: www.bhhrg.org

27. Embassy of the Republic of Belarus in the Unites States of America. (2006). *Opinion: International Observers about Presidential Election in Belarus.* March 19th 2006. Available online from:

http://www.belarusembassy.org/elections/opinion_observers.htm

28. Embassy of the Republic of Belarus in the Unites States of America. (2006). Press Release: *On Statement by President of Belarus Alexander Lukashenko at the Third All-Belarus People's Congress*. March 3rd 2006. Available online from:
http://www.belarusembassy.org/news/digests/pr030306.htm

29. Lukashenko. A.G. (2006). *The State is For the People*. Speech. Available online from: http://president.gov.by/en/press24121.html#doc

30. Shkolnikov. L. (2006). *Situation in the Republic of Belarus Today (From the Position of the Workers Democracy)*. Contribution to the 15th International Communist Seminar, Brussels 5th -7th May 2006. Available online from: www.wpb.be/icm.htm

31. Lukashenko. A.G. (2006). *The State is For the People*. Speech. Available online from: http://president.gov.by/en/press24121.html#doc

32. Cited by, Peterson. S. (2001). *US Spends Millions to Bolster Belarus Opposition*. Christian Science Monitor. September 10th 2001. Available online from:
http://www.csmonitor.com/2001/0910/p7s1-woeu.html

33. Lobjakas. A. (2006). *Belarus: EU Foreign Ministers Meet With Opposition Leader*. RFE/RL. January 30th 2006. Available online from:
http://www.rferl.org/featuresarticle/2006/01/5f66b40b-e7a6-47d8-bdbc-629c71956dee.html

34. Kessler. G. (2005). *Pressing Change for Belarus. Rice Meets With Opposition*. Washington Post, April 22nd 2005. Available online from:
http://www.data.minsk.by/belarusnews/042005/74.html

35. BHHRG. (2006). *Belarus: Brokeback Revolution. Why did Voters Reject the Denim Revolution?* Available online from: www.bhhrg.org

36. Fawkes. H. (2006). *Ukraine Still Feeling Gas Pressure*. BBC News. Monday January 1st 2007. Available online from: http://news.bbc.co.uk/1/hi/world/europe/6222355.stm

37. Milinkevich. A. (2006). *My thoughts.*. Available online from:
http://en.milinkevich.org/about/mymention/mythoughts/

38. Milinkevich. A. (2006). *Belarus: Road to the Future*. Election Platform. Available online from:

http://en.milinkevich.org/about/mymention/concept/

39. BHHRG. (2006). *Belarus: Brokeback Revolution. Why did Voters Reject the Denim Revolution?* Available online from: www.bhhrg.org

40. Myers. S. (2006). *In Belarus Expecting to Lose Then Win.* The New York Times. February 24th 2006. As reported in the International Herald and Tribune. Available online from: http://www.iri.org/newsarchive/2006/2006-02-24-News-IHT-Belarus.asp

41. BHHRG. (2006). *Belarus: Brokeback Revolution. Why did Voters Reject the Denim Revolution?* Available online from: www.bhhrg.org

42. Ibid.

43. Ibid.

44. Ibid.

45. Milinkevich. A. (2006). Cited by the press service of the European Parliament. *Steady Western Support Needed to Boost Democracy in Belarus.* Delegations 31st January 2006. Available online from: http://www.europarl.europa.eu/news/expert/infopress_page/029-4835-31-1-5-903-20060130IPR04815-31-01-2006-2006--false/default_en.htm

46. Rosenberg. S. (2006). *Daring to Criticise Belarus' President.* BBC News 11th March 2006. Available online from: http://news.bbc.co.uk/1/hi/programmes/from_our_own_correspondent/4790912.stm

47. BHHRG. (2006). *Belarus: Brokeback Revolution. Why did Voters Reject the Denim Revolution?* Available online from: www.bhhrg.org

48. McAdams. D. (2006). *How Lukashenko Won.* March 27th 2006. Available online from: http://www.antiwar.com/orig/mcadams.php?articleid=8763

49. Charter97. (2003). *Down With Tyrants!* April 3rd 2003. Available online from: http://www.charter97.org/index.phtml?sid=4&did=20030403&lang=3

50. BHHRG. (2006). *Belarus: Brokeback Revolution. Why did Voters Reject the Denim Revolution?*

Available online from: www.bhhrg.org

51. Ibid.

52. See www.Telegraph.co.uk For these and several other example, along with the 'Europe's last dictator' theme.

53. Bagdikian. B. (2004). *The New Media Monopoly*. Beacon Press. Boston.

54. Korovenkova. T. (2007). *Lukashenko Acknowledges Shortcomings Regarding Freedom of The Press*. Belaruski Novosti. 25th of January 2007. Available online from: http://www.naviny.by/rubrics/inter/2007/01/25/ic_articles_259_149491/

55. Ibid.

56. BHHRG. (2006). *Belarus: Brokeback Revolution. Why did Voters Reject the Denim Revolution?* Executive summary. Available online from: www.bhhrg.org

57. Ibid.

58. OSCE. (2006). *OSCE Parliamentary Assembly President briefs participating States on Belarus election*. OSCE Press Release 22nd March 2006. Available online from: http://www.osce.org/item/18457.html?print=1

59. BHHRG. (2006). *Belarus: Brokeback Revolution. Why did Voters Reject the Denim Revolution?* Available online from: www.bhhrg.org

60. As reported by Freedom Magazine. (2004). *Paragons of Corruption*. Freedom Magazine. Volume 27 Number 6. Available online from: http://www.freedommag.org/english/vol27I6/page28a.htm

61. OSCE. (2006). *Interim Report 2. 25th February – 7th March 2006*. Election Observation Mission. Presidential election Belarus 2006. Available online from: http://www.osce.org/odihr-elections/item_12_17899.html

62. Centre For Responsive Politics. (2004). *2004 Presidential Elections*. Available online from: http://www.opensecrets.org/presidential/index.asp?sort=E

63. Chomsky. N. (2000). *Rogue States*. Pluto Press. London. Page 119.

64. Ibid.

65. OSCE. (2006). *Interim Report 2. 25th February – 7th March 2006*. Election Observation Mission. Presidential election Belarus 2006. Available online from: http://www.osce.org/odihr-elections/item_12_17899.html

66. Ibid.

67. Embassy of the Republic of Belarus in the USA. (2006). *On Statement by the Ministry of Foreign Affairs of the Republic of Belarus on the 2006 Presidential Election in Belarus*. Press release, March 23rd 2006. Available online from: http://www.belarusembassy.org/

68. Ibid.

69. Embassy of the Republic of Belarus in the USA. (2006). *Opinion: International Observers About Presidential Election in Belarus*. March 19th 2006. Available online from: http://www.belarusembassy.org/

70. Ibid.

71. Ibid.

72. Ibid.

73. Ibid.

74. CIS (2006). *Statement of the International Observers of the Commonwealth of Independent States on the Results of Observation of the Preparation and conduction of the Elections of the President of the Republic of Belarus*. Available online from: http://www.belarusembassy.org/

75. Ibid.

76. BHHRG. (2006). *Belarus: Brokeback Revolution. Why did Voters Reject the Denim Revolution?* Available online from: www.bhhrg.org

77. Pavlovsky. G. (2006). *Interview to Sovietskaya Byelorussia*. Available online from: http://www.belarus-botschaft.de/de/pavlovsky_de.htm

78. Belaruski Novosti. (2006). *Lukashenko Reveals that Government Falsified March's Presidential Vote*. 24th November 2006. Available online from: http://naviny.by/rubrics/inter/2006/11/24/ic_articles_259_148781/

79. BHHRG. (2006). *Belarus: Brokeback Revolution. Why did Voters Reject the Denim Revolution?* Available online from: www.bhhrg.org

80. Ibid.

81. Associated Press. (2006). *Protesters Clash With Police Over Belarus Election Results*. 25th March 2006. Available online from: http://www.foxnews.com/story/0,2933,189104,00.html

82. BBC. (2006). *EU Demands Belarus Leader Freed*. 26th March 2006. BBC News. Available online at: http://news.bbc.co.uk/1/hi/world/europe/4846316.stm

83. Maksymiuk. J. (2006). *Has opposition Scored a Victory Over Fear?* Belarusian Review Volume 18 No1. 22nd March 2006. Available online from: http://www.belreview.cz/articles/3005.html

84.

Conclusion.

1. Lukashenko. A.G. (2003). *Main Points of the Lecture 'Historical Choice of Belarus'*. Press Service of the President of the Republic of Belarus. Available online from: http://www.president.gov.by/en/press14059.html#doc

2. Ibid.

3. Oxford Council on Good Governance. (2005). *Illegal US Torture Camps*. Press release. Available online from: http://www.oxfordgovernance.org/fileadmin/Press_Releases/OCGG_PRESS_RELEASE_-_Illegal_US_torture_camps.doc

4. Millies. S. (2006). *Belarus Beat Back Bush*. Workers World. March the 26th 2006. Available online from: http://www.workers.org/2006/world/belarus-0330/

Appendix.

This speech can actually be viewed online by visiting the archive of:
http://www.un.int/belarus/

Bibliography and Recommended Further Reading.

Axell. A. (2001). *Russia's Heroes*. Constable Publishers. London. (An excellent history and collection of first person accounts of the Great Patriotic war).

Bagdikian. B. (2004). *The New Media Monopoly*. Beacon Press. Boston.

Bennett. K. Et-al. (2005). *Coalfields Regeneration: Dealing with the Consequences of Industrial Decline*. The Policy Press. Bristol.

Chomsky. N. (1989). *Necessary Illusions: Thought Control in Democratic Societies*. Pluto Press. London. (Essential for beginning to understand the workings of 'independent media').

Chomsky. N. (2000). *Rogue States: The Rule of Force in World Affairs*. Pluto Press. London.

Chuev. F. (1991). *Molotov Remembers: Inside Kremlin Politics*. Ivan. R. Dee. Chicago. (A superb insight into the personalities and motivations of Soviet policy from before the Revolution until the late 1980's).

Churchill. W. & Vander Wall. J. (1990). *Agents of Repression: The FBI's Secret Wars Against the Black Panther Party and the American Indian Movement*. South End Press. Boston USA. (A superb account of actual state sponsored terror, murder and disappearances).

Commission of the C.C. of the C.P.S.U. (B) (1939). *History of the Communist Party of the Soviet Union (Bolsheviks)*. Foreign Languages Publishing House. Moscow.

Davies. R. W. (1980). *The Industrialisation of Soviet Russia I. The Soviet Offensive: the Collectivisation of Agriculture, 1929-30*. Harvard University Press. Cambridge, Massachusetts.

Gott. R. (2005). *Hugo Chávez and the Bolivarian Revolution*. Verso Books. London.

Grey. I. (1979). *Stalin: Man of History*. Abacus Books Reading UK. (A superb and rare impartial biography).

Kahan. S. (1989). *The Wolf of the Kremlin*. Robert Hale. London. (A 'biography' of Lazar Kaganovich Commissar of Heavy Industry under Stalin. Useful for its depiction of life in the Pale of Settlement).

Kudrayashov. N. (1987). *The Brest Fortress*. Raduga Publishers. Moscow.

Lenin. V.I. (1970). *What is to be Done?* Progress Publishers. Moscow. (Original Soviet translations are the most accurate, but increasingly hard to find. Can be downloaded from The Communist Party of Great Britain (Marxist-Leninist) at: http://www.cpgb-ml.org/)

Lukashenko. A.G. (1998). *Belarus Tomorrow*. East European Development Association. Geneva.

Malarek. V. (2003). *The Natashas: The New Global Sex Trade*. Viking. Canada. (An excellent study of what 'freedom' has brought east European women).

Marples. David R. (1999). *Belarus: a Denationalised Nation*. Harwood Academic Publishers. (An interesting history of Belarus, and excellent detailed summary of Lukashenko's consolidation of power 1994-1996).

Martens. L. (1994) *Another View of Stalin*. EPO. Antwerp, Belgium. (An interesting response to the commonly held beliefs concerning collectivisation in the USSR. This book is hard to find, but is available through: http://www.stalinsociety.org.uk/index.html)

Marx. K, and Engels F. (1975). *Manifesto of the Communist Party*. Progress Publishers. Moscow.

Marx. K. Engels. F. Lenin. V.I. (1967). *On Scientific Communism*. Progress Publishers. Moscow. Page 462. (Again accurate translations are becoming harder to find, a good source for original books by Marx,

Engels etc. is John Buckle Books:
http://www.rcpbml.org.uk/catalog.htm)

McAuley. M. (1977). *Politics and the Soviet Union.* Penguin, UK.

Morrison. D. (Ed). (1988). *Mikhail S. Gorbachev: An Intimate Biography.* Time Books. New York.

O'Donnell. J.S. (1999). *A Coming of Age: Albania Under Enver Hoxha.* Columbia University Press. New York.

Overy. R. (1997). *Russia's War.* Penguin Books. London. (A superb concise account of the Great Patriotic War, and also briefly covers the Russian civil War).

Palast. G. (2003). *The Best Democracy Money Can Buy.* Constable and Robinson Limited. London.

Samuel. S.P. (2003). *Belarus. Facts.* Kavaler Publishers Minsk. (Available via the Belarusian Embassy, and Ministry of Foreign Affairs. This book is regularly updated).

Stalin. J.V. (1942). *Marxism and the National and Colonial Question.* Lawrence and Wishart. London.

Stiglitz. J.E. (2002). *Globalisation and its Discontents.* W.W. Norton &co. New York.

Stuk. A. & Sapozhkov. Y. (1982). *Byelorussia.* Novosti Press agency Publishing House. Moscow.

Vakar. N.P. (1956). *Belorussia: the Making of a Nation.* Harvard University Press. Cambridge, Massachusetts.

Weinberg. R. (1998). *Stalin's Forgotten Zion.* University of California Press. Berkeley.

Zaprudnik. J. (1993). *Belarus: At a Crossroads in History.* Westview Press. USA. (An excellent detailed history of Belarus from pre-history to

1991).

Useful Websites.

Official Website of President Alexander Lukashenko. http://president.gov.by/en/ (contains speeches, interviews, and the president's daily schedule).

Embassy of the Republic of Belarus in the USA. http://www.belarusembassy.org/ (Excellent information and replies to specific accusations etc.)

Belarus News and Analysis. http://www.data.minsk.by/belarusnews/index.html (A continuously updated set of links to News stories about Belarus).

British Helsinki Human Rights Group. http://www.bhhrg.org/ (An invaluable resource for OSCE nations election monitoring and country profiles).

Cuba Solidarity Campaign. http://www.cuba-solidarity.org/ (Information on the background to the US blockade, and the campaign to remove it).

Australia Venezuela Solidarity Network. http://www.venezuelasolidarity.org/ (Excellent source for Venezuelan news and analysis).